PRAISE FOR
The Consumer's Guide to Effective Environmental Choices

"A clear and concise call to action, this book allows us to make choices that really make a difference. It is sure to create controversy in many circles."

—ED BEGLEY, JR., actor and environmentalist

"To reduce consumption wisely, we need intelligent guidelines so that what we choose to do without will substantially increase quality of life for generations to come—and for ourselves as well. This book makes a supremely useful contribution to this urgent goal. Read it and weed out your most damaging practices while keeping much of what makes life worth living."

—VICKI ROBIN, co-author of *Your Money or Your Life*

"Living responsibly means making smart choices. Here's a straightforward guide to travel, diet, and home life that demystifies the confusion over what's really best for the environment."

—ROGER SWAIN, Host of PBS's "The Victory Garden"

"If we hope to have a healthy planet for our children, we must learn to be responsible and conscious consumers. This book is a terrific guide for people who really want to do the right thing, without sweating the small stuff." —BETSY TAYLOR, Executive Director, Center for a New American Dream

"In a world of info-glut, we are constantly assaulted by often contradictory claims about many of the items we buy and use. Here is a sensible book that, instead of making us feel guilty, challenges us to think and provides guidelines to help us make ecologically wise choices." —DAVID SUZUKI, Host of "The Nature of Things"

"If you have ever wondered which of your individual actions have the greatest environmental impact (and which the least), read this book." —FRANK ACKERMAN, author of *Why Do We Recycle?*

MICHAEL BROWER, Ph.D.
AND WARREN LEON, Ph.D.

THE CONSUMER'S GUIDE TO EFFECTIVE ENVIRONMENTAL CHOICES:

PRACTICAL ADVICE FROM THE UNION OF CONCERNED SCIENTISTS

THREE RIVERS PRESS/NEW YORK

Copyright © 1999 by the Union of Concerned Scientists

Published by Three Rivers Press, a division of Crown Publishers, Inc., 201 East 50th Street, New York, New York 10022. Member of the Crown Publishing Group.

Random House, Inc. New York, Toronto, London, Sydney, Auckland
www.randomhouse.com

THREE RIVERS PRESS and colophon are trademarks of Crown Publishers, Inc.

Printed in the United States of America

Design by Rhea Braunstein

Library of Congress Cataloging-in-Publication Data
Brower, Michael.
    The consumer's guide to effective environmental choices:
    practical advice from The Union of Concerned Scientists/by
    Michael Brower, Warren Leon, and The Union of Concerned
    Scientists.
        p. cm.
    Includes index.
    1. Green products—United States. 2. Consumer behavior—
    United States. I. Warren, Leon, 1950– . II. Union of Concerned
    Scientists. III. Title. IV. Title: Consumer's guide to effective
    environmental choices.
    HF5415.33.U6L46   1999
    363.7′00973—DC21   98-27570
                                                                        CIP

ISBN 0-609-80281-X

10 9 8 7 6 5 4 3 2

CONTENTS

PREFACE

Twenty years ago one of us couldn't find a way to recycle a car full of newspapers—and this was in Cambridge, Massachusetts, supposedly a hotbed of environmental activism. We had been taking our old papers to a distant, little-used newspaper recycling station set up by the city department of public works. Once we waited a little too long between recycling trips, with the result that the newspapers not only filled the trunk but covered the car's entire backseat, spilled onto the floor, and reached up to the roof. You can imagine our dismay when we got to the recycling center only to discover that the site had been closed because of a lack of public interest.

At a loss as to how to dispose of a car full of newspapers without adding to the nation's trash problem, we called various friends and public officials for suggestions. One person told us about a neighboring city that had a government grant to carry out an experimental recycling program. With confidence that we could now do our part for the environment, we jumped into the car and drove off to the recycling center. But halfway through unloading the newspapers, an officer informed us that the center was open only to that city's residents. He ordered us to pack up our garbage and take it elsewhere. Dejected, we took everything home and, a few days later, ended up placing several hundred pounds of newspapers out on the sidewalk with the regular trash.

Recycling has certainly come a long way since then. Today curbside recycling programs have spread to many communities, and fully a quarter of the trash that households dispose of gets taken to recycling centers to be made into new paper, cans, bottles—even, in one case, clothing. Yet it is clear that recycling alone cannot solve the serious environmental problems that face America and the rest of the world.

In late 1997 many of the world's senior scientists issued a warning that human activities are inflicting "harsh and often irreversible damage on the environment and on critical resources." A substantial majority of the living Nobel prize winners in the sciences, as well as leaders of professional scientific societies around the world, signed a statement emphasizing that the scientific community has "reached a consensus that grave threats imperil the future of humanity and the global environment."[1]

It doesn't take a Nobel prize to understand that pollution and alteration of the natural world pose risks for people's health and for the maintenance of their quality of life. Americans, by and large, also realize that efforts like recycling are only partial solutions. They have consequently been left concerned but confused. No clear consensus has emerged about what else they should do to protect the environment.

As consumers, we make dozens of decisions every day about what to do or buy, but it is hard to know which of them, if any, make a significant difference for the environment. Should you worry about whether to diaper your baby in cloth or disposables? Is it wrong to purchase a microwave oven? Does it matter whether you choose paper or plastic bags at the grocery store? Faced with conflicting claims about the merits of different products, many Americans have even become cynical and discouraged, believing that no one really knows the answers.

But we are neither cynical nor discouraged, for we believe there are choices—clear, unambiguous choices—ordinary consumers can make that will truly benefit the environment. Of course, the choices are not always easy. They may involve, for example, driving a smaller car or eating less beef. But one thing we can promise you: They will make a difference.

There are four reasons to read this book:

1. *It will help you set priorities.* To move beyond recycling, you need to know which of the many hundreds of things that American consumers buy and do cause the most environmental damage. Similarly, you need to know which of the many possible changes you could make in your personal life would have the biggest benefit. This book will give you that information. It will also point out situations where the emphasis must be placed on changing the policies of governments and institutions rather than the habits of consumers.

2. *It will help you stop worrying about insignificant things.* As much as some consumer decisions should be given priority, the importance of others should be deemphasized. Our approach and advice is to focus on the big priorities and downplay subtle differences between smaller actions. By the end of the book, we hope you will never again consider purchasing a gas-guzzling car, but by the same token, you won't feel guilty about using disposable diapers, spray cans, or paper napkins.

3. *It is based on extensive analysis of how everyday household decisions actually affect the environment.* Rather than just present our personal preferences and opinions about what you should do to protect the environment, we have analyzed the links between environmental problems and Americans' individual behaviors. As you will see, we determined which of the many environmental problems in the news are most impor-

tant for consumers to pay attention to—because they are more significant than other problems and because they are caused to a significant degree by the actions of consumers. We then combined information about these problems with data on household expenditure patterns to come up with a model that can quantitatively analyze how any given set of purchases, from meat and poultry to jewelry and toys, affects the environment.

The result is a rating system that will allow you to see, at a glance, how a particular household activity compares with any other. In addition, we determine how big a difference certain possible changes—such as buying a more efficient car or reducing your meat consumption—would make in your environmental impact.

4. It is backed by the research and credibility of the Union of Concerned Scientists. In the years since its founding in 1969, the Union of Concerned Scientists has developed a reputation for presenting sound, impartial information about environmental issues. The organization's staff, in association with some of the nation's leading scientists, has studied many of the key environmental problems and has developed policy remedies for addressing them. This book builds on these earlier efforts and has benefited from the organization's resources.

Although we believe this book is different from earlier efforts to look at the relationship between American consumers and the environment, we do not want to overpromise what we can deliver. Some of our answers are tentative, based on the best currently available information. Moreover, we do not answer all questions about all consumer products. You will not be able to find out, for example, whether one type of paper towel is better for the environment than another. You won't even learn definitively whether cloth diapers are better or worse than disposables. In cases like these, where we believe the alternatives are relatively evenly matched and neither choice makes a significant difference for overall environmental quality, we do not anoint winners and losers. Because we believe that most people need not concern themselves with such choices, we don't spend time trying to make these small distinctions ourselves.

What you will learn is how to identify the things you can do that really make a difference.

Many people have helped us during the years we worked on this book, and we want to thank them.

The staff members at the Union of Concerned Scientists provided us with valuable information and support. Some of them—Peter Frumhoff, Roland Hwang, Paul Jefferiss, Margaret Mellon, Alden Meyer, Alan Nogee, and Eileen Quinn—helped further by reviewing part or all of the manuscript. We especially want to thank executive director Howard Ris for his unwavering support for this project and his useful feedback along the way.

Two other individuals—Frank Ackerman and Lee Schipper—also reviewed the manuscript and provided us with very useful suggestions for how to improve it. Of course, for any remaining errors of fact or argument, they are entirely blameless.

In doing the research, we were aided by several research assistants—Miriam Bowling, Stan Byers, Eileen Gunn, Nandana Mewada, and Rebecca Slotkin. We were helped in a quite different way by grants from the John D. and Catherine T. MacArthur Foundation and the Merck Family Fund to support the research phase of this project.

We thank historian Susan Strasser, author of such books as *Satisfaction Guaranteed: The Making of the American Mass Market* and *Never Done: A History of American Housework,* for contributing the engaging epilogue placing modern Americans' consumption into historical perspective.

Our agent, Faith Hamlin, and our editor at Crown Publishers, Laura Wood, have given us sound advice and helped us to reshape the manuscript into a more reader-friendly form.

On a personal note, we are grateful to our wives, Cynthia Robinson and Julia Scolnik, for their encouragement and helpful advice. Finally, we dedicate this book to our children: Jeremy, Sasha, and Sophie, the next generation of responsible consumers.

PART I

CONSUMERS AND THE ENVIRONMENT

1

How Many Simple Things Do People Need to Do to Save the Planet?

Amy Dacyczyn didn't start reusing vacuum cleaner bags, composting drier lint, and turning tuna fish cans into cookie cutters in order to preserve the environment, but some environmental activists have called her a hero. Instead, back in 1981, she and her husband, Jim, had decided that they needed to economize so they could achieve their dream of buying a house in the country. By shopping at thrift stores, making their own Christmas presents, and finding new uses for plastic milk jugs, egg cartons, and juice can lids, Dacyczyn was able to sock away enough of Jim's $30,000 salary so that after seven years they had $49,000 to use to purchase a Maine farmhouse. She clothed her family for $250 per year and fed them for just $42 each week.[1]

By spending less, Dacyczyn not only was able to move to Maine, but she found her day-to-day life more satisfying than when she had been spending money on movies and restaurants. She realized that she didn't want a lifestyle like that of Americans who are always "running out of the house, running to the day care center, running on the job, so they can afford candy bars, and Nintendo games, meals at McDonald's and designer sneakers."[2] Although her motives were financial and personal, her story—told through her newsletter, the *Tightwad Gazette*—has seemed to have an environmental message. Living without garbage Disposalls, VCRs, and store-bought toys, Dacyczyn has put into practice the quintessential environmentalist motto: "Reduce, reuse, recycle."

Some observers have argued that the Dacyczyns and other practitioners of simple living are blazing the path down which all the rest of us will need to travel. They argue that, in order to solve the serious environmental problems facing the world, average middle-class Americans will have to accept and even embrace a sharp across-the-board reduction in the amount of goods and materials they buy, own, use, and throw away.

But is this across-the-board approach the only way to reduce the environmental impacts of Americans' consumption? We believe a different, more targeted strategy can also be effective and will more likely appeal to a wider segment of the population. By focusing on a relatively few especially damaging aspects of their consumption, Americans can reduce overall environmental damage dramatically.

AMERICANS AS CHAMPION CONSUMERS

It is not difficult to show that Americans use a disproportionate share of the earth's resources. From the perspective of people living in the poorer countries of Africa, Asia, and Latin America, most Americans consume enormous quantities of all sorts of things: energy, metals, minerals, forest products, fish, grains, meat, and even fresh water. Compared with the average citizen of Bangladesh, for example, Americans on average consume 106 times as much commercial energy.[3]

When we look at the world as a whole, we can see that our country is responsible for a lopsided share of the total consumption of key products and materials. We use one-third of the world's paper, despite representing just 5 percent of the world's population. Similarly, we use 25 percent of the oil, 23 percent of the coal, 27 percent of the aluminum, and 19 percent of the copper.[4]

Even when we compare ourselves with people in other wealthy industrial countries, we generally emerge as the champion consumers. An average American uses twice as much fossil fuel (coal, oil, and natural gas) as the average resident of Great Britain and 2.5 times as much as the average Japanese. We consume over 3.25 pounds of boneless meat (mostly beef and chicken) each week, 1.5 times as much as the average Briton or Italian and more than 2.5 times as much as the average Japanese.[5]

The sheer production of waste in our society is astounding. The typical American discards nearly a ton of trash per person per year, two to three times as much as the typical Western European throws away. Amy Dacyczyn and others who have embraced voluntary simplicity are noteworthy precisely because they have departed so strikingly from the usual high-consumption, high-waste American lifestyle.

But does this mean that other Americans are unaware of or unconcerned about the environmental impacts of the things they buy, use, and throw away? The answer is clearly no. Our willingness to devote time, thought, and kitchen space to recycling is strong evidence that we realize that the things we consume cause environmental damage.

Admittedly, Americans have embraced recycling with varying degrees of enthusiasm. Some people get intense satisfaction from participating in a ritual that shows they are doing their part to help preserve the environment for future generations. Such individuals often take pride in the orderly systems they have established for neatly sorting and stacking their piles of paper, plastics, and glass. They vigilantly monitor their trash to make sure not one unnecessary item ends up in a landfill.

At the other extreme are a minority of Americans who

consider recycling a foolish burden imposed upon them by their overzealous children, prying neighbors, or a too-powerful government. But even if the only reason they cart their recycling containers to the curb for collection or to the dump for disposal is to avoid the reproach of those around them, they probably accept the fact that American society as a whole has come to believe that it is desirable to recycle.

In fact, the popular consensus on the relationship between environmental problems and the American lifestyle transcends an acceptance of the desirability of recycling. Even if Americans are unsure about what else needs to be done, most of them realize that recycling alone cannot adequately protect the environment. They make general connections between consumption patterns and environmental problems. In a 1995 national telephone survey conducted by the Merck Family Fund, 88 percent of Americans agreed that "protecting the environment will require most of us to make major changes in the way we live," and 67 percent acknowledged that "Americans cause many of the world's environmental problems because we consume more resources and produce more waste than anyone else in the world."[6] Nevertheless, most people interviewed had not thought deeply about the specific ecological implications of their lifestyles and did not know precisely what they needed to change.

ENVIRONMENTAL ADVICE: TOO MUCH OF A GOOD THING

Unfortunately, books on the environment have not always helped Americans develop a useful understanding of the relationship between their lifestyle and environmental problems. Environmental advice manuals have often left readers feeling that environmental damage is primarily caused by myriad small actions on the part of individual consumers and that the answer is for individuals to voluntarily change their behavior in dozens and dozens of ways.

The best-selling book *50 Simple Things You Can Do to Save the Earth* told readers that "if every American family planted just one tree, over a billion pounds of 'greenhouse gases' would be removed from the atmosphere every year." They were also asked to snip six-pack rings, use fewer plastic bags, drive less, take the flea collars off their dogs, avoid releasing helium balloons, recycle aluminum cans, and take forty-two other actions, some of which had multiple components. Suggestion number 17, for example, to "find the hidden toxics" in the American home, directly targeted shampoos, oven cleaners, air fresheners, mothballs, pens, and permanent-press clothes, but it also suggested that readers purchase a book listing hundreds of items to eliminate from the home.[7]

Responding to consumers' interest in changing their behavior, other publishers rushed out comparable compendiums of commandments with 10, 50, 100, or even as many as 1001 actions readers could take to clean up the environment.[8] To be sure, many of the ideas made sound environmental sense, but the detailed lists overwhelmed some people while producing guilt pangs in others unable to keep track of all the injunctions. Confusion mounted when it turned out that there wasn't agreement among scientists about whether some of the commands, such as to use only cloth diapers, would be of any benefit to the environment. While the books asked people to plant trees, readers were left feeling that neither they nor the authors could see the forest for the trees. None of the popular guides gave a clear answer to the obvious questions: Which of all the many suggested actions would make the most difference? And should individual action be the main focus of attention?

THE OVERUSE OF *OVERCONSUMPTION*

Established environmental organizations and environmental policymakers have tended to gravitate to the opposite extreme from the guidebook writers when discussing Americans' consumption. They have generally discussed consumption in an abstract, vague way that is disconnected from people's actual lives and unhelpful as a guide to individual action.

Environmental thinkers and leaders, both in the United States and abroad, have charged that the major sin against the environment that the rich industrial countries commit has been the practice of "overconsumption." This contention was given considerable publicity and credibility because of the highly visible 1992 Earth Summit in Rio de Janeiro. At its core, "overconsumption" remains an ill-defined political slogan that doesn't help the overconsumers know how they should change either their individual behavior or their institutions.

In the months leading up to the Earth Summit—officially titled the United Nations Conference on Environment and Development—many of the delegates from the wealthier industrial countries in the northern hemisphere were on the defensive. Environmentalists from these countries had been pushing for strong international commitments to slow rainforest destruction and reduce greenhouse gas emissions. In their concern for the gloomy future of the global environment, they did not show a similar concern for the development needs of poorer countries.

Unsurprisingly, some representatives from developing countries detested and rejected calls that their countries give priority to addressing problems that threatened the world's wealthy rather than to advancing the economic improvement of the world's poor. They felt that the industrial countries had become rich through methods of economic development that the poorer countries were now being asked to renounce. Environmentalists from Europe and the United States appeared arrogant and hypocritical when they asked developing countries to forgo the use of coal, oil, and land-clearing practices that had fueled northern industrialization.

Some northern environmentalists further infuriated those from developing countries by suggesting that rapid population growth among the world's poor was the primary driving force behind rainforest destruction, degradation of agricultural lands, and other threats to the future health of the global environment. Vocal advocates for developing countries resented being portrayed as environmental villains. Anil Agarwal and Sunita Narain of the Centre for Science and the Environment in New Delhi, India, observed, "It is ironic that those who have exploited global resources the most are now preaching to those who have been largely frugal and sparing."[9] The editors of *Third World Resurgence* added, "The poor are victims and not culprits in environmental degradation. Much of the depletion and contamination of resources have been done to meet the consumption demands of the affluent. Changing consumption habits of the affluent is thus the priority in curbing the rate of depletion or pollution of resources."[10] After all, even though the population was growing rapidly in countries like Bangladesh, each additional American consumed many times more than each additional Bangladeshi.

These criticisms certainly rang true to the now-chastened northern environmentalists and policymakers who, in their zeal to address global environmental threats, had not meant to place all the burden or blame on the developing world. When it came to reducing emissions contributing to climate change, most of them accepted that the industrial countries, which were the largest polluters, should take the first and largest steps. Conversely, most Earth Summit delegates from poorer countries acknowledged that rapid population growth was undesirable, even if it was not the sole or primary cause of the world's environmental crisis, and that developing countries should move toward more environmentally sound models of economic development.

To forge and then express an acceptable international consensus on environment and development, negotiators and policymakers became increasingly mindful to apportion blame and avoid singling out one region of the world. All the regions of the world, they pointed out, bore some responsibility for environmental problems, and all needed to contribute to the solution. To emphasize this shared responsibility, they used a carefully phrased articulation: In the South the main problem was overpopulation; in the North it was overconsumption. Both of these problems needed to be addressed.

In the years since the Earth Summit, the term *overconsumption* continues to be bandied about while only rarely being examined or analyzed. Sometimes consciously and sometimes unconsciously, those who use the term have implied that Americans need to reduce their consumption of goods and services across the board; they need to quell their materialistic lifestyle. Without further explanation or analysis, this very general decree asks Americans to accept a diminished standard of living without guaranteeing that their sacrifice will actually solve pressing environmental problems.

BAD, NOT-SO-BAD, AND EVEN GOOD CONSUMPTION

To get beyond both the vague charge of overconsumption and the mind-boggling lists of undifferentiated action suggestions, we need to start thinking about our consumption of goods and services in more complex ways. When we do, we find, unsurprisingly, that not all consumption has an equal impact on the environment. For that reason, a 10 percent across-the-board reduction in Americans' consumption would not be the most effective way to reduce environmental damage. In looking at Americans' consumption patterns, we should start by acknowledging that some consumption of food, water, and materials for clothing and shelter is necessary for survival. Although we can examine whether we are consuming more of these necessities than is desirable and whether they can be produced in less environmentally damaging ways, we cannot and should not eliminate all consumption of them.

Even if we concentrate on those items that could theoretically be eliminated, we will still see great differences in the consequences of eliminating them. The use of certain materials such as gasoline, whose burning emits air pollutants and the greenhouse gas carbon dioxide, necessarily harms the environment. If we decide we are going to consume such materials, no conceivable technology can completely avoid environmental damage, even when we take steps to minimize it. On the other hand, some things can be consumed in ways that have few consequences for the general environment. The production, use, and disposal of bubble gum, for example, can be quite benign. Given these examples, environmentally aware parents would be wiser—even if not necessarily more popular—to deny their teenage children the keys to the family car than to forbid them to chew gum.

Even if a product is environmentally damaging, it may be used in such small quantities that we shouldn't focus on trying to reduce its consumption. The popular children's toy Lego blocks are made out of acrylonitrile butadiene styrene plastic, an oil-based product. The electricity used in the manufacturing process contributes to such problems as air pollution and global warming. There is also a risk that the blocks will end up unrecycled in landfills. However, when parents consider how little material goes into the average set and the likelihood that it will be passed on to another younger child, they need not worry that they have destroyed the environment with a twenty-dollar purchase of Legos.

On the other hand, some products are so dangerous to the environment that we should eliminate them completely. The world community realized this when deciding to phase out commerical uses of chlorofluorocarbons (CFCs), a group of chemicals that had been used in automobile air conditioners, spray cans, and industrial applications. When these chemicals are released into the atmosphere, they drift up to the stratosphere, where they destroy ozone molecules that protect humans and other life-forms from harmful ultraviolet radiation. Because of this well-documented destruction of the ozone layer, scientists, governments, and ultimately even the corporations that produced CFCs realized that a 10, 20, or even 50 percent reduction in consumption would not be sufficient. The only scientifically sane course would require putting a complete end to the consumption of an otherwise useful product.

At the other extreme are items Americans should actually consume in greater quantities if they want to reduce environmental damage. For example, the owner of an old house may need to buy new water pipes to reduce the health risks from lead poisoning. We would not want to discourage that family from taking such a necessary step just because it technically involves increasing their consumption of materials.

Sometimes increasing the consumption of one product can allow us to reduce the consumption of another item that is far worse for the environment. The purchase of a microwave oven allows a family to cut its consumption of electricity, since a microwave uses one-third or less of the energy of an electric oven. If that electricity is generated from coal or oil, the microwave will have reduced air pollution and the threat of climate change. Similarly, in many parts of the country, it is not only environmentally desirable but cost-effective to add non-polluting solar hot water heaters to homes in order to reduce the use of conventional hot water systems that run on polluting fuels. Consumers may need to spend more money in the short run, but the environmental payoff will be worth it.

THE LIMITS OF CONSUMER CHOICE

Although it is essential to distinguish between the environmental impacts of different consumer products, that information alone does not provide a guide for individual action, since consumers do not have complete control over what they consume and how much damage it causes. Until the recent advent of electric utility deregulation in a few states, people who wanted to curtail the air pollution associated with electricity generation couldn't tell their electric company to stop sending them power from an especially dirty coal-fired power plant in their area. Most consumers still have limited control over where their electricity comes from, at least for the next few years. Similarly, those people thirty years ago who were concerned about the health hazards from lead in gasoline had to wait for oil companies to start producing unleaded gas.

Even when individual consumers theoretically have a better choice, they may not view it as a practical alternative. An individual who drives twenty miles to work is unlikely to switch to mass transit if the only available bus takes twice as long, comes only once an hour, and has worn, ripped, graffiti-covered seats. Homeowners are unlikely to purchase benign nonchemical forms of lawn pest control if none of the stores in their town display such products and the sales clerks do not even know how they can be ordered.

In many cases, therefore, what needs to change is the choices available to consumers. The key decisions then need to be made at the corporate, institutional, or government level rather than among individuals. Americans seeking to reduce the environmental impact of products would often be best served by pressuring their local, state, or national government to adopt policies that make it easy, or even required, for manufacturers and users of products to choose the environmentally sound option. For example, the government decision to require appliance manufacturers to list the energy costs of their products not only provided consumers with useful information but gave manufacturers a reason to improve the energy efficiency of their products. Cities that set up curbside recycling programs increase citizen participation in recycling. In the case of leaded gasoline, it was obviously much more effective for the government to ban this dangerous product altogether than to wait for every manufacturer and every consumer in the country to voluntarily switch to the unleaded alternative.

We also have to remember that, paradoxically, consumers are not the only ones who consume things, even though discussions of consumption-environment connections have most often focused on "consumer goods" and what individuals consume. Businesses, organizations, and governments also consume things as part of their activities, and sometimes they are more responsible for pollution than are individuals. We therefore should not assume that the decisions of individual consumers cause most environmental damage. Instead we should focus some of our attention on changing organizations rather than individuals.[11]

Nevertheless, the role of individual Americans and their personal consumption choices remains large. Just as we vote with our ballots on election day, we vote with our dollars when we choose to buy or not to buy particular products. Not only do we send important messages to manufacturers when we buy their products, but we let our family, friends, and neighbors know something about our values. Recycling, for example, would not have become widespread if individuals had not embraced it and begun to practice it in their homes, schools, and offices well before any governments mandated it or even made it convenient. In retrospect, the triumph of recycling is especially impressive because so much of the change in attitudes and individual behavior was instigated by seemingly powerless children and teenagers who prodded their families, schools, and colleges into action.

THE FORGOTTEN IMPACT OF INDIVIDUAL CONSUMERS

The far-reaching impact of individual consumers acting to preserve the environment can be easily overlooked or forgotten. If we turn again to the story of the chlorofluorocarbons that destroy the ozone layer, the main actors may initially seem to be scientists, governments, and chemical companies. Back in 1985, after scientists concluded that human-produced chemicals would destroy ozone but still did not have definitive proof that the ozone layer was actually thinning, representatives of forty-three countries met in Vienna. The resulting document—the Vienna Convention for the Protection of the Ozone Layer—did not commit the signatory nations to phasing out use of the chemicals suspected of destroying ozone, but it was nevertheless a significant achievement. As chief U.S. negotiator Richard Benedick observed, it was "the first effort of the international community to deal with an environmental danger before it erupted."[12]

Over the next few years, as evidence mounted that ozone was actually being lost in the atmosphere, the international community took concrete steps to phase out ozone-depleting substances. In 1987, with the Montreal Protocol on Substances That Deplete the Ozone Layer, thirty-seven signatory nations agreed to limit their release of CFCs and Halons, and for industrial countries to halve CFC emissions by the year 2000. The protocol was revised and strengthened in 1990 and then again in 1992. Chemical companies responded by substituting other chemicals in refrigerators, automobile air conditioners, and other products that formerly required CFCs. Because individual consumers no longer have the choice of selecting products that damage the ozone layer, the ozone layer should heal itself over time. Governments rather than individual consumers bear responsibility for overcoming the remaining obstacles blocking this hopeful scenario—continued CFC production in countries that cannot afford to switch and the smuggling of illegal CFCs by unscrupulous businesses.

So where do individual consumers fit into this story? Well before governments acted, consumers had taken the matter into their own hands. Back in the mid-1970s, in response to scientists' first published articles about threats to the ozone layer, millions of Americans stopped using aerosol spray cans of deodorant and hair spray. Since about half of all fluorocarbons produced at the time went into these cosmetic products, this was not an insignificant step. A 1976 public opinion survey, just two years after publication of the first scientific reports of the CFC threat, showed that more than one-fifth of Americans had shifted from spray cans because of concern for the environment.[13] By demonizing the spray can, environmentally concerned consumers made it financially appealing for cosmetic manufactures to switch their products to other containers and easier for the federal government, in 1978, to ban ozone-depleting chemicals from spray cans. The actions of individual consumers were central to solving what, at the time, was half of the problem.

Then in the 1980s individuals, especially young people, focused their attention on another humble but destructive product—the polystyrene (styrofoam) cup. Environmental activists and environmentally aware high school students heaped scorn on colleagues, family members, and friends caught drinking from polystyrene. Reeling under bad publicity for its heavy use of foam containers and fearing loss of business, the McDonald's fast-food chain appeased an important segment of its target audience by abandoning foam made with CFCs. Other companies followed suit, again showing the impact of individual consumer action.

Unfortunately, the CFC story also reveals the difficulty of trying to solve environmental problems solely through voluntary consumer action. After the demise of the CFC-filled spray can and the polystyrene cup, still other consumer uses of CFCs remained, but most people were reluctant to do anything about them. About 140 million cars and trucks on the road in the early 1990s had CFC-carrying air conditioners that were prone to leaks. As much as half of the CFCs could escape before the car owner noticed a loss of performance. On top of that, car repair shops servicing the systems generally did not worry if the rest of the CFCs escaped into the atmosphere. Although some consumers tried to find service shops that recycled the CFCs, few considered giving up their car air conditioners.

We can see that individual consumer action works best when it does not require significant consumer sacrifice. As Lydia Dotto and Harold Schiff's book on the ozone controversy observes, "Giving up spray cans was a change in life-style that was not particularly hard to live with; it had the perhaps unique advantage of being a virtually painless exercise in environmental responsibility."[14] Unfortunately, there are few such painless exercises.

Moreover, it can be hard to educate millions of consumers about the specific impacts of their consumption choices, and it is easy for them to be confused. Most often Americans do not fully understand the dangers associated with particular products, but sometimes they also remain unaware of developments enhancing product safety. Seventeen years after CFCs were eliminated from spray deodorants and hair sprays, many people still think those products destroy the ozone layer. Similarly, a significant share of the environmentally concerned public is unaware that foam cups are no longer responsible for ozone destruction.

Much of the confusion stems from the difficulty in getting accurate information about problems with consumer goods out to people who are being bombarded by a much larger number of messages encouraging them to buy and cherish particular products. The average American is exposed to about three thousand advertising messages a day, and globally corporations spend over $620 billion each year to make their products seem desirable and to get us to buy them.[15] No wonder it can be hard for people to focus their attention on the environmental dangers of gas-guzzling cars or lawn pesticides.

Although this book alone cannot counterbalance the efforts of the entire advertising industry, it can provide clear information about which American consumption patterns cause the most damage to the environment and what should be done about them. By focusing on the biggest problems and pursuing the solution strategies most likely to work, Americans can make sure that they provide a safe, healthy environment for themselves and future generations.

2

Media Makes the Message—Garbage as a Case Study

R emember the *Mobro 4000*, the barge that in 1987 wandered for months looking for a place to unload its cargo of stinking garbage from Long Island? Making perhaps the most famously ill-fated voyage since the *Titanic*, the barge came to symbolize what many people thought—and still think—is America's most serious environmental problem: trash. Politicians decried a growing shortage of landfill space, while environmentalists accused consumers of throwing too much stuff away. "This barge really dramatizes the nationwide crisis we face with garbage disposal," one reformer said in a typical talk-show appearance.[1]

One result of all this attention was to give a big boost to a nationwide campaign to get households to recycle. Driven by pressures from environmental groups and ordinary consumers, the number of curbside programs around the country soared from under a thousand in 1988 to almost nine thousand in 1996.[2] Curbside programs now serve about 135 million people. And the fraction of household trash—what the professionals call municipal solid waste—now being recycled reached a national average of 27 percent in 1995, up from about 10 percent in 1987, the year the *Mobro* set sail.[3]

The problem is, there was never a real trash crisis. What people took to be a crisis was largely an illusion created by a news-hungry media and some wrong-headed analysis. The trash saga, in fact, is symptomatic of how American consumers, in their eagerness to do the right thing, are sometimes led to focus their attention and energies on issues that have little connection to the real environmental threats we face.

That does not mean that most recycling programs are garbage, as a *New York Times Magazine* article described them in 1996.[4] Not only are they extremely popular, but most actually do good for the environment without taxing town budgets very much. But the events surrounding the *Mobro* crisis—and the great attention paid to the trash problem—raise troubling questions about how America sets its environmental priorities and point to the need for cold, hard facts to guide consumer decisions.

A BRIEF HISTORY OF TRASH

Benjamin Franklin said that nothing is certain in life except death and taxes. He might just as well have added garbage, which is something humans have always produced and have always had to figure out what to do with. In this sense little is new about America's trash problem. We produce more trash than ever before, to be sure, but none of the ways we might deal with it—dumping it, burning it, recycling it, or reducing the amount produced—are fundamentally different from what has been practiced for thousands of years.

For much of history people mostly just dropped their garbage on the ground wherever it suited them. Many ancient cities and even some modern ones literally rose above their garbage by building on top of it.[5] The ancient Trojans, for example, left litter on the floors of their homes and merely covered it with dirt periodically, no doubt to keep down the smell and limit the mess. Over time the floor level rose high enough that roofs had to be raised and doors rebuilt. One engineer has estimated the rate of accumulation of Trojan garbage at 4.7 feet per century.[6]

We may smile at this bit of ancient history, but much the same thing occurred in Manhattan, where the ground level today is six to fifteen feet higher than it was in colonial times, the result of enormous amounts of garbage and other materials being used as fill for construction projects.[7] The practice of "reclaiming" land from the sea in New York and other coastal cities of the United States can be seen as a time-honored exercise in solid waste management.

Dumping has never been the only method of handling human refuse, however. Recycling and reuse were always important in preindustrial societies, as they are today. Before this century much of recycling was done in an informal fashion by roving scavengers who collected the materials people threw out and either burned them for heat, reused them, or sold them. Entire industries were based on recycled products. For example, paper used to be made from recycled fabrics collected from households and fabric manufacturers. The U.S. paper industry originally gravitated to the northeastern United States because it was a concentrated source of cloth rags. It was only when the process for making paper from wood fiber was developed and imported from Germany in the 1860s that the industry began moving west, to be closer to the vast forests that were its new source of raw material.[8]

Or take the case of food waste, which people throughout history have recycled by feeding it to domesticated animals. This practice was quite common in the United States right up until the middle of the twentieth century, when it became incompatible with modern urban lifestyles and health standards. The main problem was that the use of raw garbage as an animal feed caused frequent outbreaks of trichinosis poisoning and other diseases. One such epidemic led to the forced slaughter of hundreds of thousands of pigs in the mid-1950s and resulted in government regulations banning the practice.[9]

THE CHANGING NATURE OF TRASH

So what *is* new or different about the trash problem today? The total quantity of municipal solid waste now generated is certainly larger than it once was. According to figures published by the federal government, the generation of municipal solid waste grew from 88 million tons per year in 1960 to 208 million tons in 1995.[10] (These figures include household waste as well as waste from businesses and a small amount from industry; but household waste accounts for the majority.) Unfortunately, data from before 1960 are not available, but the trend was probably the same.

Surprisingly, though, the amount of waste produced *per person* has not increased as much as many people assume. In 1995 the rate of municipal solid waste generation was about 4.3 pounds per person per day. Yet according to one estimate, residents of Manhattan between 1900 and 1920 were getting rid of an average of twelve hundred pounds of coal ash per person per year, or about 3.3 pounds per person per day. Add to that food wastes and other garbage, plus manure from the millions of horses stabled in American cities at the turn of the century, and it appears that urban dwellers back then (at least in northern cities, where coal and wood were burned for heat) may have produced slightly more waste per person, on average, than Americans do today.[11]

This conclusion at first seems hard to reconcile with the image of Americans consuming and wasting more than ever before—until one realizes that most of the wastes generated in our society have merely moved "upstream" from households to industry. If 200 million tons seems like a lot of stuff for towns and cities to throw away, consider that seventeen industries surveyed by the EPA in the 1980s reported 7.6 *billion* tons of waste generation a year, most of which came from iron and steel production, electric power generation, and the paper and pulp industries. An additional several billion tons of wastes from oil and gas extraction, mining, and manure from agricultural livestock were also reported.[12]

Needless to say, neither horse manure nor coal ash figures very prominently in today's municipal waste stream, and food waste has also declined dramatically in importance (thanks in part to refrigeration, packaging, and garbage Disposalls). In their place the major new addition—accounting for a little over a third of municipal solid waste by weight—has been packaging.[13] This catchall category includes glass bottles and jars, metal drink and soup cans, cardboard boxes and milk cartons, and (since around 1960) plastic containers of all types. The sudden rise of disposable packaging in the 1940s and 1950s attracted so much attention that in 1955 *Life* magazine gave the United States the not-so-flattering label of "the throw-away society."[14]

Several forces were responsible for making packaging such an important part of our national image.[15] One was that improvements in manufacturing processes and the declining cost of natural resources such as wood and aluminum made it cheaper to put products in containers. This packaging mode had clear advantages for the distribution and storage of goods. Another factor was that many industries of the period were busy consolidating their operations into a smaller number of larger factories. Cheaper and more durable packaging made this possible by allowing firms to store products longer and ship them over longer distances.

Even more fundamentally, business was in the process of

forging a new relationship with its customers in which packaging played a more central role than ever before. Fast disappearing were the small general stores and markets offering individual attention to buyers. In their place arose ever-larger and more anonymous supermarkets and department stores. How a product appeared on the shelf consequently became one of the principal methods by which manufacturers attracted customers. As one packaging industry figure put it, packaging became the producer's "sole representative at the sales decision point."[16]

New kinds of packaging encouraged a throwaway lifestyle. Plastic bottles and containers were meant to be discarded, not reused or recycled. The advent of this new consumer convenience put pressure on other container manufacturers to market disposable products as well. As late as the 1940s, virtually all glass bottles were refillable—some of us even remember the time when we put empty milk bottles on the stoop for collection in the morning when the milkman made his rounds. By the 1960s the "no deposit, no return" era of packaging had arrived.

Other materials and products besides packaging also began taking up a larger share of the urban waste stream. Disposable diapers, for example, were practically nonexistent thirty years ago but accounted for about 1.4 percent of solid waste in 1995 (measured by weight). In the same period the share of waste coming from paper and plastic plates and cups more than doubled, from 0.3 percent in 1960 to 0.8 percent in 1995. Office paper and commercial printing soared from 3.1 percent to 9.1 percent (linked no doubt to growth in the use of computers, word processors, and bulk mail).[17] Actually, none of these figures should be taken as very precise, since we have no direct ways to accurately measure how much of each kind of trash is being thrown away. They are all derived from estimates of materials flowing into and out of the economy. But packaging and other disposable items have undoubtedly become much more important in the past fifty years.

RECYCLING, INCINERATION, AND DISPOSAL

One thing that did not change very much until the 1980s was how American cities and towns disposed of their trash. Almost without exception dumping remained king. Of course, the method of dumping was not nearly as haphazard as it had been a few decades earlier, when most garbage and other human and animal wastes were routinely just tossed into streets. By the 1930s virtually all major cities collected their citizens' trash and disposed of it in landfills.

And yet the new collection approach was still not very satisfactory in many respects. Most of the so-called landfills used for dumping trash were really just open pits, which naturally attracted flies and rats and produced many noxious smells and air pollutants. Fires were commonly set to reduce the volume of trash, creating still more pollution. As public complaints about the disposal sites grew, waste engineers in the 1940s and 1950s began promoting the "sanitary" landfill, which was advertised as environmentally safe. But in practice the improvement was not great. Most early sanitary landfills were merely the same old pits, over which a layer of dirt was thrown each day to try to keep down odors and reduce health hazards. Furthermore, only a small fraction of cities and towns adopted this technique. According to a survey by the U.S. Environmental Protection Agency (EPA), as many as fourteen thousand communities were still using open dumps in 1972.[18]

To cope with public complaints and the rising volume of trash, some cities experimented with incineration and recycling. After some false starts incineration became quite widespread, handling an estimated 30 percent of wastes by 1960, while recycling took care of another 6 percent or so.[19] Many apartment buildings and homes had small incinerators in their backyards to take care of yard wastes, paper goods, and other combustible items. But with nothing in the way of pollution controls, the many incinerators in operation around the country aroused even more public consternation. A government report from the mid-1960s described the scene in stark terms: "billowing clouds of smoke drifting from hundreds of thousands of antiquated and overburdened incinerators, open fires at city dumps, wholesale on-site burning of demolition refuse . . . acres of abandoned automobiles that blight the outskirts of our greatest cities."[20]

What is important to recognize is that the public outrage over unsanitary trash disposal methods reflected not so much a worsening of the problem for American cities—although growing waste production certainly put additional stress on the system—as a heightened sensitivity among ordinary people to health and environmental issues. No one who reads what it was like to live in an American city in the late nineteenth century could dispute that conditions in the 1960s were incomparably improved. Visitors to New York around the turn of the century described the city as "a nasal disaster," in which "some streets smell like bad eggs dissolved in ammonia." Hogs by the thousands used to be herded through Cincinnati streets to slaughterhouses, leaving their pungent wastes behind.

But merely eliminating those appalling conditions was not good enough. By the 1960s Americans were learning a great deal about how their society was damaging the environment through books such as Rachel Carson's *Silent Spring*. They were also learning that air and water pollution from cars, industry, wastes, and other sources posed a real hazard to their health. And as the rapidly growing middle class moved out to the suburbs, the greener surroundings they sought proved incompatible with existing waste-disposal methods. Maybe it was because life on the whole had become much less dangerous that people began focusing on problems that had received little attention before. Whatever the reason, Americans began demanding that waste managers do better. And that ultimately set the stage for the *Mobro*.

THE *MOBRO* SAGA

Few people over the age of thirty will forget the sight of the immense barge loaded with more than 3,100 tons of trash that in 1987 wandered from New York to the Gulf of Mexico in search of a place to unload. Almost overnight it made the town of Islip, Long Island, famous throughout the country, no doubt much to the chagrin of its town supervisor, Frank Jones. "We are decent folk who want to solve our own problems," he was quoted as saying, somewhat plaintively, at the time.[21]

The barge quickly became a symbol of what the media and the general public saw as a nationwide garbage crisis. The most widely quoted statistics of the time indicated that the country was quickly running out of space in which to dump its trash. Newspapers cited a survey sponsored by the EPA that found that at least twenty-seven states would face severe landfill problems in the coming three to ten years. The same survey said that half of all municipalities would run out of landfill space within ten years, and a third would run out within five.[22] Encouraged by such statistics, people saw the barge as the window to a future in which their lives would be overrun by foul, smelly garbage.

The amazing thing was how easily both professional analysts and the general public were fooled. It is not that the facts were wrong—many landfills were being shut down, and fewer were being built to replace them. And yes, in some places like New York, this was causing an acute shortage. However, according to archaeologist William Rathje (who runs a project at the University of Arizona that does nothing but study garbage), the United States has probably always been within a few years of a landfill shortage because most landfills are designed to be used for only ten years or so before they are filled up.[23] Furthermore, the new dumps that have been built from the 1980s onward have been much larger than the ones being closed, so even though the number of operating landfills in the country has dropped more than 60 percent since 1988, landfill capacity overall has not decreased.[24] Indeed, were that not so, we would be seeing garbage piling up all over the place.

If a shortage of landfill space was not the cause, why then did the *Mobro* set sail? A tightening of state and federal environmental standards, coupled with some bad decisions by Islip town officials and commercial trash haulers, conspired to launch the ship on its ill-starred voyage. Here is how it happened.

Since the 1970s the federal government had been steadily raising the health and environmental standards for both existing and new landfills. With the passage of laws such as the Air Quality Act of 1967, the Resource Recovery Act of 1970, and the Resource Conservation and Recovery Act of 1976, the old ways of dealing with waste were rapidly becoming unacceptable. Even so-called sanitary landfills came under attack because of observed problems such as toxic chemical leaks into groundwater. Responding to these issues, the EPA's Office of Solid Waste quickly became one of the largest divisions of the government's environmental bureaucracy and began issuing reports advocating urgent reforms.[25]

Prodded by these federal initiatives, individual states also took action to clean up their dumps and landfills. This sensible policy led the New York State Department of Environmental Conservation to order that all landfills on Long Island be shut down by 1990. (The reason Long Island was singled out was its relatively high water table, which meant that chemicals leaking out of trash dumps posed a serious threat to drinking water.)

The new restrictions on dumping left Islip in a dilemma. Hauppauge landfill, Islip's dump, was nearly full, and the town was blocked by the state from expanding the dump while it waited for two new trash incinerators to be completed. In an attempt to conserve the remaining landfill space, the town board voted in November 1986 to bar the dumping there of all trash from businesses. Naturally, this caused the price of commercial trash disposal to soar as haulers demanded a premium to truck the stuff elsewhere.[26]

Seeing an opportunity to make a quick profit, trash haulers in the area banded together to finance a scheme by an Alabama native named Lowell Harrelson, who planned to use a fleet of barges to take Long Island trash to dumps in the South, where disposal prices were very low. The first barge trip to be financed was that of the *Mobro,* which left in March 1987 with 3,186 tons of Islip trash.

The problem was, Harrelson had not secured agreements with southern dumps to accept the trash before the barge departed. A North Carolina dump at first agreed to accept the load, but by the time the barge showed up at the port, state regulators began questioning the deal. The trash owners seemed to be in such a hurry that it was suspected the trash might contain hazardous wastes. And so the barge and its tug were abruptly ordered back to sea. As it resumed its voyage, the news media caught wind of the problem, and publicity about the trip snowballed. Communities along the East Coast and the Gulf of Mexico let it be known they would not accept the trash. Citing national pride, Mexico—which had accepted wastes from the United States before—also turned down the barge's load. Six thousand miles and six months later, the *Mobro* returned to New York, where its cargo was finally off-loaded and incinerated. Ironically, the four hundred tons of ash produced by the incineration wound up back in the Hauppauge landfill, where it had first been rejected, after state regulators finally agreed to allow the landfill's expansion.[27]

Throughout the *Mobro* saga the availability of landfill space was never a problem, although that fact was hard to discern amidst the heated news coverage. To be sure, landfills were in short supply in the Northeast because of recent closures and the difficulty of building new facilities in that densely populated region. However, thousands of tons of trash were already being hauled by truck from the Northeast to dumps in other parts of the country. It was not the amount of trash the *Mobro* carried but the bad publicity associated with it—and suspicions about its hazardous content—that forced the barge back to New York.

On a national scale there was certainly no landfill shortage. Nor is there one today: in 1995 forty-eight states had landfill capacity sufficient to last at least five years, six more than in 1986.[28] Partly this is because of recycling programs and trash incineration, which have managed to stop the growth in the amount of waste being put into landfills each year. But even without such programs most parts of the country would have no difficulty finding places to dump their waste. The basic reason is that the U.S. population density is fairly low—much lower than that of most other industrial countries. Consequently, there are a great many open spaces located far enough from where people live, where carefully designed and operated landfills can be placed.

What about the soaring costs of landfill disposal? This was another factor widely cited at the time as proof of a garbage crisis. Again, the numbers are not in dispute. Back in the 1960s and 1970s, it cost just a few dollars to dispose of a ton of waste at a typical town dump. By 1994 state average tipping fees at landfills ranged from $8 per ton in New Mexico to $75 per ton in New Jersey, with a national average of $31 per ton.[29]

The higher cost, however, was due primarily not to a shortage but rather to the changing economics of the trash hauling business. The cost of waste disposal is driven by two main factors. One is the cost of hauling the trash to the landfill. As the number of landfills has dropped, the average hauling distance has gone up, and with it the price. Much of the trash produced in the Northeast and Mid-Atlantic states is now trucked to places as far away as New Mexico, giving these states by far the highest hauling fees.

The second factor is the cost of building and operating landfills to meet the latest environmental standards. New facilities have clay or plastic linings to prevent chemicals from seeping into groundwater, and they often have underground piping systems to collect noxious gases and liquids that might otherwise escape. Furthermore, every day's load of garbage must be covered with a layer of dirt six inches thick to discourage odors, pests, and bird scavenging. And when a landfill is closed, it must be capped by a clay or plastic layer and covered by topsoil at least six feet deep. All of these items cost money, and the disposal cost is raised further because the extra materials take up space—about a fifth of the available volume.[30] Finally, to obtain permits to site new waste facilities, companies building landfills must pay legal and other fees amounting to hundreds of thousands of dollars. While there may be no physical shortage of landfill space, it is certainly not always easy to win the support of communities potentially affected by them.

At bottom, therefore, the higher cost of waste disposal today is the result of higher environmental standards. Rather than an indication that things are getting worse, they are really a sign that things are getting better: communities are now safer, and people are paying closer attention to the full cost of safe trash disposal. Somehow, though, in the *Mobro* affair this message got lost amidst the media hoopla over the meandering trash barge.

DUMPING ON RECYCLING

Still, you might ask, what harm did the media hype do if the end result was to give a big boost to recycling programs? Critics of recycling—who seem to be getting more numerous in today's antiregulatory political environment—have a lot to say on that subject. Their argument is that recycling programs are not as beneficial as they appear to be and actually may distract from more useful things consumers might do to protect the environment. A *New York Times Magazine* article about recycling, entitled "What a Waste," claimed, "Recycling may be the most wasteful activity in modern America: a waste of time and money, waste of human and natural resources." The *Wall Street Journal* argued, "Curbside Recycling Comforts the Soul, But Benefits are Scant." Other recent books and articles make clear that dumping on recycling is a fashionable trend.

Adversity is nothing new to the recycling movement. The emergence of environmental politics in the late 1960s and early 1970s at first gave a shot in the arm to then-languishing efforts to tame the throwaway society. A hallmark of the period was the rise of community-based recycling programs, which were mostly run by volunteers. According to one estimate, as many as three thousand recycling centers were organized in the months before and after Earth Day in 1970. In 1976 passage of the Resource Conservation and Recovery Act lent even more impetus to the movement by putting the EPA in charge of regulating waste facilities. By the late 1970s the EPA Office of Solid Waste was calling for a national recycling target of 25 percent. At the time only about 5 to 7 percent of city trash was being recycled.[31]

In the early 1980s, however, the recycling movement seemed to come to a halt. One reason was that the focus of official policy shifted from recycling to converting trash to energy in incinerators. Much of this shift can be attributed to the attitudes of solid waste professionals, most of whom did not take recycling seriously, seeing it as complicated, inconvenient, and too dependent on voluntary household participation to make much of a dent in the waste disposal problem. High-tech incinerators capable of burning almost everything in the waste stream and producing steam and power at the same time seemed a far better solution. Wildly fluctuating prices for recycled materials also forced some early recycling programs to shut down or cut back. In the end, despite the success of numerous community-based recycling programs, the average rate of recycling in the country in the early 1980s rose no higher than about 10 percent.[32]

THE SUCCESS OF RECYCLING PROGRAMS

The *Mobro* episode was one of many events that combined to rejuvenate the recycling movement in the mid-to-late 1980s. Most involved conflicts over proposed landfills and waste-to-energy incinerators. A prominent example of the latter was community-based opposition to the LANCER (Los Angeles City Energy Recovery) project. Despite initially enjoying strong support from many political and businesses leaders, including L.A. mayor Tom Bradley, the incinerator proposal foundered in the face of loud complaints about both its $235 million price tag and its possible impacts on the health of residents in the community where it was to be located. One of the most critical issues was uncertainty about the toxicity of the ash that would be produced by the facility and dumped in a landfill. Chemical tests of ash samples seemed to support classifying the ash as nonhazardous, but no record was kept of the kinds of materials that had gone into the tested ash, leading to suspicions that the test was rigged. As Gilbert Lindsay, a leading backer of LANCER on the city council, in the end observed ruefully about his constituents: "They are just frightened to death."[33]

In the wake of widely publicized events like these and growing public enthusiasm for recycling, cities and towns throughout the country moved with amazing speed to institute recycling programs. Different communities adopted different strategies. Many passed mandatory recycling statutes requiring homeowners to place materials like newspapers and aluminum cans in colored bins for collection at curbside. Although rarely backed by stiff fines or other enforcement measures, the statutes seemed to be effective at getting households to participate in curbside recycling programs. For example, the participation rate in a Fitchburg, Ohio, program tripled after it became mandatory, reaching 66 percent after only a few months.[34] Some states and communities chose to ban the disposal in landfills of certain kinds of waste, particularly yard trimmings such as grass, leaves, and branches. And still others imposed fees on homeowners or created other incentives like bottle deposits to encourage greater recycling and a reduction in the weight or volume of discards.

The results are undeniably impressive. The national average recycling rate jumped from around 10 percent (1985) to 27 percent (1995) in the space of just ten years.[35] The current level exceeds the EPA's national recycling target of 25 percent, reestablished in the late 1980s. The leading state, Minnesota, boasted a rate of 46 percent in 1995, a remarkable achievement considering that solid waste engineers used to predict that no more than 10 or 15 percent of trash could be recycled.[36] Many states aim to go even higher, although in many cases their self-imposed deadlines have already passed. California plans to recycle half of its waste by the year 2000; New Jersey's goal was 60 percent by 1995 (the reported 1995 rate was 42 percent); Texas was seeking a more modest 25 percent recycling rate by 1995 (its 1994 rate was 14 percent).[37] (These figures are not entirely comparable, since the states and the federal government define and measure wastes in different ways.)

Even more striking is how our culture has wholeheartedly adopted the recycling ethic. Elementary schools and television programs like *Sesame Street* hammer home to children the virtues of reusing milk cartons, soda bottles, paper, and other household items. Probably most parents at one time or another have received humbling lectures from their children after being caught tossing a glass jar or newspaper in the trash can. And by and large parents share their children's commitment. Indeed, much of the success of recycling programs can be attributed to the quasi-religious support they receive from ordinary consumers. In a 1990 Gallup poll, 80 to 85 percent of people said they or their households had participated in some aspect of recycling; no other identifiable environmental action even came close to this level of support.[38]

That recycling's popularity has endured is all the more surprising considering the many glitches and inconveniences that have accompanied the start-up of curbside programs. Many of us have experienced the annoyance of trying to satisfy complicated rules about what can and cannot be recycled. Glass jars—but not their tops? Plastics number 2 and 3—but not number 1? Can glossy color catalogs go in the bin with black-and-white newsprint? Still, there is no sign that the public is becoming impatient, so convinced are people of the virtues of recycling.

THE CRITICS' CASE AGAINST RECYCLING

There is nothing so tempting to gore as a sacred cow. And so, ironically, it may be the very popularity of recycling programs and the halo of political correctness surrounding them that account for the wave of criticism directed at them in recent years. What are the critics saying? And do their criticisms make sense?

The critics have adopted three main lines of attack. The first is to say that the problem that recycling programs were mainly intended to solve—the famous garbage crisis—was largely a media-generated illusion. On this point the critics are mostly right. Certainly that is true about landfill space. As the *New York Times Magazine* article pointed out, "The *Mobro*'s saga was presented as a grim harbinger of future landfill scarcity, but it actually represented a short-lived scare caused by new environmental regulations."[39] For their part, recycling supporters say landfills are not running out of space precisely because recycling programs have been so successful at diverting waste from them. However, it seems unlikely that the 17 percent increase in the recycling rate since the 1980s really spelled the difference between yesterday's crisis and today's complacency.

Another "mythical tenet of the garbage crisis" that the critics gleefully skewer is the notion that ordinary city trash presents a serious health risk for the general public. By and large it does not—and whatever risk it does pose will diminish with time as new landfill regulations take effect. Most of the materials discarded in landfills are fairly innocuous—paper, yard waste, construction debris. Even the notorious plastics are safe for precisely the reason they have been condemned: They do not degrade with time. A small percentage of truly toxic materials, such as solvents, paints, cleaners, and mercury- and lead-filled batteries, are present in household waste, but most of these are likely to remain within landfills, especially the modern clay- or plastic-lined ones. In any case, most curbside recycling programs do nothing to eliminate these hazardous substances from the waste stream, concentrating instead on glass, paper, plastics, and steel and aluminum cans.

That is not to say that currently operating municipal landfills pose no threat at all; and some, like Staten Island's Fresh

Kills landfill, are thoroughly detested by nearby residents. But it is well to remember that any hazards posed by the three thousand or so municipal landfills now in operation are utterly dwarfed by those created by industrial waste facilities. There are more than 200,000 industrial waste dumps of various kinds in the country, most of them "surface impoundments," which are basically natural or man-made ponds containing liquid wastes. Although officially judged to be "nonhazardous," many of these sites contain a veritable soup of compounds that could seriously harm the environment, such as oil and gas drilling wastes, fertilizers and other agricultural chemicals, and residues from organic chemical and plastics production.

Lending support to the critics, an EPA study released in 1987 classed sixteen thousand municipal landfills, sludge and refuse incinerators, and surface impoundments as only a "medium" health risk, far down the list of environmental hazards.[40] Most of the sites in this group, in fact, were either already closed or have since closed, indicating that the problem today is mainly one of identifying the most dangerous ones and cleaning them up. About a sixth of sites slated for Superfund cleanup are former municipal waste dumps, largely old ones with no liners, leachate collection systems, or other environmental controls, and containing a mix of both hazardous industrial wastes and ordinary household wastes.

Another EPA study suggested that if municipal solid waste landfills continued to operate under federal regulations, the overall cancer risk would average fewer than 0.08 cases per year, or about one case every twelve years.[41] And federal regulations that went into effect in 1997 are far more strict than those in place when this estimate was made in the late 1980s. "I find it hard to argue that waste management is our most urgent environmental problem," says Frank Ackerman, a solid waste expert who used to work for the Tellus Institute, an environmental consulting firm. "At most, it is one among many issues that clamor for our attention. Other problems pose more serious threats to our well-being than the disposal of solid waste."[42]

DOES RECYCLING PAY?

Even if the garbage crisis was a weak motivation for recycling programs, that does not automatically mean they should now be abandoned. Still, the critics make the case that it means just that. They rely on two other arguments: one, that recycling programs are too expensive ("At least by any practical, short-term measure, curbside recycling doesn't pay," according to *The Wall Street Journal*[43]); and two, perhaps most provocatively, that they actually hurt the environment. On these two points, however, the critics are on much shakier ground.

One problem is that, in attacking the costs of recycling, the critics often focus on a few egregious (and suspect) cases while ignoring the bulk of experience. Writing in *Issues in Science and Technology*, a magazine for Washington policymakers, two engineers and an economist give the example of Pittsburgh, where they claim it cost $470 per ton to recycle but only $94 per ton to collect and dispose of ordinary garbage.[44] Even if true— and other evidence indicates that, whatever problems the Pittsburgh program suffered early on, it is now recycling at a much lower cost than the article claims—the case is not representative of the cost of recycling in most towns and cities, and it ignores revenues from selling recycled materials.

A more systematic comparison shows that recycling is indeed more expensive, on average, than ordinary trash disposal, but in some years it saves money, and overall the excess cost is not great. Here are the three main factors that lead to that conclusion:

- **Cost of recycling programs.** According to Ackerman, the nationwide average cost of curbside recycling programs is about $123 per ton for collection and a further $50 per ton for separation and processing of recyclable materials, giving a total of $173 per ton. (Individual program costs can deviate widely from this average.)

· **Value of recycled materials.** The market price for scrap materials varies greatly in response to supply and demand. In 1993 there was a glut of recycled materials such as paper, so the average selling price was just $46 per ton. But in 1995 there was a jump in demand, resulting in an average selling price of $165 per ton. Prices have since dropped back to more like 1993 levels.

· **Cost of ordinary trash disposal.** Recycling programs reduce ordinary trash disposal costs by an average of $31 per ton (the national average landfill tipping fee). In some places the avoided trash disposal cost is a lot higher than $31 per ton—in Seattle, Washington, for instance, it is $70 per ton. In others, of course, it is much lower.[45]

If we assume that the average long-term selling price of recycled materials is about $70 per ton, then on a national average basis, curbside programs lose about $72 per ton of materials collected.[46] With the average household recycling about a fifth of a ton of waste each year, the excess cost per household appears to be about $15 per year, hardly a major drain on town or family budgets.

Another important factor overlooked by the critics is that the cost of recycling tends to go down as more people participate and recycle more things. The main reason is that the more stuff there is to pick up, the fewer houses each truck has to visit before it is full and heads off to a recycling center, which means lower fuel, maintenance, and labor costs per truckload. In the highest-cost cities the problem is often that household participation rates are very low. In the Pittsburgh example, where the recycling cost was estimated to be $470 per ton, the recycling rate was reported to be only about 7 percent of household waste collected and about 5 percent of all municipal solid waste. An independent survey showed that in communities with recycling rates comparable to this, the average recycling collection cost was $285 per ton. But in communities where the recycling rate was over 20 percent, the collection cost averaged $93 per ton, or two-thirds less.[47]

The recycling critics go even farther astray when they charge that curbside programs actually hurt the environment. Some of them argue that because recycling programs cost more than traditional waste disposal, they most likely have greater environmental emissions: "The variety of activities associated with the two- to four-fold increase in costs associated with recycling is almost certain to result in a net increase in resource use and environmental discharges," according to the *Issues in Science and Technology* article. But even if the cost figures were correct—and as we have seen, they are not representative of most programs—money is a crude yardstick, at best, with which to measure pollution.

A much better approach is to examine the pollutant emissions of the different waste disposal strategies directly. Virtually all studies that have done this have come down decisively on the side of recycling. A recent one performed by Franklin Associates indicates that curbside recycling programs reduce energy use and many kinds of air and water pollution. In no respect was ordinary trash disposal deemed environmentally superior. According to the report, a typical curbside recycling program that collects steel and aluminum containers, newspapers, glass, and certain kinds of plastic will eliminate, for every ton of waste processed, 620 pounds of carbon dioxide, 30 pounds of methane, 5 pounds of carbon monoxide, 2.5 pounds of particulate matter (soot and ash), and varying amounts of other pollutants. The greatest benefits come from replacing virgin raw materials such as wood and petroleum in manufacturing processes with recycled materials. It takes less than 25 percent as much energy to make aluminum cans from recycled cans as from virgin ore, for instance.[48]

SETTING PRIORITIES

Despite the many weaknesses in their case, the critics of recycling make one telling point: A single-minded emphasis on recycling may distract consumers from other, possibly more effective strategies for protecting the environment. As we have seen, the problem that recycling programs were originally trumpeted as solving—the garbage crisis—was exaggerated and magnified by a lot of media hype. If the programs turned out to be worthwhile, that may be largely an accident.

Certainly, plenty of other consumer obsessions—many involving trash—have turned out to be a waste of time. A classic example is the brief glorification of cloth diapers. (We deal with the cloth-versus-disposable-diaper debate in chapter 6.) Such episodes demonstrate that consumers need far more solid, factual information about the choices that confront them than they usually get.

The problem is not just that consumers may waste a lot of time and effort on supposedly "green" actions that do not benefit (or may even hurt) the environment. Perhaps even more important, repeated instances in which wrong or misleading information is given can turn even the most enthusiastic and committed green consumers into cynics. Like the boy who cried wolf, environmental activists who loudly trumpet dangers that later prove false or exaggerated risk turning off the very constituents they are trying to mobilize.

Then there is the issue of setting priorities. Curbside recycling has been the most successful consumer-oriented environmental strategy by far. But what other things might individual consumers and communities be doing? What about establishing alternative transportation to cut air pollution? Or instituting new zoning standards to reduce the impacts of housing developments? And what should we do about things we buy that cannot be recycled but are manufactured with large amounts of energy and large releases of toxic chemicals? At the moment there is little information to help individuals and communities figure out which of the many actions they could take deserve the most effort.

3

The Real Impacts of Household Consumption

Americans spend their money on many different things—from apples and armchairs to zinnias and zip drives. Which of all these things cause the greatest problems for the environment, and which are relatively benign? One lesson of the *Mobro* saga is that American consumers need more and better information about the actual impact of their various activities on the environment. That's what we will try to provide in this chapter.

We will divide all consumer spending into categories and show which cause serious problems and which do not. In perhaps our most striking finding, we will show how just seven spending categories are responsible for most of the environmental damage attributable to consumers.

The first step in reaching this conclusion was to determine which environmental problems pose the greatest threat to human health and the earth's ecology. We have chosen to focus on just four problems. Here they are in alphabetical order:

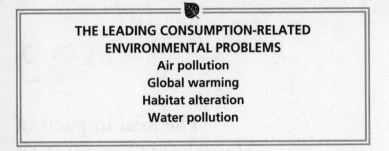

**THE LEADING CONSUMPTION-RELATED
ENVIRONMENTAL PROBLEMS**
Air pollution
Global warming
Habitat alteration
Water pollution

How did we arrive at this list? The process is described in detail in Appendix A of this book, but to summarize it briefly, we relied mainly on two comprehensive environmental studies, or risk assessments, one conducted by the EPA, the other by the California Comparative Risk Project.[1] These studies collected all available scientific data on the health and ecological impacts of a wide range of human activities and ranked them according to severity (high, medium, or low). We selected only the problems that ranked as medium or high risks in either study. We then whittled the list down further by excluding problems not linked to *current* household consumption or activities. That meant dropping, in particular, pollution from inactive hazardous waste sites and mines, as well as from chemicals such as PCBs that have already been banned or whose use is greatly curtailed. It also meant excluding stratospheric ozone depletion, since most of the chemicals that damage the ozone layer are being phased out under international treaties and are no longer sold in the United States. Of course, we do not mean to imply that these problems are insignificant, but decisions made by consumers from this day forward will do little either to alleviate or exacerbate them.

The resulting list of environmental problems is deceptively short, as each category actually includes a wide variety of impacts and sources:

Air Pollution

Two common outdoor air pollutants, ozone and fine particulate matter, pose an especially high risk to public health.[2] Most are generated directly or indirectly by the burning of fossil fuels, such as gasoline in cars and coal in power plants. The California report estimates that as many as three thousand deaths each year in California alone are caused by particulate matter, with an additional 60,000 to 200,000 cases of respiratory infections in children and up to 2 million nonfatal asthma attacks due to both particulates and ozone. A more recent national study indicates that fine particles with a diameter of less than 10 micrometers (PM_{10}) cause about 64,000 extra deaths every year, corresponding to an increase of about 31 percent in the mortality rate from cardiopulmonary causes in the most polluted cities.[3]

Certain highly toxic air pollutants, although not as widespread as ozone and particulate matter, also pose a serious health risk. The toxic pollutant category includes many chemicals not under federal regulation, such as evaporated pesticides and emissions from chemical plants, metallurgical processes, and sewage treatment plants. Although the health effects of most of these chemicals are not well known, the EPA risk assessment estimated about two thousand cancers a year nationwide from just twenty of the unregulated substances.

Although we think of it mainly as a scourge of densely populated cities, air pollution also affects plants and wildlife in rural areas. Pollutants such as ozone, nitrogen oxides, and sulfur dioxide are known to damage coniferous trees and may harm other plants as well. A closely related problem that occurs mainly in the East is acid deposition ("acid rain"), which arises when sulfuric and nitric acids are formed in the atmosphere and precipitate as rain or snow. These chemicals affect trees and change the acid balance of lakes and streams. About twelve hundred lakes in the United States, or 4 percent of vulnerable lakes, have become fully acidified because of acid rain, and little can now live in them. Another 5 percent are sufficiently acidified that some aquatic life is threatened.

Global Warming

Scientific data indicates that the earth has gotten warmer over the past 100 years. Not only have global average temperatures increased, by an average of 0.5 to 1.1 degrees Fahrenheit, but glaciers have retreated, the mean sea level has risen, and other unmistakable signs of warming have been detected. Have these changes been caused, at least in part, by human emissions of greenhouse gases, most notably carbon dioxide? Are even more dramatic changes in store for the future?

Ten years ago hundreds of scientists around the world began to work through the Intergovernmental Panel on Climate Change to evaluate all the research that has been done on global warming and to reach conclusions about what is known and what remains to be determined. Over time they have become more confident in their projections. Although no one can predict the future with absolute certainty, the scientists believe that the climate has very probably already begun to change because of human activities and they expect a temperature rise of a few degrees in the coming decades.[4] For this reason many climate experts have called for strong international action to reduce human emissions of greenhouse gases. This view has been supported by the world's leading senior scientists, including the majority of living Nobel prize winners in the sciences, who in 1997 called global warming "one of the most serious threats to the planet and to future generations."[5]

A temperature change of a few degrees may not seem like a lot, but it could be enough to alter the range of natural habitats and affect the distribution of the species within them. It would also likely cause changes in precipitation patterns, resulting in more summer dryness in some places but less in others, for example. Rising sea levels caused by melting glaciers and thermally expanding sea water would inundate coastal areas and harm coastal wetlands. Under the best scenarios these changes will occur gradually, but there is a risk of abrupt shifts in climate that could have catastrophic results not only for plants and wildlife but also for the global economy.

Scientists are only just beginning to assess the potential impacts of global warming on human health. A recent study by the World Health Organization, the World Meteorological Organization, and the UN Environment Programme points to a variety of potential health concerns, including increased heat stress, higher air pollution (because heat promotes certain pollution-forming chemical reactions), and increased incidence of certain waterborne and food-borne infections.[6]

In addition, a sense of fairness to the citizens of other countries should dictate that a high priority be given to reducing U.S. emissions of greenhouse gases. With only about 5 percent of the world's population, the United States produces about 20 percent of global emissions from human sources. Furthermore, it is the poorest developing countries that are likely to suffer the greatest health consequences because they have less institutional capacity and fewer financial resources to adapt to changing climate.

Habitat Alteration

Although poaching and the trade in endangered species are significant concerns, the greatest threat to wildlife by far is the human destruction or alteration of natural habitats. Within the United States the most serious habitat disturbances arise from activities such as logging, mining, agriculture, marine fishing, diversion of water for agriculture, and suburban sprawl.

As an example, in the past few decades in many areas, wildlife biologists have observed a decline in the numbers of neotropical migratory birds. At first it was assumed that this decline was caused mainly by deforestation of the birds' winter habitats in Central America and the Caribbean. But research has found that land development in the United States may be as much to blame. As people move into formerly wooded areas, for example, they are usually accompanied by cats, raccoons, squirrels, chipmunks, blue jays, cowbirds, and other animals that harass and kill smaller birds. In one study using fake nests, "[t]he eggs were raided constantly by a dozen or so different types of predators . . . most of them animals that live near human communities, feeding on garbage or handouts."[7] For other types of birds, such as prairie warblers, agriculture is to blame for disrupting their habitats. Still others, such as vultures and eagles, are threatened by toxic chemicals that are present in the food they eat and cause problems such as sterility and embrittled eggs.

When it comes to the alteration of freshwater habitats, hydroelectric dams, reservoirs, and water diversions of all kinds are often to blame, as they can radically change the salinity, sedimentation, and other characteristics of rivers. This can affect many threatened species, as well as migrating fish. For instance, water diversions caused the winter run of Chinook salmon in the Sacramento River system to drop from nearly 120,000 in 1968 to an estimated 100 in 1991.

Preserving natural habitats is not only good for plants and animals, but it also directly benefits people. In recent years scientists have become increasingly conscious of the many valuable services these ecosystems perform, including purifying air and water, controlling floods, detoxifying wastes, pollinating crops and natural vegetation, and helping to control potential agricultural pests.[8] The economic value of these services to humans is large and doesn't even count the emotional and psychological benefit many people feel they get from coming in contact with nature.

Water Pollution

The category of water pollution covers many different chemicals and compounds from a variety of sources. Despite tightened regulations over the years, some industries still discharge toxic chemicals into water, which can contaminate drinking water, kill plant life, and contaminate fish. Leading examples include mercury, cadmium, and other heavy metals released in mining and various industrial activities, numerous organic compounds discharged from petrochemical factories, and pesticides washed off agricultural fields and urban yards.

In addition to such highly toxic pollutants, various more common water pollutants can be harmful to humans and wildlife in substantial quantities. For example, soil eroded from cropland, range land, recently logged forest land, and construction sites frequently winds up in lakes, streams, and coastal waters, affecting the penetration of sunlight and choking off plants. Fertilizers that are washed off of cropland, as well as wastes from livestock, also frequently contaminate water bodies. (In one shocking case, according to a U.S. Department of Agriculture report, "a dike around a large hog-waste lagoon in North Carolina failed, releasing an estimated 25 million gallons of hog waste—twice the volume of the oil spilled by the Exxon Valdez—into nearby fields, streams, and a river. The spill killed virtually all aquatic life in a 17-mile stretch of river between Richlands and Jacksonville, North Carolina."[9]) Improved treatments notwithstanding, discharges from municipal sewage facilities and storm drains can cause elevated bacteria and nutrient levels.

THE CONSUMER'S ROLE

After determining the environmental problems to focus on, we created a set of environmental indexes so we could quantify the contribution of various activities to each problem area. The indexes included the number of tons of greenhouse gases, common and toxic air pollutants, and common and toxic water pollutants emitted each year. To represent sources of habitat alteration, we created indexes of consumptive water use (in gallons per day) and of "ecologically significant" land use (in acres, adjusted to take into account the relationship between different types of land use and species endangerment patterns).

Then we set about investigating how the environmental impacts are linked to household purchases and activities. We created a model of the U.S. economy that traces environmental impacts from all kinds of industrial and agricultural activity down through the production chain to individual consumer products and services. We added the direct effects of household activity, such as air pollution produced by home furnaces. We then used this model to calculate the impacts of household spending in 134 categories, including items as diverse as cheese and carpets. These categories were aggregated into fifty major categories (e.g., dairy products, furnishings), and then into ten broad activity areas (e.g., food, household operations). (In Appendix A, we will explain our research method in detail and assess its strengths and limitations, but here we want to focus on our results.)

We discovered that just seven out of the fifty major categories account for a majority of the environmental impacts (except toxic water pollution) linked to consumer behavior. The list of the seven most damaging kinds of consumption is given in the box below, in rough order of decreasing importance. Through the rest of this chapter, we will show you why these seven cate-

---

THE MOST HARMFUL CONSUMER ACTIVITIES
Cars and light trucks
Meat and poultry
Fruit, vegetables, and grains
Home heating, hot water, and air conditioning
Household appliances and lighting
Home construction
Household water and sewage

gories are so significant and why other items don't make the list. We will also give you an overall picture of how the spending of the average American impacts the environment.

THE BIG PICTURE

Before we discuss some of the most important and interesting findings, we want to give you an overview of the relationship between consumer spending and environmental problems. The percentages in table 3.1 show the fraction of environmental impacts due to each of the ten broad activity areas: transportation, food, household operations, housing, personal items and services, medical, yard care, private education, financial and legal services, and "other." Again, they are listed in rough order of decreasing overall impact.

You will notice a surprising degree of variation in the

Table 3.1. Environmental Impacts per Household

	Global Warming	Air Pollution		Water Pollution		Habitat Alteration	
ACTIVITY AREA	GREENHOUSE GASES	COMMON	TOXIC	COMMON	TOXIC	WATER USE	LAND USE
Transportation	32%	28%	51%	7%	23%	2%	15%
Food	12	17	9	38	22	73	45
Household operations	35	32	20	21	14	11	4
SUBTOTAL	80%	77%	80%	67%	59%	86%	64%
Housing	6	7	4	10	10	2	26
Personal items and services	6	7	6	7	12	6	5
Medical	6	6	6	4	13	3	3
Yard care	0	1	2	9	3	3	0
Private education	1	1	0	0	1	0	0
Financial and legal	1	1	1	1	1	0	1
Other	1	1	0	2	1	0	0

impacts of the ten household activity areas. Transportation and household operations (heat, hot water, lighting, and appliances, among other things) account for thirty times as much common air pollution as yard activities or education expenses, for instance, while food purchases cause five times as much common water pollution as transportation.

The variation is important because it shows that how households spend their money does indeed matter. Nothing would be more discouraging than to discover that no matter what we do (short of living in a cave), about the same amount of environmental damage will result. This table demonstrates, on the contrary, that some kinds of consumption are *much* worse for the environment than others.

Furthermore, just three of the household activity areas— food, household operations, and transportation—account for the majority of environmental impacts. The reason is not simply that people spend more money in these areas than in others. We spend as much on medical care and personal items as we do on household operations, yet the latter produce six times the emissions of greenhouse gases. Rather, something about the way these services are provided or used results in a much greater impact on the environment.

Now let's look at some of the details behind the numbers. What are the main contributors to environmental harm in each area? And why? For example, within household operations, how do air conditioners stack up against refrigerators, wood stoves, electric lights, and furniture? We will focus on six of the ten areas on the table: transportation, food, running a household, housing, some personal items and services, and yard care. We will not talk about the impacts of medical expenses, which although substantial are not something over which consumers have very much control. The impacts of the other expenditure categories (private education, financial and legal, and other) are too small to bother with here.

TRANSPORTATION

We have all heard something of the evils of the automobile—pollution, the blight of highways, junkyards filled with wrecked cars and tires. But when analyzed objectively, how does it stack up against the other sources of environmental harm?

For the most part, unfortunately, transportation, particularly automobiles, deserves its bad reputation. Our findings indicate that household use of transportation, ranging from recreational boating to cars to passenger air travel, is responsible for 28 to 51 percent of greenhouse gases and air pollution and 23 percent of toxic water pollution. Our use of transportation even poses a significant threat to wildlife through the use of land for roads and highways.

To see how these problems are distributed among different modes of transportation, we can divide the transportation sector into the following broad categories:

- Personal cars and light trucks (including minivans and pickup trucks)
- Personal aircraft, recreational boats, and off-road vehicles
- Passenger air, intercity rail, ferry, and intercity bus travel
- Other (includes motorcycles, trailers, mass transit)

The impacts in each case include both vehicle operations and manufacturing. (As in other consumer categories, impacts from the disposal of cars, tires, batteries, and similar items by households are not counted here, but are folded into the impacts of household solid waste.)

Figure 3.1 shows how the impacts are distributed across the categories. The total length of each bar shows the proportion of total consumer-related environmental impacts due to that form of transportation. This lets us focus our attention on the areas where transportation is a significant part of the overall problem. We can see at a glance, for instance, that it accounts for 50 percent of toxic air pollution and almost 30 percent of

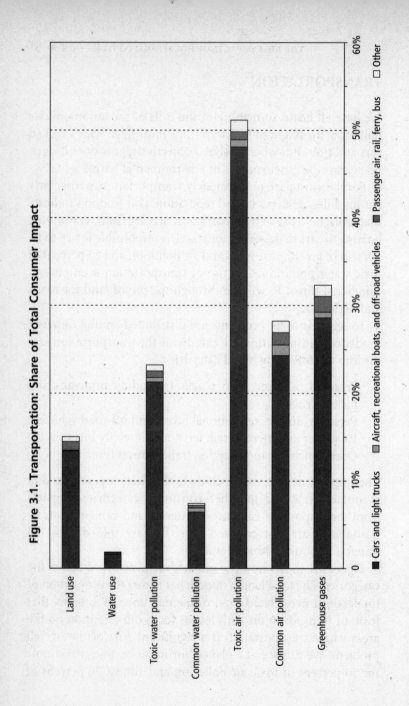

Figure 3.1. Transportation: Share of Total Consumer Impact

Categories along horizontal axis: Land use, Water use, Toxic water pollution, Common water pollution, Toxic air pollution, Common air pollution, Greenhouse gases

Legend: Cars and light trucks · Aircraft, recreational boats, and off-road vehicles · Passenger air, rail, ferry, bus · Other common air pollution, while it contributes very little to water use.

Not surprisingly, among the transportation modes, automobiles and light trucks, including minivans and sport utility vehicles, dominate every sector, mainly because they account for the vast majority of personal vehicle travel (about 84 percent, measured by passenger miles[10]). Because this is such a significant category, it is instructive to look at the kinds of impacts cars and trucks produce and how they are distributed between manufacturing, maintenance, and fuel use.

In terms of greenhouse gases, the average new car is responsible for about 2 metric tons of carbon emissions each year. But because many households own more than one vehicle, and when emissions in the production of maintenance items (fuel oil, batteries, and so on) are counted, the average emissions per household amount to 3.7 tons per year, just over one-fourth of all greenhouse gas emissions linked to household purchases. About 15 percent of the emissions can be traced to the manufacturing of the vehicles and maintenance items, while the remaining 85 percent is caused by their use (primarily from the burning of gasoline).[11]

The data on common air pollution tell a similar story. Household ownership and use of cars and light trucks account for about a quarter of all such emissions; the impacts of driving contribute about four-fifths of the automobile total. An even greater proportion of *toxic* air emissions—over 45 percent—comes from cars and light trucks, with all but 10 percent of the automobile contribution attributable to driving.

The automobile's impact on water pollution is more intriguing. What could be the source of the large toxic chemical releases? Here the problem lies squarely with car manufacturing, in particular with the production of steel, batteries, paints, plastics, aluminum, lubricants, fluids, and other items. When the manufacturing of items for car maintenance is included, batteries become easily the most important source of toxic water pollution. Indeed, our analysis suggests that about 4 percent of toxic chemicals released into water come solely from factories manufacturing batteries for household vehicles.

About a third of the automobile's contribution to common water pollution is from runoff of salt and other chemicals applied to roads. The substantial automobile share of land use is also due to the damage caused by roads and highways to ecosystems. This is one case where the impacts are clearly not in the consumer's direct control, so it is tempting to ignore them. We need to recognize, however, that the tremendous emphasis on automobiles in our society is behind much road construction, and that roads have a major impact on wildlife in one way or another. Including the effects of roads in our analysis helps remind us of our responsibility for how our society meets its transportation needs.

As indicated in figure 3.1, all of the other categories of transportation make a fairly small contribution to our environmental problems overall. This is not to say that every one of these alternative modes of transportation is better than automobiles for the environment; it's just that they are not used nearly as much. To make a head-to-head comparison, we can divide the impacts of each mode by the number of miles passengers traveled. Table 3.2 shows this comparison using intercity bus travel as the baseline.[12]

The data in this table have to be treated with some caution, since the emissions and passenger mile data come from different sources and may not be entirely consistent. Also, we don't have passenger-mile data for subways and urban light rail systems, personal boats and aircraft, off-road vehicles, and ferries and cruise ships. Nevertheless, the table suggests that overall, intercity bus travel is the winner, while motorcycles and automobiles have the greatest impacts in most categories relative to the service they provide.

The finding for motorcycles is perhaps surprising at first glance. Although motorcycles get over twice the average fuel

Table 3.2. Impacts per Passenger Mile by Transportation Mode, Compared with Bus Travel

TRANSPORT MODE	Global Warming GREENHOUSE GASES	Air Pollution		Water Pollution		Habitat Alteration	
		COMMON	TOXIC	COMMON	TOXIC	WATER USE	LAND USE
Cars and light trucks	3.0	1.6	4.2	1.8	2.7	1.2	4.4
Motorcycles	3.0	3.3	9.1	3.9	11.1	4.2	5.9
Passenger air travel	1.7	0.7	0.6	1.0	0.8	1.0	3.5
Passenger rail travel	1.2	2.2	0.2	0.6	1.5	0.7	7.8
Intercity bus travel	1	1	1	1	1	1	1

economy of cars and light trucks, their small engines have no catalytic converters or other pollution controls, resulting in high air emissions. Also, the proportion of steel and other metals in motorcycles is high compared with their total weight, resulting in relatively high toxic air and water pollutant emissions. In addition, motorcycles usually carry only one passenger, which raises the impact per passenger mile.

The high common air pollution emissions from intercity passenger rail service (meaning Amtrak) is a consequence of two facts: most passenger trains are pulled by diesel engines that have few emissions controls,[13] and ridership is relatively low on many train routes.[14] The extensive track network, which is not as heavily used as highways, also makes land use impacts relatively high. Nevertheless, in most categories, intercity rail travel, as well as air and intercity bus travel, have lower impacts than automobiles and motorcycles. This may be particularly surprising for air travel. However, modern jet aircraft are relatively efficient in fuel use, while average aircraft load factors are quite high—65 percent. By comparison, cars carry an average of only 1.9 passengers, which for a five-person car implies a load factor of just 37 percent.

Although we could not include personal aircraft, recreational boats, and off-road vehicles in this table because of a lack of passenger-mile data, all of them are well known to generate disproportionately large amounts of air pollution. Off-road vehicles, including snowmobiles, dirt bikes, go-carts, and the like, have small, uncontrolled engines and are often operated under conditions (slow speeds, up and down hills) that greatly increase their emissions. EPA data suggest that the emissions rate for two-stroke off-road vehicles may be as much as ten times that of four-stroke on-road motorcycles and fifteen times that of ordinary cars.[15] Recreational boats—and to a lesser degree, personal aircraft—have similar characteristics. Expensive toys, both for the consumer and the environment!

FOOD

Food production has a pervasive impact on the environment. About 60 percent of our country's land area is devoted either to crops or to livestock grazing, often greatly diminishing its ability to support natural wildlife. Then there are the effects of fertilizers, pesticides, animal wastes, and erosion on water quality, not to mention methane emissions from rice production and ruminant livestock and air pollution and greenhouse gas emissions from energy use. All of these factors combine to make food second perhaps only to transportation as a source of environmental problems.

To analyze the consumer's role in these impacts, we've divided food purchases into the following broad categories:

- Meat and poultry
- Fruit, vegetables, and grains
- Dairy products
- Other (including seafood, alcohol, soft drinks, specialty foods, and tobacco)

All four categories include food purchased for consumption outside the home. The distribution of environmental impacts across these four categories is shown in figure 3.2. (Note that the horizontal scale is different from that of figure 3.1.)

Meat and poultry consumption has a large impact on common water pollution, water use, and most important, land use. About 800 million acres, or 40 percent of the U.S. land area, is used for grazing livestock, most of which is for household food consumption. An additional 60 million acres is used to grow grain for feeding livestock. Although cropland can support some wildlife, and range and pasture can support considerably more, our index of ecologically significant land use nonetheless indicates that household meat and poultry consumption alone is responsible for about a quarter of threats to natural ecosystems and wildlife.

Raising livestock for meat consumption has other impacts as well. Irrigating crops for feed production puts a major drain on water resources. (About 18 percent of total consumptive water use is attributable to feed for livestock.) Animal wastes are responsible for about 16 percent of common water quality problems traceable to household consumption. The sheer quantity of animal wastes generated is astounding—some 2 billion tons of wet manure a year, over ten times the amount of municipal solid waste generation. The danger posed by such wastes to aquatic habitats and drinking water was highlighted by the case of the failed North Carolina dike we mentioned earlier in this chapter that released an estimated 25 million gallons of hog waste into the surrounding environment.

Among the different kinds of livestock, beef cattle appear to pose the most serious problem, with chickens coming in second and pigs third. In 1995, 103 million cattle (including about 10 million milk cows), 60 million hogs and pigs, 10 million sheep and lambs, and about 7 billion chickens were being raised in the United States.[16] The cattle account for about 45 percent, chickens for 34 percent, and pigs for 12 percent of animal waste

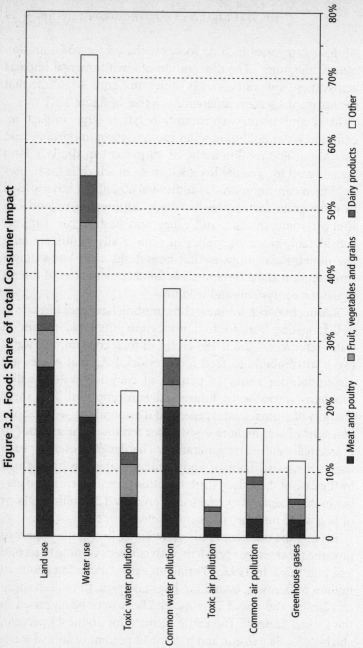

Figure 3.2. Food: Share of Total Consumer Impact

Land use

Water use

Toxic water pollution

Common water pollution

Toxic air pollution

Common air pollution

Greenhouse gases

0   10%   20%   30%   40%   50%   60%   70%   80%

■ Meat and poultry   ■ Fruit, vegetables and grains   ■ Dairy products   □ Other production. The remaining 9 percent comes from turkeys, sheep, goats, and other livestock. Cattle are also responsible for most livestock land use.

Although raising cows to produce milk involves similar kinds of activities as raising beef cattle, the overall impacts on the environment are much smaller. According to our analysis, dairy production accounts for 4 percent of common water pollution and 7 percent of water use, whereas meat production is responsible for 20 percent and 18 percent of these impacts. The difference is especially striking when you consider how much more food energy and nutrition milk and milk products provide to the average diet. The average American consumed 570 pounds of dairy products in 1995, nearly ten times the consumption of beef.

Growing fruit, vegetables, and grains also has a major impact on the environment, most noticeably in water use. Irrigated crop production for human consumption takes an enormous amount of water (about 30 percent of the total). Food crops in general also use substantial amounts of land and produce some water pollution, mainly because of fertilizer and pesticide use and soil erosion.

Our model does not show consumption of seafood ranking high in causing environmental damage, in part because Americans eat much less seafood than meat, dairy, fruit, vegetables, or grains. However, we need to acknowledge that our analysis did not factor in several serious problems with seafood production, including depletion of particular fish species from overfishing, the impact of excessive fishing on other sea life, and the environmental damage caused by unregulated fish farms in other countries. For that reason, it is hard to reach a general conclusion about whether it is better or worse for the environment to eat fish rather than something else.

We do know, however, that there are significant differences in the environmental impacts of eating different types of fish. Consumers should shun some fish species and instead choose from among those types that are not depleted, whose fisheries are managed well, and whose fishing does not cause major damage to ocean ecosystems. Various organizations have begun publishing information evaluating the relative impacts of eating different types of seafood. The National Audubon Society in the May–June 1998 issue of its magazine *Audubon* featured a useful guide to 21 species of fish and seafood. Although consumption of sharks, swordfish, and orange roughy should be avoided, squid, mackerel, and striped bass, for example, appear to be much less problematic.

How about food processing, transportation, and packaging? Do they cause substantial harm to the environment? Alan Durning's popular book *How Much Is Enough?* asserts that food packaging absorbs "mountains" of metal, glass, paper, cardboard, and plastic. It also stresses the environmental impacts of shipping food long distances from where it is grown to where it is sold.[17]

Our findings suggest that although food processing, packaging, and transportation play a significant role, they are not the leading cause of environmental problems due to food consumption. For the fruit, vegetables, and grains category, we broke out the environmental impacts of crop cultivation, food processing, packaging, transportation, and retail stores.[18] (The fruit, vegetables, and grains category includes both highly processed and packaged foods such as boxed cereals, and relatively unprocessed foods such as fresh vegetables and fruits.)

We find that in five out of seven environmental impact categories (and especially the dominant water-use category), the majority of the impacts come from the cultivation stage rather than the packaging, processing, transportation, and retail stages. Moreover, in those cases where packaging, processing, and transportation account for a significant share, the *total* impacts due to fruit, vegetables, and grains are modest. For example, although transportation accounts for 26 percent of

Is It Better for the Environment to Avoid Beef?

A natural question to ask is how the impacts of different types of food we buy compare for the same amount of nutrition delivered. Beef production, in particular, has come under a great deal of criticism as excessively damaging to the environment. At first glance that criticism seems justified, but let's look more closely at how the impacts of red meat, poultry, and grains compare.

Our unit of comparison will be one pound of animal protein (beef or chicken), which has the nutritional value of about 1.4 pounds of grain. We'll use pasta to represent the grain. In 1994 the average price of a pound of ground chuck was $1.84, the average price of chicken was about $1.48 per pound (boneless equivalent), and spaghetti and macaroni cost $0.87 per pound. The table below shows what we get when we put these figures into our model. Using pasta as our baseline and calling it 1, you can easily see how poultry and red meat compare.

Table 3.3 Impacts of Red Meat, Poultry, and Pasta

	Global Warming	Air Pollution		Water Pollution		Habitat Alteration	
	GREENHOUSE GASES	COMMON	TOXIC	COMMON	TOXIC	WATER USE	LAND USE
Red meat	3.4	2.2	1.9	17.5	4.5	4.9	19.9
Poultry	1.4	1.4	1.1	11.2	1.7	1.4	1.6
Pasta	1	1	1	1	1	1	1

As expected, pasta has the lowest impact in every category, and red meat the highest. In most cases the difference is quite large. For instance, compared with pasta, red meat is responsible for 20 times the land use (because of cattle grazing), seventeen times the common water pollution (because of animal wastes), five times the toxic water pollution and water use (from chemicals applied to feed grains and water for irrigation and livestock), and three times the greenhouse gas emissions (from greater energy use). Only in the air pollution categories are the impacts at all comparable. Poultry comes surprisingly close to pasta in water use, land use, toxic and common air emissions, and greenhouse gases, but it resembles red meat in the amount of common water pollution produced.

greenhouse gas emissions from the fruit, vegetables, and grain category, it represents only 0.6 percent of all greenhouse gas emissions traceable to consumer purchases.

HOUSEHOLD OPERATIONS

Running a household involves consuming many things, from heat and electricity to toilet paper and dishwashing detergent. All of these items entail some environmental impact, and cumulatively the impact from household operations is very large.

There are innumerable ways to divide up and classify the operations of running a household. We've adopted the following broad categories:

- Heating, hot water, and air conditioning
- Appliances and lighting
- Furnishings (including furniture and metal, glass, paper, and plastic products)
- Cleaning products, paints, and other chemicals
- Water, sewage, and solid waste disposal

Figure 3.3 shows how the environmental impacts of household operations are distributed among the categories. Three areas of household operations appear to place by far the greatest burden on the environment: (1) heating, hot water, and air condition-

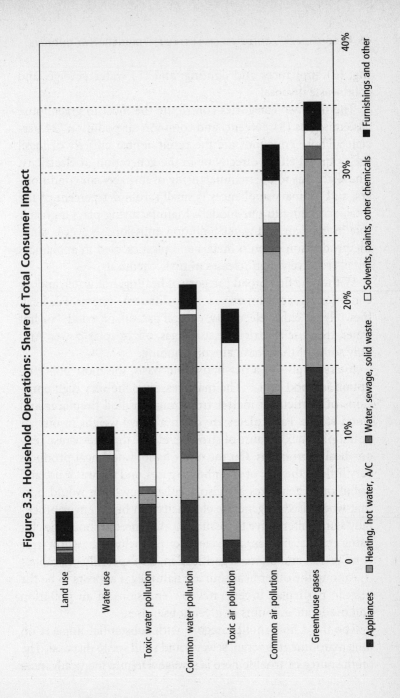

Figure 3.3. Household Operations: Share of Total Consumer Impact

Land use

Water use

Toxic water pollution

Common water pollution

Toxic air pollution

Common air pollution

Greenhouse gases

0   10%   20%   30%   40%

■ Appliances   ■ Heating, hot water, A/C   ■ Water, sewage, solid waste   □ Solvents, paints, other chemicals   ■ Furnishings and other ing; (2) appliances and lighting; and (3) water, sewage, and solid waste disposal.

The first two categories contribute the most to greenhouse gas emissions (31 percent) and common air pollution (24 percent). Those emissions are the result almost entirely of fossil fuels burned either directly or in the generation of electricity. The share due to the manufacturing of furnaces, air conditioners, and ordinary appliances is small (around 1 percent of the total, according to our model). Manufacturing plays a greater role in toxic air and water pollution emissions, however, since the production of both metals and plastics used in appliances entails relatively high releases of toxic chemicals.

Within the first broad category of heating, hot water, and air conditioning, consumers use many different systems. For heat, they rely on either electricity, natural gas, oil, or wood. For hot water, they use electricity, natural gas, oil, or solar power. And only some of them have air conditioning.

Interestingly, on a per-household basis, the most polluting option is wood heat.[19] The main reason is the very high emissions of particulate matter from uncontrolled fireplaces and wood stoves. Particulates are given a heavy weight in our air pollution index because of strong evidence that they cause serious health problems. On the other hand, wood heat produces very little in the way of greenhouse gases, and the water use and pollution it generates are also relatively low. (We would note that wood used to generate electricity can be an environmentally sound alternative to fossil fuels. Advanced technologies for using plant matter for electricity, including whole-tree combustion and biomass gasification, are especially desirable.)

Among the other heat sources, natural gas appears to be the best; in particular, it generates low emissions of air pollution and moderate amounts of greenhouse gases.

The third household category with substantial impacts on the environment is water, sewage, and solid waste disposal. The main source of trouble here is sewage. Despite many advances in sewage treatment, ordinary municipal sewage remains a major source of water pollution, especially in coastal areas and estuaries, and it accounts for about 11 percent of the total in our common water pollution index. Most of that is directly attributable to households. Of course, short of taking themselves off city sewer systems and installing septic tanks in their backyards, there is nothing consumers can do in their personal lives to reduce this form of pollution—it is up to government to improve waste treatment. Individual citizens can, however, prod their local governments to take action.

It may surprise readers to note that home water use accounts for only about 5 percent of total water consumption. As we have seen, the vast majority of water consumption actually goes to irrigated agriculture and livestock, not to households. However, high household water use can still be a serious problem in communities where water is in short supply.

Solid waste disposal contributes to environmental problems mainly through the air pollution generated by trash incineration. Before anyone leaps to blame commercial trash-burning facilities, however, it should be noted that about three-fourths of the pollution in this category comes from open trash burning by individual households.

Although household operations account for a relatively small share of toxic air and water pollution, some useful things can be learned from the data. Cleaning products and services turn out to be the leading sources of toxic air pollution in household operations and are responsible for about 9 percent of all emissions in this category linked to consumer purchases or activity. This finding may be surprising but is easily explained. First, dry-cleaning establishments—which sell most of their services directly to households—emit more than ninety thousand tons of toxic compounds into the air each year (out of a total of around 3.5 million tons from all sources). Second, the evaporation of commercial and consumer solvents (which are used mainly for cleaning but also in paints and other house-

Which Appliances Use the Most Electricity?

Electricity seems clean and nonpolluting when it's used in the home, but most of that electricity is generated by burning polluting fossil fuels, especially coal. For that reason, the more electricity an appliance uses, the greater its environmental impact. So it is instructive to know which appliances use the most electricity in the typical household. The figures in the first column of table 3.4 compare the electricity consumed by several kinds of appliances, as well as lighting, at average rates of use. Since some appliances are far more common in households than others, the per-unit consumption must be multiplied by the average number of units owned by a household to arrive at the average household's electricity consumption (last column). For example, even though swimming pool pumps consume an enormous amount of electricity—twice as much as refrigerators, in fact—they contribute little to overall elec-

Table 3.4. Electricity Use by Household Lighting and Appliances*

	Average Electricity Use per Unit (kWh/yr)	Average Number of Units per Household	Average Electricity Use per Household (kWh/yr)
Refrigerator	1,155	1.20	1,383
Lighting	940	NA	940
Television	360	2.05	739
Electric dryer	875	0.57	495
Stand-alone freezer	1,240	0.35	429
Range/oven	458	0.60	276
Microwave	191	0.84	161
Waterbed heater	960	0.15	145
Dishwasher	299	0.45	135
Swimming pool pump	2,022	0.05	96
Electric washer	99	0.77	76
Computers	77	0.23	18

*Electricity use is per appliance unit, except lighting, which is per household.

tricity demand because only about 5 percent of households own them.

Overall, the top contributors to the environmental impacts of household lighting and appliances turn out to be, in descending order of importance, refrigerators, lighting, televisions, and, far down in impact, electric dryers and stand-alone freezers.

hold chemicals) contributes an additional 500,000 tons, of which perhaps a third is due directly to household use.

Cleaning products and services contribute much less to toxic water pollution, probably because most of the chemicals poured down household drains get removed in sewage treatment plants. It should be stressed, though, that the risks to family members, especially children, from direct exposure to solvents and other potentially toxic chemicals can be significant but aren't counted in our environmental indicators.

The main sources of toxic water pollution are the manufacturing of appliances (4 percent) and furnishings (3 percent). In the case of appliances, the pollutants are mostly generated in steel production, the manufacturing of printed circuit boards and electron tubes, wiring, plastics, copper drawing and rolling, and surface coatings. In the case of furnishings, it is the manufacture and application of preservatives, adhesives, paints, dyes, and other chemicals used in wood furniture and carpets, drapes, and other fabrics that are mostly to blame.

HOUSING

Buying a home is the largest single investment most of us will ever make, and renting a home or apartment is one of the largest expenses. We're extremely conscious of the financial implications of these decisions, but what about their environmental implications?

Overall, housing as a category—which includes rental and owned housing—is not one of the most important sources of environmental damage, primarily because the most environmentally harmful activity, the construction of new homes, involves only a relatively small share of the population in any given year. Nevertheless, housing has a significant impact in a few areas, particularly water pollution and land use, because of the wood, stone, and other materials, as well as energy, used in its construction and upkeep. To investigate those impacts we divided housing into the following categories:

- Home construction
- Maintenance and repair
- Mobile homes

The home construction category includes new houses and apartments for both rental and individual ownership. Everyone who lives in a house or apartment shares responsibility for the impacts of home construction, even if we don't actually own the dwelling we occupy. You can't escape the environmental responsibility of living in a mansion just because you rent it.

The maintenance and repair category includes remodeling and additions as well as exterior and interior repairs paid for both by homeowners and by landlords on behalf of renters. The mobile homes category covers only the impacts of manufacturing, not of driving the homes around. Land occupied by housing lots is included in the home construction category; indirect land use (such as forest land harvested for wood for home construction) is distributed among all categories as calculated by our model.

Figure 3.4 shows how the impacts of housing are distributed among these categories. The most noticeable feature of the chart is that about 26 percent of ecologically significant land use is linked to home construction, or put another way, this category is the source of about a quarter of threats to wildlife and natural ecosystems from land use. Some of this impact is due to the direct use of land for housing lots. Roughly 36 million acres of land in the United States are devoted to residential use, or a third of an acre per household on average.[20]

But the materials that go into home construction also play a significant role. Building a house takes an enormous amount of wood and wood products. In 1991 about two-thirds of the timber harvested in the United States went to structural lumber of one kind or another, and most of that was for home construction. Of course, houses last a long time, so it is appropriate to spread the impact over many years.[21] Residential construction is also the leading source, within the housing category, of greenhouse gases, air, and water pollution. Where common water pollution is concerned, the main cause is soil disturbance in construction, with forestry operations (to produce the wood) a distant second. When land is cleared, a lot of erosion often results, and the sediments eventually find their way into lakes and rivers, where they can affect plant and fish life. Road construction and clear-cutting produce similar effects in forests.

Toxic water pollution is produced in the manufacture of materials that go into new houses, including steel, paints and preservatives, plumbing, plastics, paperboard, and copper wiring. Another source is landscaping for new homes, which uses abundant amounts of fertilizers. (The fertilizers themselves are not counted as toxic, but toxic chemicals are produced in their manufacture.) As for air pollution and greenhouse gases, electricity used in the production of materials for new houses, trucks bringing materials to housing sites, and construction vehicles such as backhoes and bulldozers are the largest sources.

The maintenance and mobile homes categories appear to be

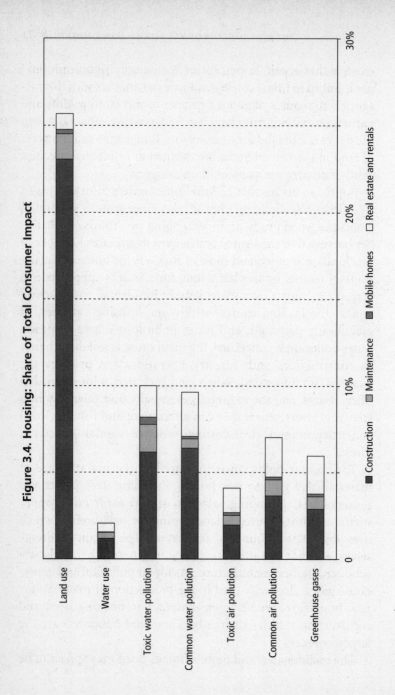

Figure 3.4. Housing: Share of Total Consumer Impact

Legend: Construction | Maintenance | Mobile homes | Real estate and rentals

Categories: Land use, Water use, Toxic water pollution, Common water pollution, Toxic air pollution, Common air pollution, Greenhouse gases

X-axis: 0, 10%, 20%, 30%

much less important. That is mainly because expenditures in these areas are much smaller than expenditures for new home construction. When compared on an equal footing, however, the impacts of mobile homes in particular can be substantial. Although a typical mobile home is responsible for only one-sixth the common water pollution of the typical single-family home, its manufacture causes a third the greenhouse gases and common air pollution and over half the toxic air and water pollution.[22] The explanation for these differences lies in the different mix of materials in each type of construction. Single-family houses are built mainly of wood and wood products, stone, or brick, while mobile homes (like cars) are constructed mainly of metal and plastics. The manufacturing of metal and plastic materials produces relatively more toxic air and water emissions but uses relatively less land.

A key difference between the two that is not reflected in these figures, however, is that single-family homes provide a great deal more living space than mobile homes. If the comparison were made on the basis of comparable living space, single-family houses would probably come out better than mobile homes in almost all categories.

PERSONAL ITEMS AND SERVICES

This category of expenditure is far more diverse than the others we have looked at so far. Thus, although its impacts overall are quite significant, no single item within the category is terribly important, and indeed none of them appear in our top seven list. Nevertheless, we will take a look at a few of the items, since some of the results are surprising.

We've divided this category into four broad groups:

• Clothing
• Personal services

- Paper products
- Other

Clothing includes boots, shoes, handbags, luggage, and leather goods. The personal services category spans a wide array of things, including the U.S. Postal Service; religious, civic, and business organizations; photographic studios and developers; beauty and barber shops; and child care agencies. Also included are sports clubs, golf memberships, race tracks, and other entertainment. Newspapers, magazines, books, notebooks, stationery, greeting cards, and sanitary products are covered under paper products. Under "other," we have placed jewelry, clocks and watches, toys, musical instruments, and small arms and ammunition.

Figure 3.5 shows that among these categories, purchases of clothing have consistently the most serious impact, followed closely by personal services. In one or two categories, paper products and "other" are significant, though never dominant. This general distribution reflects, in part, the relative expenditures for these categories. The largest expense category is clothing, for which consumers spent roughly $230 billion a year, or $2,400 per household in 1995. That is followed by personal services ($207 billion), entertainment ($103 billion), jewelry, toys, and instruments ($87 billion), and paper products ($79 billion).

These categories are still so broad, however, that it is difficult to know where the impacts come from, so it is useful to consider smaller subcategories (see table A.5 in Appendix A for details).

Under clothing, for example, apparel is the leading source of environmental damage. The production of these products is surprisingly energy intensive, and perhaps because unfinished cloth and finished apparel take up a lot of space for their weight, motor freight transportation also ranks high on the list of pollution sources. One reason clothing contributes to toxic

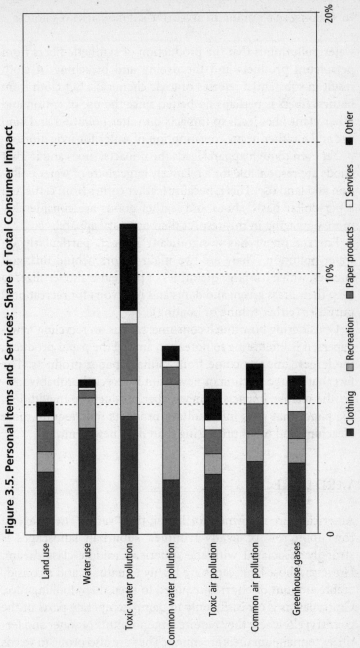

Figure 3.5. Personal Items and Services: Share of Total Consumer Impact

Land use

Water use

Toxic water pollution

Common water pollution

Toxic air pollution

Common air pollution

Greenhouse gases

0   10%   20%

■ Clothing   ■ Recreation   ■ Paper products   □ Services   ■ Other water pollution is that the production of synthetic fibers from petroleum products and the dyeing and bleaching of cloth result in substantial releases of toxic chemicals. But cloth from natural fibers is perhaps no better, since the use of cotton and other plant fiber leads to impacts on water pollution and land use and a rather heavy consumption of water for irrigation.

Yet even though apparel leads the impacts, shoes and leather goods are responsible for a relatively large share of water pollution and land use. This is because leather comes from cattle. On a per-dollar basis, shoes and leather goods are considerably more damaging in this respect than ordinary apparel.

Entertainment has a significant impact, particularly on water pollution. There are two main factors behind this: golf courses, which use large quantities of pesticides and fertilizer to keep their grass green; and dams and reservoirs for recreational purposes (either fishing or boating).

Considering how much consumers focus on recycling newspapers, it is interesting to note that, among the paper products, the largest impacts come from sanitary paper products. The fact that a large fraction of newsprint is recycled probably lowers the relative impacts of newspaper production. In addition, the paper that goes into sanitary products may require more bleaching and other processing than does newsprint.

YARD CARE

Americans are renowned for loving their yards. The image of row upon row of neatly trimmed suburban landscapes is strongly associated with the American middle-class dream. However, those landscapes are highly unnatural, and a considerable amount of effort is required to keep them looking nice. Grassy lawns grow easily only in damp, temperate parts of the country; elsewhere they require large amounts of water and fertilizer to maintain their greenness. They are also prone to weeds and pests, with the result that homeowners frequently apply relatively large amounts of pesticide to them.

How do these impacts stack up against other sources of environmental harm we have examined? Overall, they are fairly modest, primarily because total spending on yards is much smaller than for some of the other categories we have looked at. In this case, we have divided the category into the following main elements:

- Fertilizer and pesticide use
- Water use
- Lawn and garden equipment and use
- Other (including landscaping services and materials)

Fertilizers and pesticides include those purchased by households or applied to residential yards, whether by the homeowner, a landlord, or a landscaping service. Water use is that portion of household water consumption that is used outdoors to water lawns and gardens. The lawn and garden equipment category (which includes lawn mowers, weed wackers, chain saws, and the like) covers both the impacts of manufacturing and the air pollution generated during their use. Landscaping materials include mainly stone and concrete products for such things as patios, walkways, and retaining walls.

As figure 3.6 shows, the most serious problem linked to yard care is water pollution (both common and toxic) from fertilizers and pesticides. Rainfall tends to wash chemicals applied to lawns and gardens into streams and rivers. This urban runoff accounts for about 14 percent of common water pollution on our index, and just over half of that, or 9 percent, is due to residential use of fertilizers. Pesticides are the main factor in toxic water pollution, as residential use of pesticides accounts for about 8 percent of all pesticide applications. (The impact on human health is probably larger than this low number indicates, since people frequently come into close contact with common yard pesticides.)

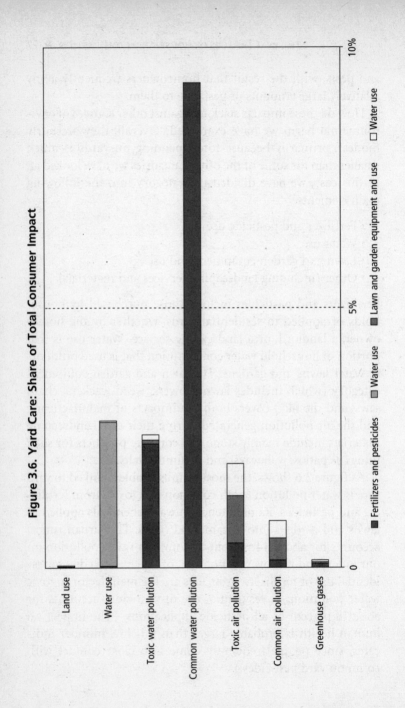

Figure 3.6. Yard Care: Share of Total Consumer Impact

Land use
Water use
Toxic water pollution
Common water pollution
Toxic air pollution
Common air pollution
Greenhouse gases

0   5%   10%

■ Fertilizers and pesticides   ▨ Water use   ▧ Lawn and garden equipment and use   □ Water use

Direct use of water in the yard, of course, dominates water consumption for yard care. (Other, minute water use is mainly for manufacturing fertilizers and pesticides.) On average, about 35 percent of household water use goes to tending yards, and the proportion may be as high as 50 or 60 percent in hot, arid climates such as the Southwest.[23] Most of this is for watering lawns. Simply switching from a landscape dominated by grass to one dominated by trees and shrubs could reduce outdoor water use by as much as 80 percent. Still, water use in the yard is a fairly small fraction of total water consumption, since the great majority of water is used in agriculture.

Another finding to consider is that, within the yard category, lawn and garden equipment is the main source of common and toxic air pollution. The reason the overall share is so small is that lawn and garden equipment is very seldom used. An EPA study indicated that leaf blowers, for example, are used by homeowners an average of just nine hours a year, and homeowners run their lawn mowers only one-sixteenth as often as professional landscaping services do.

The air pollution generated per hour of use of such equipment is actually very high, since the equipment has nothing in the way of pollution controls. The EPA estimates that running a new lawn mower for an hour produces the same emissions as driving a used car fifty miles, while running a new chain saw for an hour has the same impact as driving two hundred miles. These figures may well understate the case, as there is evidence that in-use emissions from lawn mowers and similar equipment are at least twice as bad as emissions from new equipment.[24]

CONCLUSIONS

Now that you have seen which household spending categories cause the most environmental damage, we can focus on what consumers can do about them. In part, we need to know whether alternatives would allow them to reduce the damage attributable to spending on the seven "worst" kinds of household consumption shown in the table at the beginning of this chapter. That's what we'll turn to next. Which things can consumers change, and at what cost in money and convenience?

PART II

WHAT YOU CAN DO

4

Priorities for
Personal Action

B eing an environmentally responsible consumer is all about
making sound choices. Should you move into a bigger
house? Buy a second car? Eat less meat? No one can make these
decisions for you, but with the information provided in this
book, we hope you will be able to strike a balance that suits
your conscience and your needs.

The list of the "seven most harmful consumer activities" in
the last chapter can get you started on this road by helping you
set priorities. But recognizing the most environmentally harmful things that American consumers collectively do is only the
first step. What to do next?

Alas, many of the things that cause the most damage are
pretty fundamental to the American middle-class way of life.
Nowhere is that fact more evident than in our reliance on the
automobile: We use it to get to work, take the kids to school,
shop for groceries, go out on the town, go on vacation. Visitors
from other countries are frequently shocked to discover that in
many American communities it is almost impossible to get
around without a car.

Likewise, middle-class Americans have grown accustomed to

living in large houses. (The average floor area of a newly constructed single-family home grew almost 40 percent from 1970 to 1994.[1]) With those houses come lots of lighting and electric appliances, not to mention manicured lawns requiring fertilizers and pesticides to stay green and weed-free. We don't mean to imply that everyone lives this way, of course. There are many lower-income families who do not enjoy such comforts. Having less money to spend, they tend to drive less (if they own a car at all), live in smaller houses or apartments, have fewer appliances, and so on. At the same time, a small but perhaps growing number of middle-class and wealthy Americans are voluntarily choosing to live a simpler life, giving up at least some of the income and luxuries they have grown used to.[2] Their motivation, by and large, is not to save the environment but to slow down the pace of life. Nevertheless, spending less money (whether voluntarily or not) usually results in a lower impact on the environment.

But most Americans happily embrace a middle-class lifestyle. Should that be cause for feeling guilty (if you are among that group) or assigning blame (if you are not)? Not necessarily, for it is important to recognize that protecting the environment is only one of many factors people must weigh in making their life choices. You may decide to live in a suburb because the schools are better and safer there than in the city you left. Who is to say that is wrong? You might like to ride the train to work but find it would take an hour longer each way than if you drove; that's two hours a day less time to spend at home with your family. Why should you feel guilty about choosing to drive?

Our choices, in other words, are frequently shaped and constrained by circumstances. Into that breach must step some form of collective action at the community, state, or federal level to ease the barriers to responsible consumption. Chapter 7 will discuss the many ways government and communities can reshape the choices consumers have.

Despite the constraints and trade-offs we all face, it is possible to become much more responsible consumers without wholly abandoning the lives we have grown used to. The key is to focus on reducing our environmental impact in a few areas where we know the benefits will be greatest. That's where this chapter comes in. Here we present and discuss eleven personal actions that would make a major difference if American consumers undertook them. The eleven actions are listed below:

PRIORITY ACTIONS FOR AMERICAN CONSUMERS

TRANSPORTATION
1. Choose a place to live that reduces the need to drive.
2. Think twice before purchasing another car.
3. Choose a fuel-efficient, low-polluting car.
4. Set concrete goals for reducing your travel.
5. Whenever practical, walk, bicycle, or take public transportation.

FOOD
6. Eat less meat.
7. Buy certified organic produce.

HOUSEHOLD OPERATIONS
8. Choose your home carefully.
9. Reduce the environmental costs of heating and hot water.
10. Install efficient lighting and appliances.
11. Choose an electricity supplier offering renewable energy.

By pursuing these few actions, Americans can help solve the most serious *national* environmental problems linked to consumer behavior. Of course, your particular community may have a *local* environmental problem—like a leaking landfill, a polluting incinerator, or a threat to a particular endangered species—that deserves priority attention. We would certainly encourage you to get involved in solving such problems. But in this chapter we will offer suggestions that make sense to follow no matter where you live.

You should also consider whether your household participates in any out-of-the-ordinary activities that happen to have a very high environmental impact. For example, do you go snowmobiling or dirt-biking every weekend, or own a power boat? In the next chapter we will discuss some activities that seem to us to be especially desirable to avoid. Appendix A lists a larger number of activities that have relatively high impacts per dollar of expenditure.

TRAVELING LIGHT

Although we have resisted assigning an overall ranking to the different categories of personal consumption, it is hard to avoid the conclusion that personal use of cars and light trucks is the single most damaging consumer behavior. It is a major direct cause of greenhouse gases and many types of air pollution, and indirectly it is also a major source of water pollution (through manufacturing of cars, oil and gasoline production, and runoff from highways) and ecologically harmful land use (for the road network). What can ordinary consumers do about it?

First we need to ask why Americans drive so much; why, in fact, individual use of cars, sport utility vehicles, and other light trucks is increasing. Many factors are involved, but here are three leading ones:

• **Driving is affordable.** On the one hand, average household income has been rising, which means more households can afford to own one or two cars and drive them greater distances. At the same time the costs of owning and operating a car are lower in the United States than in most other countries because of efficient markets and relatively low fuel and import taxes. And once a car is purchased, it is inexpensive to operate. A typical trip of ten miles costs about one dollar, including expenditures for gasoline, oil, maintenance, and tires.[3]

- **Communities are spread out.** Americans are living in ever more spread-out communities that make it virtually inevitable that they will drive a lot. Between 1980 and 1990, while our central cities lost 500,000 people, the suburbs gained 17.5 million people.[4] Since suburbs have a lower population density than inner cities, people must normally travel farther to work, shop, and play. What is more, it is much more difficult and costly to maintain an adequate system of public transportation in a suburb than in a city. In a suburb with, say, half the population density of a city, half as many people live within a reasonable distance of any bus stop or subway station. It is not surprising then that suburban residents average about 50 percent more vehicle-miles of travel than residents of urban centers.[5]

- **Driving is often convenient and satisfying.** Drivers enjoy access to an extraordinarily extensive road network that makes travel between any two points convenient and quick compared with most alternatives. Not only that, many people like driving their own car because it makes them feel safe and comfortable and gives them a high degree of personal control. No waiting for a scheduled bus or hunting for a taxi—just hop in your car and go. Given our culture's emphasis on personal freedom and independence, this psychological motivation may be as important as any other.[6]

As a consumer, how can you counteract these powerful forces and learn to "travel light"? The first thing you might do is take a quick inventory of your travel habits and how they compare with the average household. Look back through your car maintenance records and estimate how many miles you drove in the previous year. Tally up your plane trips and estimate the distance flown. Also count up the approximate number of train and bus trips and the distances traveled. Then compare the results with the following travel statistics for an average household:

Table 4.1. Your Household Travel Profile

Category	Your Household	Average Household
Number of members of household		2.7
Number of cars/light trucks owned		1.8
Annual distance traveled (all cars/LT)		21,000
Average miles per gallon		22.6
Annual distance traveled by air		3,150
Annual distance traveled by intercity train		60
Annual distance traveled by intercity bus		300
Total annual distance traveled		24,510

(You should not count school bus trips or commuter rail or bus trips; just intercity bus and rail travel. Also, your air travel should not include business travel paid by your employer, only personal travel or self-employed business travel.)

Where your household stands with respect to the average on this chart could help you decide how much priority to give to transportation and what areas need the most attention. If your household already travels much less than the average *and* uses relatively less harmful forms of transportation (like buses or an exceptionally fuel-efficient car), then you might reasonably decide to concentrate on other aspects of your consumption.

If your household's travel profile is more typical, however, there will be many ways you can significantly reduce the burden on the environment. The most significant actions involve making the major decisions, such as where to live and what cars to own, that commit your household to certain patterns of consumption for years to come. There are also many small, everyday actions that can have a large cumulative effect. Here are some examples of both:

If you move, choose a place to live that reduces the need to drive.

Of course, most of us don't move every year, but it is surprising how often households do relocate. The next time this happens to you, make sure you consider the implications of your decision for your driving habits. If you have a stable, long-term job, try to move as close to it as you can. Just as important, try to be near public transportation and places to shop and run errands. (Commuting and trips for family and personal business accounted for 58 percent of person-miles traveled for the average household in 1990; social and recreational travel accounted for most of the rest.)

The benefits of such a move for your overall health and sense of well-being could be substantial. People spend on average an hour a day in their cars, and for regular commuters it is often two or three hours a day. If you lived closer to work and stores, you would have more time for yourself, and also probably more opportunities to walk and bicycle. At the same time, the environmental benefits could be huge.

Think twice before you purchase another car.

Most households now own two cars, and quite a few own three or four. Sometimes that is necessary—if there are two wage-earners, for example, and both have to commute by car because no other options are available. But if you want the extra car only because it will be a little more convenient, stop and consider two things.

First, the mere purchase of a car harms the environment because it encourages the manufacturing of more automobiles. When you picture that new car in your driveway, imagine instead the four tons of carbon and nearly 700 pounds of ordinary pollutants pumped into the atmosphere as a result of its manufacture.

Second, not having an extra car will discourage you from making unnecessary car trips and force you to make more effective use of the car you have. This suggestion is a bit like advising a smoker who is trying to quit to keep cigarettes out of the house, or a dieter to buy no sweets. Without that car always at hand, you just might find yourself doubling up with your spouse on trips to the store, hitching rides with friends, perhaps even bicycling or walking.

If you are buying a car, make sure it is the right size for your everyday needs and is the most fuel efficient and least polluting in its class.

Along with where you live and how many cars you own, the type of car you drive has major implications for the environment. The first mistake to avoid is buying a car that is bigger or more powerful than you really need. These days light trucks (including sport utility vehicles, passenger vans, and pickups) are all the rage among affluent consumers. (The fraction of vehicles sold that are light trucks grew from 16.5 percent in 1980 to 40 percent in 1996.[7]) The bad news for the environment is that the average new light truck gets only 20.5 miles per gallon, while the average new passenger car gets 28.5. Even more important, both cars and light trucks have gotten much heavier and more powerful in the past decade. If it weren't for this trend, fuel consumption by personal cars and trucks would be 15 percent lower than it is today.[8]

The key is to choose a car that meets your regular or typical needs, not your extraordinary needs. Television ads notwithstanding, most of those who own four-wheel-drive all-terrain vehicles rarely drive through blinding rainstorms on muddy hillsides. If you plan on going camping in the outback two or three times a year, consider renting a four-wheel-drive vehicle for those few occasions.

Once you have decided on the appropriate size, look for the most fuel-efficient and least-polluting cars (often the two go hand in hand) in that class. The range of performance is wide—usually a 50 percent difference or more between the most and least fuel-efficient vehicles in a class. Even between vehicles of the exact same size and weight, the differences between the best and worst choices can be 20 percent or more. So a little research can make a big difference.

Living Without a Car

In 1992, Katie Alvord embarked on an experiment in car-free living. She had long been aware of motor vehicles' significant environmental impact, so she had avoided unnecessary car trips and often took the bus. But then she met some people who had chosen to go car free. Inspired by them, she decided to try it.

At the time, Katie was not living in the easiest place to be without a car, since her home in the northern California countryside was three miles from the nearest bus stop. Despite her somewhat inconvenient location, Katie realizes she ultimately had an easier time giving up her car than most people would, since she worked at home and therefore didn't need to commute to a job. Conveniently, the local buses included a rack for her bicycle. She also bicycled once or twice a week into town. In addition, she took taxis and occasionally rode in neighbors' cars.

She believes her experience holds lessons for others. She found that she did not need a car nearly as much as she thought she did. When you have a car, you stop considering other options, even when they are better.

In 1994, Katie moved to rural Michigan. Because of long distances and harsh weather, she hasn't been able to go completely car free, but she has continued to minimize her automobile use. She even puts snow tires on her mountain bike so she can keep biking in the winter. She and her husband have also recently purchased a used electric car.

You should also look into buying a "low-emissions" car, to reduce your contribution to air pollution. Under new standards developed in California and adopted in some northeastern states, automakers are now producing cars that meet more stringent standards than the minimum national standard. Low-emission cars meet one of four standards: transitional low-emission, low-emission, ultra low-emission, and zero-emission. (The last refers to electric and hydrogen fuel cell cars.) If you live in California or one of the northeastern states, you should be able to buy an ultra-low-emission or zero-emission vehicle directly. In other states you may be able to order one specially through a local car dealer.

Each year the U.S. Department of Energy tests the fuel efficiency of new cars and light trucks. Most car-buying guides for consumers include the results, but they are also available from the Department of Energy. The Union of Concerned Scientists provides information on its web site (www.ucsusa.org) about some of the environmentally best and worst vehicles. For a more in-depth look at your car choices, you may want to consult the annual *Green Guide to Cars and Trucks,* published by the American Council for an Energy-Efficient Economy.

Set concrete goals for reducing your travel.

Most of us have a household expense budget. Why not a household travel budget? It's not hard to keep track of how much you drive on a weekly or monthly basis. Keep a log of daily trips, and note the odometer miles at the end of each week or month. Set your household a goal—perhaps a 20 percent reduction will seem appropriate in your case. You could then try to reduce the total miles driven by 5 percent (about fifty miles, on average) each month until you reach your goal. If your driving habits right now are about average, you would have the satisfaction of knowing, once you reduce driving 20 percent, that you are lowering your household's total contribution to global warming and air pollution by about 5 percent. Don't forget to count other kinds of trips as well, especially air travel, the second most common form of fuel-driven transportation.

One trick to motivate yourself to reduce your driving is to imagine that gasoline is much more expensive than it really is. Burning a gallon of gasoline generates a lot of pollution and contributes to global warming. Those "external" costs are not reflected in the price we pay at the pump. But why not pretend that they are? If you imagine that every ten-mile trip costs not one dollar but three, you may find yourself coming up with creative ways to reduce your driving. For instance, you could make it a habit to plan carefully before you go shopping, so you can cover all of your errands in one trip. You might inquire at work to find colleagues to commute with, for having two or three people in a car reduces the "cost" proportionately.

Whenever practical, walk, bicycle, and take public transportation instead of driving.

Although walking and bicycling cannot substitute for much of the driving people do, it would be remiss of us not to mention these two utterly benign forms of transportation. If only we lived in a society where we could walk easily to most destinations! Unfortunately, as communities become more spread out, people find fewer opportunities to walk and bicycle regularly. Only about 4 percent of the U.S. population walks to work, down from 5.6 percent in 1980. (Yes, the government collects statistics on this sort of thing.)[9] And many newer communities are practically designed to make walking difficult, providing few safe walking paths and grouping houses and stores in different areas.

If walking and bicycling aren't serious options in your neighborhood, then at least consider taking the bus or train instead of driving. That applies to both short-distance commuting trips and long-distance vacation and business travel. In all cases your trips will have a much smaller impact on the environment.

EATING RIGHT

The production of food for household consumption is a very significant cause of environmental problems, with two main classes of foods—meat and poultry; and fruits, vegetables, and grains—making their way onto the top seven list. (Keep in mind that our model cannot effectively assess the comparative impacts of eating seafood.) Consumption of these foods is responsible for most water use and contributes heavily to land use and to both common and toxic water pollution. This finding seems to pose an insurmountable difficulty: How can we substantially reduce the amount of food we eat? Although many of us could perhaps benefit from a little dieting, we are not going to suggest that cutting back on your caloric intake is the way to save the environment; do it for your health instead.

Producing food will always be a resource-intensive activity, but its impacts could be reduced considerably. Most of the changes must be systemic ones undertaken by farmers with the assistance and prodding of governments. But individual consumers can help move things in the right direction in two key ways.

Eat less meat.

Our results show that meat production causes more environmental harm than other food production, so it is desirable to try to reduce the amount of meat you eat.

It may be helpful first to compare your household's consumption of meat and other foods with the average. It is a bit harder to figure out how many pounds of beef or chicken you consume a year than how many miles you drive, but if you first estimate the number of times a week your family eats each type of meat, and the average serving size, you can quickly arrive at a rough estimate. You could also keep track of your food purchases over several weeks. (If you buy chicken on the bone, then multiply the weight you purchase by 0.7 to get the approximate boneless-equivalent weight.)

Table 4.2. Your Household Food Consumption Profile

Item	Your Household	Average Household
Number of members of household		2.7
MEATS		
Hamburger/beef/steak (boneless)		
Times each week		
Amount each serving (lbs.)*		
Weekly consumption (lbs.)		3.2
Pork, ham, lamb, mutton (boneless)		
Times each week		
Amount each serving (lbs.)*		
Weekly consumption (lbs.)		2.6
Chicken and turkey (boneless)		
Times each week		
Amount each serving (lbs.)*		
Weekly consumption (lbs.)		3.1
Total weekly meat consumption (lbs.)		8.9
FRESH FRUITS AND MELONS (lbs.)		6.5
FRESH VEGETABLES AND POTATOES (lbs.)		13.3
GRAINS AND SWEETNERS (lbs.)**		17.5
MILK AND MILK PRODUCTS (lbs.)		29.7
SEAFOOD (lbs.)		0.8

*Boneless-equivalent weight. **Includes grains in processed foods such as baked goods and pasta.

Both the total amount of meat and the type of meat you consume matter when it comes to the environment. As we saw in chapter 4, poultry production is substantially less harmful, per pound of meat consumed, than beef or pork production. However, for the same amount of nutrition, fruits, vegetables, and grains are less environmentally harmful than poultry. According to our model, cutting the average household's meat consumption (both poultry and red meat) in half and replacing it with the nutritional equivalent of grains would cut food-related land use and common water pollution—two of the three most serious environmental consequences of food

Eating for the Environment

Carolyn Hottle, like a growing number of consumers, has found several ways to reduce the environmental damage associated with food consumption. She started by avoiding meat and poultry, primarily for health reasons. For the past ten years, she has also tried to buy organic foods whenever she can. It has become much easier in recent years as the quality of organic products has improved and food stores have carried more of them. Even though she can't always buy organic, she estimates that two-thirds of her fruits, grains, and vegetables are now organic.

Carolyn tries to support organic food efforts by shopping at stores that seem most committed to carrying such foods and by asking managers at the other food stores in her community to stock more of these products. An avid gardener, she grows some of her own fruits and vegetables, without using any pesticides or chemical fertilizers.

Because of taking these several steps, the environmental impact of her food consumption is much less than that of the average American.

production—by 30 percent and 24 percent, respectively. But water consumption, the other major food-related environmental issue, would be reduced by just 3 percent.

Perhaps more surprisingly, a shift from red meat to dairy products would also help the environment, even though milk comes from cows. The reason is that a dairy cow can produce many times its own weight in milk in a single year. Only 10 percent of cattle in the United States are dairy cows, but their production of milk, by weight, is 3.5 times greater than the production of beef and beef products.

Buy certified organic produce.

The other strategy for reducing the environmental impacts of your food consumption is to buy certified organic produce.

Although usually somewhat more expensive than traditional produce, it is produced using techniques that are far less harmful to the environment.

What exactly is organic farming? It is part of a larger movement toward environmentally sustainable agriculture. Unlike industrial agriculture, which looks at the farm as an outdoor factory, with inputs entering one end and outputs exiting the other, sustainable agriculture views a farm as an integrated system made up of elements like soil, plants, insects, and animals. Farmers who take a sustainable approach reduce or eliminate traditional inputs such as pesticides and fertilizers. Rather than concentrate on a single crop, they use crop rotations and other adjustments of the agricultural system to manage problems such as pests, diseases, and poor soil quality.

It used to be that consumers who wanted to buy organic produce would have little confidence that what they were getting was really superior to the traditional supermarket fare. But in recent years the sustainable agriculture industry and various states have launched third-party certification programs that assure that organic produce meets clear production standards. These standards aim for as few synthetic inputs as possible. The market for organic produce has also grown rapidly, and food stores carry it in many communities.

The critical question is how big the environmental benefit is when you switch from conventional to organic or low-input produce. Unfortunately, the answers are hard to define precisely, and reliable data are scarce. It is safe to say that a shift to organic agriculture would vastly reduce toxic water pollution, since few synthetic inputs are used. It could reduce common water pollution as well because of lower inputs of fertilizer (whether synthetic or natural) and reduced soil erosion due to cover crops and low and "no-till" practices. Low-till farms may also use less motorized equipment, resulting in lower air pollution. Water use is likely to be lower as well, since on organic farms that use cover crops and crop rotations, the soil retains more moisture and requires less irrigation.

The yields of organic crops, on the other hand, tend to be lower than those of conventionally grown crops, so more land might be needed to grow the same amount of food.[10] Although land use is a very important issue, we don't think it should stop you from buying organic produce, for two reasons. First, the organic farming industry is still young, so many farms are still in transition from conventional to full organic farming. It is well known that crop yields during this transition often decline, but over time they tend to rise again to close to those of conventional crops as soil quality improves. Several long-established organic farms actually report higher yields than the average for conventionally grown crops in the same counties.[11] Second, the higher quality of soil and the greater diversity of plants grown on well-established organic farms suggest that, acre for acre, organic farms may be less harmful to wildlife.

From the consumer's perspective, the main drawback of organic produce is that it usually costs more. The price premium ranges anywhere from 10 percent to as much as 100 percent in some areas. The reason is partly that strong consumer demand for organic produce allows organic growers to charge more than others do. Also, since organic yields are usually lower, prices have to be higher for farmers to earn the same income. In addition, conventional farms tend to benefit from cheaper distribution systems and from some economies of scale.

Over time the price gap should narrow as the organic farming industry matures. Perhaps the best reason for consumers to buy organic produce now is to help support this fledgling industry so that, over the long run, many more people will be able to buy its products.

Consumers can also become producers of organic food by growing some of their own. Home gardening can have many environmental benefits. To help you get started using organic gardening techniques, we have listed in Appendix B a few of the many good books and magazines on this topic.

LIVING WELL

Three of the categories in our table of most harmful kinds of household expenditures have to do with the home: home construction, household lighting and appliances, and heating and cooling.

Choose your home carefully.

One of the most important decisions you can make is the type of home you live in. Your first task should be to avoid moving to a bigger house than you really need. It is shocking at times to drive around new residential developments and see how enormous modern houses have become. Even though the average household size has dropped in recent decades, many upper-middle-class Americans are becoming accustomed to living in veritable mansions, often with over four thousand square feet of living space, four or more bathrooms, and five bedrooms. This trend is made possible by rising affluence, relatively low land and material prices, and an extensive highway network that makes commuting easy.

The implications of such oversize houses for the environment are twofold. First, they require more energy to heat and cool. All other things being equal (such as the amount of insulation in the walls), annual fuel or electricity use for climate conditioning is approximately proportional to floor area. Thus, if you pick a house that is 25 percent larger than you need, your fuel bills, greenhouse gas emissions, and air pollutant emissions will be about 25 percent higher than they could be.

Second, larger houses require more building materials and energy inputs than smaller houses. This becomes an especially important consideration if you are contemplating purchasing a new house rather than a resale. We saw in the last chapter that wood for new home construction is one of the largest sources of timber demand and therefore a major cause of habitat disturbance and species endangerment. Home construction

Choosing Where to Live

It can be hard to decide where to live, especially when you want your choice to be good for the environment. Jim and Dana Snyder-Grant weighed many options—some having to do with the environment, others with other considerations—when they and some friends decided they wanted to move together to the same community. Because they were looking for a number of homes next to each other, they concluded that they should build a new small development, even though this would eliminate the option of moving to existing housing. For Dana and Jim, it also meant they would have to move from their current home in Boston to a suburb, where there was land available to build but where they ran the risk of becoming more dependent on their car.

Having made this choice, Dana and Jim found many ways to minimize its environmental impact. Foremost they made sure that their house would be in a community with good commuter rail service so that Jim would not have to drive to work in Boston.

For the house itself, Dana and Jim chose an energy-efficient design and environment-friendly building materials. At just 1,350 square feet, the home is much smaller than the average new house and ensures that their ongoing environmental impacts will accordingly be less than average. Perhaps most unusually, they and their friends clustered their houses on one part of the property, leaving more than two-thirds of the land permanently undeveloped. This has preserved a beautiful, wildlife-rich natural landscape that would have otherwise been entirely converted to house lots.

uses many other materials that are also responsible for environmental damage. A mansion of 7,500 square feet may weigh several hundred tons, while a small house of 1,500 square feet weighs just thirty-five.[12] And if we consider all the materials used for a mansion's extra features—swimming pools, in-ground sprinkling systems, long driveways, patios, and decks—the differences between an oversize house and a modest one become even greater.

It is also best to avoid buying a house with a large yard in a new residential development. As we saw earlier in this chapter, suburban sprawl encourages more driving, but in addition, the push of residential development into currently unpopulated areas is a major cause of habitat disturbance. Some 35 percent of land-based endangered species are threatened by expanding residential housing and the associated commercial development and roads.

If you are lucky enough to be buying a custom-built house, you can make a huge difference by insisting that the architect or builder install superefficient features. According to the *Consumer Guide to Home Energy Savings,* a handy little guidebook published by the American Council for an Energy-Efficient Economy, state-of-the-art energy-efficient houses typically require less than a quarter as much energy for heating and cooling as most existing houses. With more insulation in walls and ceilings than standard new houses, high-efficiency windows, and heat-recovery ventilation systems, such homes usually cost $5,000 to $10,000 more to build. However, the extra cost can be recovered in a few years through savings on fuel and electricity expenses.

On a smaller scale, if you are moving to an apartment, you can try to get the landlord to make improvements—insulation, weather-stripping, storm windows—that will both save you money on your utility bills and help the environment.

Take steps to reduce the environmental costs of heating and hot water.

First of all, if you have an old heating or hot water system, consider installing a new, efficient one. Once again a little forethought can go a long way. If the home you live in now has a very old furnace or steam boiler (one installed more than twenty-five years ago), it is probably not very efficient and not

Building an Affordable, Environmentally Sound House

The Barritt House, a new home near Carson City, Nevada, disproves the notion that the best environmental design features and technologies can be found only in expensive custom homes. This modest fifteen-hundred-square-foot dwelling, designed by Union of Concerned Scientists senior scientist Donald Aitken, shows that an environmentally superior house can be affordable and attractive.

Despite high summer temperatures in Nevada, the house doesn't need air conditioning. Light-colored roof shingles reflect the sun, while high-performance windows and special shades keep the heat out on hot days (but in on cold ones) while still allowing light in. Ceiling fans, vents, and the room layout all enhance air circulation. The garage is placed on the south end of the house to provide a buffer between the living quarters and the strongest, most direct summer sun.

In typical houses, incandescent lights produce considerable unwanted heat, but in this one sunlight provides almost all of the light needed during the day. At night or when it's cloudy, there are efficient fluorescents. For all these and other reasons, the house uses 60 percent less electricity than the average house of its size in the region.

The Barritt House also features cutting-edge solar-electric (photovoltaic) roof tiles that convert sunlight into electricity. During the summer this system produces more electricity than the house needs and sells the excess to the local electric company. During the winter the photovoltaic tiles produce about 20 percent of the house's electricity. Although this sort of system is still not normally cost effective, it shows that clean solar power could provide a significant share of the energy we need for our homes without requiring any additional land.[13]

only produces more pollution and CO_2 than it should but also adds unnecessarily to your heating bills. A new furnace or boiler could cost $2,500 or more (installed), but if it substantially improved the efficiency of your heating system, you might save $200 or more annually on your heating bills, and you will certainly reduce your household's environmental impact.

There are also less expensive tricks you can use to improve the efficiency of an older heating system without replacing the furnace or boiler, such as installing flue dampers to keep heat from escaping out of the house when the furnace or boiler switches off.

If you have the option to change the type of fuel your heating system uses, you should probably choose either natural gas or an electric heat pump. Gas burns more cleanly and efficiently than oil, and gas furnaces (which heat air, as opposed to boilers, which heat water) can be as much as 95 percent efficient, meaning that 95 percent of the energy from the gas gets transferred to the air and sent through the house.

Electric heat pumps work like refrigerators, pumping heat from the outside into the house or (during warm weather) from inside out, like air conditioners. Exceptionally good heat pumps can deliver more energy than they consume, even considering the large amount of energy lost in electricity generation. Heat pumps that transfer heat from the outside air are not efficient in very cold weather, though. Where winter temperatures frequently drop below freezing, you may want to consider a ground-source heat pump (which transfers heat to and from the ground, where temperatures are steadier). They cost more but are even more efficient than standard heat pumps.

Whether or not you are installing a new heating system, it always makes sense to use heat wisely. Turn down the thermostat at night, keep it below 68 degrees Fahrenheit during the day, insulate, make sure your windows are well sealed, and upgrade windows and doors to energy-efficient varieties. These are just a few of the steps that can cumulatively reduce your home heating use and fuel bills substantially.

Many of the same considerations apply to home hot water systems. In addition, you can also consider solar water heating.

If your present water heater uses electricity, then adding a solar collector and an extralarge storage tank (to handle cloudy days) can both reduce your electricity consumption for water heating (by 40 to 90 percent) and make economic sense. A typical solar water heating system costs $3,000, a hefty sum, but it can save $150 to $350 per year, depending on the local climate. (Because natural gas is so much less expensive than electricity, it usually will not pay to add a solar system to a gas water-heating system.) Solar systems can make especially good sense for including on a new house since, if the price of the system is added to the purchase price of the house, the monthly savings on electricity bills will often be greater than the increase to mortgage payments.

Every situation will be different, however. To find out what options you may have for improving or replacing your current heating and hot water systems and otherwise saving energy, you will have to consult an expert. Many electric utilities and gas companies offer free home energy audits, or you can pay a modest amount for one yourself.

Install efficient lighting and appliances.

The key source of environmental harm from household appliances and lighting is electricity use. Although it is helpful to train yourself to use your appliances and lighting as sparingly as possible, the easiest way to make a really big difference is to buy the most efficient types to begin with. We can illustrate this point well by looking at refrigerators and freezers.

Refrigerators and freezers account for about a quarter of electricity use in the home, on average. A new refrigerator or freezer is a big investment, but you might want to consider getting a new one. New models are much more efficient than older ones, especially if your old refrigerator no longer has tight seals and otherwise performs worse than when you bought it. You may be able to save fifty dollars or more annually on your electric bills by buying a highly efficient replacement refrigerator. If it turns out to make sense to buy a new refrigerator, keep in mind that it is usually a bad idea to keep the old one around for extra food storage. If you really need more storage space, it is more efficient to have one big refrigerator than two smaller ones. On the other hand, you shouldn't purchase a larger refrigerator than you really need, since the bigger it is, the more electricity it will use. Like houses, refrigerators have been getting bigger even while families have been getting smaller. Lastly, pay close attention to the energy labels that appear on all new refrigerators and freezers. They compare that model's electricity consumption (in kilowatt-hours per year) with that of other models of a similar size.

When you think about other home appliances, such as stoves, clothes dryers, and air conditioners, you can apply the same suggestions as for refrigerators—consider whether it's time to replace your existing appliance, don't buy a larger one than you need, and read energy labels carefully to find the most efficient model for your needs. Clothes washers are a partial exception to these rules: although some new front-loading, energy-efficient, water-saving washers use just one-third of the water of traditional top-loaders, the most effective way to reduce energy use from clothes washing is to switch from hot water to cold water washes. All but 10 percent of the energy used for washing clothes goes to heating the water.

Along with assessing your use of appliances, you should consider lighting. Most lighting in homes consists of ordinary incandescent light bulbs, which convert electricity to light by heating a filament. The technology has not changed much since Thomas Edison. They are horrendously inefficient, however: only about 10 percent of the electricity used produces visible light, while the rest goes into heat.

Since the 1980s compact fluorescent lighting has provided an alternative to conventional lighting that is three to four times more efficient. Like standard fluorescent light bulbs, they work by running a high-voltage current through a gas. Compact fluorescents are designed to fit into conventional lighting fixtures, making them suitable for home lighting. Their environmental benefits are impressive: Replacing just one 75-watt incandescent bulb with an 18-watt compact fluorescent will save about 570 kilowatt-hours of electricity over the fluorescent's ten-thousand-hour lifetime. That means, if the mix of fuels used to produce the electricity is typical, just one compact fluorescent bulb will eliminate the combustion of three hundred pounds of coal. Also, compact fluorescents pay for themselves in two or three years in normal use, both through reduced electricity charges and (since compact fluorescents last about ten times as long as regular bulbs) savings on replacements.

However, compact fluorescents also have some disadvantages that have made them less than popular with most consumers. (They are widely used in commercial lighting, though.) Shoppers often balk at their high retail price of ten dollars or more. Also, the quality of light, though much improved over garish conventional fluorescent bulbs, is still not always as pleasing as the warm light from incandescents (which, after all, mimic the spectrum of sunlight). Furthermore, compact fluorescents have bulky fittings that do not fit in some conventional fixtures. Although several companies are marketing lines of lamps and fixtures designed for compact fluorescents, they have been slow to penetrate the market.

But considering their environmental benefits, it is worth going to some trouble to make them work.

Choose an electricity supplier offering renewable energy.

This last recommendation could not have been made even three years ago because ordinary household consumers used to have no choice of where to purchase their electricity. However, many states are now far along the process of creating competition in electricity supply. This means that consumers will be able to choose which company to buy their electricity from. As a result, there is a movement afoot by some independent power companies and utility companies to offer consumers "green" power generated from renewable resources such as wind and solar. In just a short time the movement has gathered surprising momentum, as market research and pilot projects have demonstrated that a significant number of households are willing to pay a little extra for renewable electricity.

Different companies will present very different kinds of green power. To find the best, you should demand a detailed breakdown both of the sources of electricity a company proposes to use and of the amount of pollution produced per unit of energy delivered (with a comparison to the regional average). The greenest packages will probably contain substantial amounts of wind energy, solar energy, hydropower, and energy from plant matter, and little or no coal or nuclear energy (the latter because of radioactive waste generation and safety risks). But different gradations of green power may be offered for different prices. The key to making a decision will be to compare the characteristics of the package offered against the standard package. Are you willing to pay two dollars per month extra to get 20 percent of your electricity from wind? Three dollars per month for a 50 percent drop in greenhouse gas emissions?

So keep an eye out! If you start seeing advertisements for green power and the price seems reasonable and the offer serious, it would be an excellent way to reduce the environmental impacts of your household's electricity use. Most important of all, you will be encouraging the growth of an industry that has the potential to greatly reduce air pollution, greenhouse gases, and other harmful impacts of electricity generation.

5

Avoiding High-Impact Activities

W hen we first started doing the research for this book, some of our friends jokingly told us that we had increased their anxiety level and that it would remain high until our results were in. They confessed that they engaged in certain activities that they suspected were bad for the environment but didn't know for sure how bad. Because they wanted to be responsible consumers, if our findings were to confirm their suspicions, they would feel obliged to cut down or eliminate the suspect activities.

In truth, we too have had these sorts of suspicions. And indeed the conclusions from our analysis suggest that we should reduce our own use of wood fireplaces, for example.

In this chapter we discuss some of the consumer practices that have an especially high environmental impact. We will try to present our findings in an objective, straightforward way, even though this may mean exposing some quite enjoyable activities as environmentally harmful. Because these activities represent only a small share of total consumer spending, they did not make it onto the priority lists in chapters 3 and 4, but they are quite harmful on a per-dollar or per-use basis. This means that, from an environmental standpoint, it would be best if you spent your money in other ways. In some cases you should try to avoid these activities completely. In other cases, you should just make sure to keep your use to low levels. (The concluding table in Appendix A allows you to compare the environmental impacts per dollar of 134 consumer activities.)

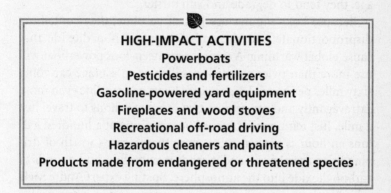

HIGH-IMPACT ACTIVITIES
Powerboats
Pesticides and fertilizers
Gasoline-powered yard equipment
Fireplaces and wood stoves
Recreational off-road driving
Hazardous cleaners and paints
Products made from endangered or threatened species

POWERBOATS

When we rank the ways in which consumers cause environmental damage, motorboats do not come out very high on the list. But that is only because relatively few people use them, compared with the number who drive cars, eat meat, or heat homes, and because they use their boats only a relatively few hours a month. About 12 million marine engines—on everything from large ferries and barges to yachts, fishing boats, and dinghies—currently operate in the United States.[1] Most of these engines are used for recreational boating.

The average marine engine causes considerably more environmental damage than a car engine for each hour it operates, because car engines have much more effective emissions controls. Gasoline marine engines produce high amounts of air pollution, especially hydrocarbons, which then react to form smog.

For this reason, an hour of water skiing can create nearly as much smog as driving from Washington, D.C., to Orlando, Florida.[2]

Marine engines also cause water pollution, since a share of their fuel goes out their tailpipes unburned into the water, and fuel leaks are common. Many of these engines are old, since boats are kept in operation many more years than cars. As they age, they tend to degrade and run dirtier.

Because boat engines use lots of gasoline, they contribute disproportionately to the emissions of carbon dioxide that cause global warming. A typical seventeen-foot powerboat will use more than twice as much gasoline as an average car going sixty miles per hour.[3] Large luxury boats use gasoline even more extravagantly and can require two or more gallons to travel just a mile. Just ten hours of luxury boat cruising at a hundred gallons an hour is equivalent to more than a year's worth of driving in an average car, and it sends twenty thousand pounds of carbon dioxide into the atmosphere. Boating expert Andre Mele asks, "Is there any other form of transportation more profligate?" He concludes, "Only a fighter jet consuming over 600 gallons during half an hour of supersonic combat flying, might get worse mileage [per passenger] than a large pleasure boat."[4]

We do not mean to suggest that consumers need to stay out of boats completely. After all, because they are used few hours, the high hourly emissions do not necessarily add up to all that much pollution. However, we do believe you should avoid purchasing a large gas-guzzling yacht or an oversize speedboat. You should also make sure that any smaller vessel you own operates as cleanly as possible.

Unfortunately, boat manufacturers provide little information on engine efficiency and air pollution emissions, so it is hard to get the information needed to make wise decisions. The government does not require boats to bear the same sorts of energy-use labels that cars and appliances do. But the situation should get somewhat better over time. In 1996 the EPA finally established emission standards for new boat engines, which aim to reduce hydrocarbon emissions 50 percent by 2020 and 75 percent by 2025.[5] Perhaps government-required labels and incentives for fuel efficiency will come next.

PESTICIDES AND FERTILIZERS

The use of pesticides and fertilizers on lawns and gardens is responsible for nearly 10 percent of the common water pollution attributable to consumers, and it causes about 3 percent of toxic water pollution. We need to remember that pesticides—whether they are herbicides, insecticides, or fungicides—are expressly designed to kill living things. When used improperly (and sometimes even when used as intended), they can endanger people and harm living things other than their intended victims.

About 70 million pounds of pesticides are applied to home lawns and gardens annually. Although chemical manufacturers have tended to reduce the toxicity of lawn chemicals over time, they remain inherently dangerous products.

Given this danger, it is alarming to realize that, according to a study by the EPA, half the people who use pesticides on their yards do not read the warning labels. Both intentionally and unconsciously, homeowners also often exceed manufacturers' recommended doses. Partly as a result, some homeowners use up to ten times more chemical pesticides per acre than farmers do.[6] (They often also frequently apply too much synthetic fertilizer, which can not only contaminate groundwater and have other negative environmental consequences but also damage their lawn.) Most lawn care companies are more careful, but some operate under the principle that, when it comes to chemical applications, the more the merrier.

You should always keep in mind that pesticides and fertilizers can be dangerous and avoid applying them in unnecessarily high quantities or in a cavalier, reckless manner. You should consider whether there is a nonchemical method for dealing

Remaking the Backyard

Sara and Marty Stein followed all the conventional advice when they moved to a Pound Ridge, New York, house with a large unkempt backyard covered by "brambles, bushes, vines and grasses."[7] To produce a neat, manicured landscape, they cleared the brush, moved rocks, and planted flower beds. They pulled up plants that were thriving under local conditions and replaced them with ones selected from horticulture magazines and plant catalogues. They hired a lawn care company to apply regular fertilizer treatments and prescribe a heavy watering schedule.

But then, having transformed their yard, the Steins realized they had made a terrible mistake. They had created a landscape that could be maintained only with heavy inputs of chemicals and water. The land now needed "feeding, watering, planting, cultivating, and pest control, whereas before it managed all these things itself."[8] They especially regretted that their yard no longer supported all the wildlife that had been there when they first moved in.

Sara Stein began to look at her yard afresh, from the perspective of an ecologist. She sought to understand the roles that different plants and animals played in the wild habitats in her area and tried to create a backyard ecosystem that would welcome butterflies, pheasants, hummingbirds, snakes, bats, shrews, toads, and other animals. She planted native plants, reduced her use of pesticides, and replaced some of the lawn with prairie meadows. Her goal was to "restore nature's abundance."

The Steins' yard is still landscaped and still serves the needs of the people living there, "but less is mowed, the choice of plants is different, and thickets have replaced some open beds."[9] Sara Stein now advocates reforming suburban landscaping to better preserve natural ecosystems.

with a lawn or garden problem. If you conclude that you need to use a pesticide, investigate the potential hazards of alternative ones and make sure to choose the one that poses the least risk. Then, when you apply it, you should take all the precautions recommended by the manufacturer and stay within the recommended dose. You should be especially careful to keep children and pets away from treated areas.

It is also well worth thinking about what sort of landscaping you want and need. In most parts of the country, a flawless, lush green lawn requires repeated applications of pesticides and artificial fertilizers. The first, but perhaps psychologically hardest, change you can make is a change in mindset. Rather than aspire to have a perfect, uniform lawn, you can instead accept one that has a few uneven spots, weeds, and differences in coloration. In addition, you can make sure to use those grass seed mixtures that will require the fewest pesticide applications in your particular climate. In recent years seed companies have brought such products to market in response to some homeowners' desire for lawns that take a smaller toll on the environment.

Over time you can also redesign your yard so that it requires fewer inputs. Many books and magazines, some of which we have included in the resource guide in Appendix B, provide useful advice on this sort of low-impact landscaping. In general they will encourage you to limit the amount of grass and instead use other ground covers, like ivy, and plant more shrubs and trees. This sort of landscaping will also generally have the side benefit of reducing water use. If you live in an arid climate where water is in short supply, you can go further than this and landscape with native plants that require relatively little water.

GASOLINE-POWERED YARD EQUIPMENT

Lawn mowers and other yard equipment, such as chain saws and weed wackers, don't use very much gasoline but still produce high quantities of air pollution for every hour they are used. Because they tend not to have effective pollution controls, a five-horsepower lawn mower can produce more air pollution than a 200-horsepower car.

We will not suggest that you eliminate the use of yard equipment entirely, since that would likely be impractical. You can instead try several approaches to reducing the environmental harm associated with it. For one thing, you can tune and maintain your equipment regularly, since that will keep it running as cleanly as possible. You can also choose electric equipment, rather than gasoline, when feasible.

Some partial relief from high-polluting gasoline equipment is on the way. In great part because of concern in the Los Angeles area about smog caused by lawn mowers, some cleaner models are starting to be sold. The next time you need a lawn mower or similar product, you can make sure to choose the least-polluting one available.

The air pollution from lawn mowers and yard equipment is another reason to consider relandscaping to reduce the size of your grass lawn. Just think how nice it would be not to have to mow and edge all that grass.

FIREPLACES AND WOOD STOVES

Few things are cozier or more comforting on a cold winter's evening than to sit in front of a wood fireplace. For this reason most people who purchase a new home want it to have one. Unfortunately, although it pains us to admit this, fireplaces are quite bad for the environment. As we saw in chapter 3, fireplaces (as well as wood stoves) produce unusually high emissions of air pollutants.

Old-fashioned fireplaces are the worst offenders. They are remarkably inefficient devices that generally burn with less than 10 percent efficiency. When the fireplace is not in use, cold air can enter the house or heated inside air can escape. When it is used, the smoke that goes up the chimney sends large quantities of pollutants into the atmosphere. Because some of the smoke inevitably stays inside the house, indoor air quality can also suffer, especially in a highly insulated, tight house with limited air circulation.[10]

If you have a fireplace in your house, you can reduce some of these problems by installing and using a damper (rooftop ones tend to work best) and glass doors. A high-efficiency fireplace insert will help more but will be expensive. If the main reason for using your fireplace is for aesthetics and atmosphere, you can use artificial firelogs, which provide little heat but reduce air pollution emissions by up to 80 percent.[11] Even if you make these changes, your fireplace will still produce some air pollution. Nevertheless, we don't think you need to brick it over. We ourselves have a hard time imagining never again building a fire on a cold winter's night. However, we do urge you to think about limiting the amount of wood you burn in your fireplace. We're going to try to do this and hope you will too.

Older wood stoves represent a greater problem for the environment than fireplaces. They produce only about half the emissions of a traditional fireplace and don't normally harm indoor air quality, but most people who have a wood stove use it many more hours than the typical fireplace. Most wood stoves cause far more air pollution and land use than conventional furnaces that burn the equivalent amount of oil or natural gas. True, wood burning contributes relatively little to global warming, and it poses no risk of oil spills (the latter a fairly minor source of water pollution overall). But these benefits, in our opinion, are far outweighed by the large quantities of pollutants emitted into the atmosphere. If you have an older stove, you should certainly take all possible steps to reduce emissions, by making sure that you only use seasoned wood, building the most efficient types of fires, and maintaining the stove and chimney regularly.

Even better, you could consider shifting to some other heating source or upgrading to a newer, more efficient wood stove. Because of the problems associated with wood stoves, the EPA in 1988 enacted regulations requiring new models to burn wood more cleanly and efficiently. In comparison to older stoves, which generally burn at no more than 50 percent efficiency, newer EPA-certified stoves test on average at 70 percent efficiency, and sometimes up to 80 percent efficiency.[12] According to the Combustion and Carbonization Research Laboratory of the Canadian government's CANMET-Canada Technology Centre, EPA-approved stoves have less than half the pollutant emissions of older models. More impressively, the best systems have less than one-sixth the emissions of an old wood stove and less than one-twelfth the emissions of a typical fireplace.[13] These advanced-combustion systems are available as fireplaces—well worth considering if you are building a custom house and want to include a fireplace.

Even the best wood stoves will produce more air pollution than heating with natural gas, but if you live in a rural area where wood is cheap and air pollution is not a major concern, a new, efficient wood stove could be a reasonable choice.

RECREATIONAL OFF-ROAD DRIVING

It sure looks like fun to race across the desert in a four-wheel-drive sport utility vehicle or to bounce over sand dunes in a dune buggy. To some people, off-road travel also looks like a good way to enjoy nature. After all, you are outdoors, far from urban life, able to see places that might otherwise be inaccessible.

Unfortunately, off-road driving can cause serious environmental damage. Experiments in the Mojave Desert have shown that a single pass by a four-wheel-drive vehicle over damp desert land can cause enough soil compaction to significantly reduce the density of various plant species.[14] Similarly, one pass over a salt marsh or tidal flat can so compress the sand or mud that it becomes useless as habitat for clams and other animals that reside below the surface. Driving over sand dunes can endanger small animals who live there and damage vegetation, thereby allowing wind to erode the sand.

As awareness of the problems with off-road vehicles has increased over the past two decades, governments have placed more land off limits to them and have otherwise regulated their use. In many places, for example, off-road vehicles are allowed only on specially designated roads and trails. But because of pressure from off-road enthusiasts, keepers of public lands, such as the U.S. Forest Service and state parks agencies, still sometimes allow drivers to go places where ecosystem damage will be inevitable. In other places, because no clear rules have been established, inappropriate vehicle use continues. Anyone who leaves established trails to drive off-road for pleasure over a sensitive natural landscape shows a willful disregard for the need to conserve natural ecosystems.

Beyond the danger to fragile land, off-road vehicles pose other problems for the environment. Snowmobiles, dune buggies, dirt bikes, and most other similar vehicles all produce high air pollution emissions, because they have poor pollution controls. Until improved engines with better controls are in place, it is best to avoid these vehicles, even in situations where you would not be harming the land.

HAZARDOUS CLEANERS AND PAINTS

Although neither cleaning products nor paints and preservatives are among the main causes of environmental damage, they rank high on a per-dollar basis in terms of their air pollution or water pollution impacts (see table A.5 in appendix A). In some cases, these products pose a considerably more serious direct risk to their users than they do to the general environment. But because literally hundreds of different products are encompassed by these categories of household spending, it can be quite confusing for consumers to figure out which ones to use or not use. To help you, we offer a few simple, common-sense guidelines.

The most significant risks to both users and the environment come from the misuse or improper disposal of products. More than anything else, you should become a label-reader when buying cleaners and paints. By just reading labels carefully and faithfully following their instructions, you can reduce much of the risk. If you take all the precautions that manufacturers suggest, occasional use of commercially available products will be unlikely to cause serious problems for either you or the environment.

However, if you want to take an even more cautious and safer approach, you should avoid the more hazardous products. Latex paints are safer for both users and the environment than oil-based ones, for example. In general, you can again use product labels as the starting point for information. The more serious the safety warnings and precautions—such as wearing masks and gloves or keeping windows open for ventilation—the greater the likelihood that the product poses significant risks to you and to the environment. When less risky alternatives are readily available, you should use them. Products sold in environmental catalogues and health food stores as safer for the environment are generally that way, but you should be cautious about words like "natural" or "biodegradable" that don't necessarily increase a product's safety.

Obviously, the more toxic a product, the more you need to worry about how you dispose of it. Rather than provide lengthy lists of how to get rid of various chemicals, cleaners, and paints, we suggest you find out which items your town or city collects on hazardous waste collection days and then follow their guidelines. You can find more specific advice on disposing of various hazardous materials on the Environmental Protection Agency's web site at www.epa.gov/grtlakes/seahome/housewaste/house/mainmenu.htm.

Dry cleaning represents a different sort of problem than cleaning products used in the home. Commercial dry cleaners, on a per-dollar basis, are responsible for very high levels of toxic air pollution. Government regulations are prompting dry cleaners to take steps to reduce these levels, but, for the foreseeable future, dry cleaning will remain a relatively high-polluting activity. For that reason, from the standpoint of the environment, it's better to launder clothes than to dry clean them. Luckily, most people don't use dry cleaners all that much, and occasional trips to get sweaters, suits, or dresses cleaned are not environmental sins. However, if you are a heavy user of dry cleaning, you should try to cut down. You can also try to find out which dry cleaners in your area are doing the most to reduce the pollution caused by chemicals.

PRODUCTS MADE FROM ENDANGERED OR THREATENED SPECIES.

This should be a no-brainer. yet a few people think it can't possibly make a difference if they only have one or two stuffed rare birds, a single ocelot skin, an exotic pet, or an occasional container of sturgeon caviar. And how much damage can it do to pick just a few unusual wildflowers? The fact of the matter is that when a plant or animal species is endangered, or even threatened, every single loss to its population counts.[15]

A SPECIAL CASE: HAVING CHILDREN

When we started working on this book, we were conscious of the fact that many people view population growth, not household consumption, as the root cause of the world's environmental problems. After all, they argue, if there were fewer people, not as much would be consumed and less pollution would be produced. In a 1994 article four scholars at the College of Environmental Science and Forestry of the State University of New York estimated that every baby born in the United States would lead to an average lifetime production of "one million kilograms of atmospheric wastes, ten million kilograms of liquid wastes, and one million kilograms of solid wastes." They also found that, at current use rates, each new American would eventually consume 700 kilograms of minerals and 24 billion BTUs of energy. The authors therefore concluded that "the most effective way an individual can protect the global environment, and hence protect the well being of all living people, is to abstain from creating another human."[16]

Is this analysis correct? Given the subject we chose for the book you are reading, you probably will not be surprised to discover that we do not advocate a sole focus on limiting births, as a matter of either public policy or personal choice. For one thing, the U.S. population at its current size already causes serious environmental damage that would not end or diminish just by stabilizing the population. Even a 10 or 20 percent reduction in the number of Americans would not lead to a long-term significant improvement in environmental quality and public health unless it were accompanied by the sorts of policy and behavioral changes discussed elsewhere in this book. And it would take decades to accomplish.

The number of people matters, but so does how and where they live. For this reason population growth is only one of several causes of most environmental problems. Earlier in this book, for example, we have shown that suburban sprawl tends to exacerbate habitat alteration, air pollution, and global warming. Initially, one might assume that population growth is the primary cause of this sort of development. However, even in metropolitan areas where the population has been falling, large tracts of land on the outskirts continue to be developed for housing and business. In greater Philadelphia, even though the population fell 3 percent from 1970 to 1990, the amount of land used increased 32 percent.[17]

Nevertheless, it is clear that having fewer children is better for the environment in the long run than having more children. But this certainly does not mean that people should stop having children altogether. The decision to have a child is qualitatively different from the choice of whether to eat an extra steak or purchase a gas-guzzling automobile. Many people view parenthood as essential to their happiness and sense of self-worth. No one should expect people to decide on having fewer or no children solely, or even mainly, on environmental grounds.

What Americans should ask of themselves and others is that the decision to have a child be made thoughtfully and carefully. People should understand that for population to stabilize, the *average* fertility rate will need to be roughly two children per woman. They then need to make a very personal and important decision about how many children to have. And if they choose to have children, they should make it a priority to teach and model the sorts of environmentally responsible behaviors described in this book.

Collectively, Americans should also support efforts that educate and help people, both in the United States and elsewhere, to exercise control over their own fertility and have no more children than they really want. The United States leads the industrial world in numbers of unwanted births and teen pregnancies. In 1996 the Population and Consumption Task Force of the President's Council on Sustainable Development made its core population goal "to stabilize U.S. population promptly, through universal access to voluntary reproductive health and family planning services and the empowerment of women." The task force argued strongly that voluntarism must always remain "the foundation for promoting population stabilization," but that education, especially of adolescents, was essential if people are to make informed, thoughtful family planning decisions.[18]

6

Seven Rules for Responsible Consumption

So far, we have tried to help you focus on those consumption categories that have the biggest impact on the environment and to give you information about some consumer practices that have a disproportionately high environmental impact every time someone engages in them. However, the advice of the previous two chapters does not cover all the thousands of consumer decisions you are faced with in a given year. Moreover, while we have tried to be clear about what you *should* worry about, we haven't yet told you what you *should not* worry about. That is equally important—for lowering your anxiety level as well as for increasing your effectiveness.

In this chapter we offer seven simple rules that you can apply to all of your consumer decisions. You can think of these rules when you are faced with a choice that is not covered in the previous chapters or when you want a reminder not to feel unnecessary guilt about your consumer actions.

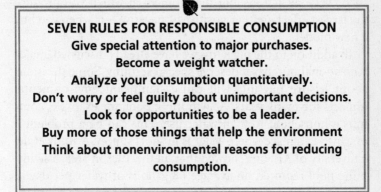

SEVEN RULES FOR RESPONSIBLE CONSUMPTION
Give special attention to major purchases.
Become a weight watcher.
Analyze your consumption quantitatively.
Don't worry or feel guilty about unimportant decisions.
Look for opportunities to be a leader.
Buy more of those things that help the environment
Think about nonenvironmental reasons for reducing consumption.

GIVE SPECIAL ATTENTION TO MAJOR PURCHASES

Major, out-of-the-ordinary purchases have an especially important impact on your overall environmental profile. By being careful when making such consumer decisions, you can generally (even if not always) reduce environmental damage faster and more easily than through smaller, everyday actions. That's why, when describing priorities in chapter 4, we emphasized these sorts of decisions—which house or apartment to select and which car, appliances, and heating system to buy.

Refrigerators provide a clear example of how this principle works. Let's assume that you want to purchase a eighteen- or nineteen-cubic-foot refrigerator. By buying the most efficient model, you will use about 40 percent less electricity for refrigeration than if you buy the least efficient model, thereby causing 40 percent less of the air pollution and greenhouse gas emissions associated with electrical generation.[1] You can't achieve anywhere near this large a reduction by taking ongoing conservation measures, such as regularly vacuuming refrigerator condenser coils or making sure not to unnecessarily open the door. This doesn't mean that you should ignore or abandon such everyday actions, but the moment at which you produce the largest effect—either positive or negative—is when you buy a new model.

In addition to the big items we have already discussed, major recreational purchases deserve special scrutiny. Some decisions about leisure pursuits will cause significant environmental impacts for many years. A swimming pool, for example, commits a household to high water use. This can be a problem if one lives in a place where water is in short supply. A study at the University of Arizona showed that, in the Tucson area, a swimming pool required on average 68 gallons of water per day in March and 84 in the summer for refilling the pool to compensate for evaporation, for cleaning the pool filter, and for pool maintenance.[2] A pool with a pool pump will also significantly increase a households' electricity use, contributing to air pollution and global warming.

Among other major recreational choices, snowmobiling will do more damage than cross-country skiing. A fifty-foot power yacht or jet ski will do much more environmental harm than a sailboat or canoe. We are sure you can think of other similar sets of recreational choices.

BECOME A WEIGHT WATCHER

In asking you to think about weight when making consumer decisions, we are referring not to your own body weight but to the weight of the things you buy. All things being equal, the purchase of a heavy item will have a larger impact than the purchase of a light one. Of course, everything isn't always equal. If it were, we would not have had to do any analysis to write this book; we could have just taken out a scale. Chemical pesticides are so toxic, for example, that even a few pounds can have a much greater impact than a ton of bricks. The production of

Investigation Pays Off

It was lucky Kim Stone was on the board of her condominium association when it came time to replace her building's roof. She and her family live in one of 25 units in an old Chicago factory that was converted to housing ten years ago.

All buildings need to have their roofs periodically replaced, but for one this size the cost can be quite high—about $100,000. The environmental implications of roofing alternatives can also be significant. But when Kim saw the proposed contract for the work, she was surprised and disheartened to discover that energy efficiency and the comfort of the building's occupants hadn't been considered. Although the top floor was often too hot in the summer, the roofing plans didn't address this problem and only called for minimal insulation.

Kim decided to do some investigation to see what could be done. For starters, she learned that a light-colored roofing membrane could be substituted for a typical black one. This would mean that less heat would get transmitted to the rooms below in the summer, and it wouldn't cost a cent more!

Increasing the insulation would, of course, add to the project's cost, but Kim's research showed that this would be good for the residents' pocketbooks as well as the environment. By combining information she obtained from a national environmental group with data about her building's roof, she determined that spending an extra $14,000 on insulation would pay for itself in just three years. After that, residents would continue to save on their energy bills. The reduced energy use would also eliminate as much air pollution and greenhouse gas emissions as normally produced by heating and air-conditioning an entire apartment. With solid information in hand, Kim was able to convince the condominium board to support her recommendations.

virgin aluminum is so energy intensive, and its mining has such great impacts, that recycling light aluminum cans is more important than recycling heavy glass.

In many situations the obvious environmental differences between two products are not so large, and the table of impacts per dollar in Appendix A will not be able to help you. You should then assume that the more weight, the greater the environmental impact.

For this reason, it's more important to recycle a three-pound Sunday newspaper than a one-ounce plastic yogurt container. Even if a hundred-pound clothes dresser is made from wood grown in an environmentally responsible manner, it will have a larger environmental impact than a half-pound videotape made from human-produced materials, once we factor in the energy required to harvest the wood, turn it into a dresser, and ship it to the consumer. This does not mean that you need to avoid purchasing all heavy products, but you should scrutinize those decisions more carefully, unless you use the light items in high quantities.

We aren't suggesting that you need to carry around a precision weighing instrument when you go to the store. Instead, we hope you will think in large-scale weight terms. If you use eight thousand pounds of gasoline in your car each year, but only seventeen pounds of plastic trash bags, it is clear which represents a bigger problem and where you can have a more dramatic impact on improving the environment. Moreover, by remembering the small weight of many consumer products, you can reduce your guilt and anxiety levels dramatically. Light nontoxic products, such as plastic trash bags, paper napkins, and leather wallets, do not deserve to be high priorities for environmental concern.

ANALYZE YOUR CONSUMPTION QUANTITATIVELY

You can take the dictum to watch the weight of your consumption one step further and analyze your consumption quantitatively. Let's imagine, for example, that you live in a southwestern community where water is relatively scarce and comes from depletable wells. To protect future water supplies, you decide you want to reduce your water consumption. Rather than try to remember the dozens of suggestions you may have heard for saving water and randomly implement those that you can recall, you should start by analyzing how you use water. Then try to identify two or three changes that will make a big difference. This will be easier than trying to implement a dozen new water-saving measures. You may discover, for example, that a hundred gallons of water a day go to watering your lawn and garden, while only two gallons go to brushing your teeth. If you change your plantings, settle for a less lush landscape, and alter your watering system, you may be able to reduce your water use by fifty gallons a day, whereas reducing the water you use when you brush your teeth by the same proportion would save a mere gallon a day. It is obvious that you should give priority to changing your lawn. Although it might be ideal to be a more frugal tooth brusher, the impact would be so small that you shouldn't feel guilty if you prefer not to change or just do not want to think about it.

When analyzing your consumption quantitatively, it is also useful to think in terms of the total payback from each particular action you might take. To use our water example again, you may conclude that the best place to cut down on water use is with showers, since there are five household members who each take a seven-minute daily shower, collectively using 175 gallons of water a day. Two ways to cut down on this use would be by asking everyone to shorten their shower from seven to five minutes or by installing a low-flow showerhead. Assuming you have an old five-gallon-per-minute showerhead, the former action would save ten gallons each time a family member remembered to be quicker, but a new 2.5-gallon-per-minute showerhead can be installed once, thereby saving half of the water, or 31,938 gallons in the first year alone. Installing the showerhead would clearly be the more effective and important action.

DON'T WORRY OR FEEL GUILTY ABOUT UNIMPORTANT DECISIONS

Both to increase your environmental effectiveness and to avoid unnecessary guilt or confusion, we would like to see you remain focused on those environmental choices where your actions can make the greatest difference. Our advice up to now has tried to help you do this.

What should you do if you are faced with a consumer choice that is not covered in our list of priorities in chapter 4 or by the principles in this chapter? If you do not know for sure whether it seriously damages the environment, don't worry about it. Concentrate instead on more obvious problems. There are certainly enough cases where it is crystal clear that the actions of Americans cause serious environmental damage that you should not devote much energy to matters where the evidence is inconclusive or the harm is small.

To help you avoid both unnecessary actions and unnecessary guilt, we want to point out several products that are not especially harmful and some consumer choices that are not especially important. But please keep in mind that this does not mean we are endorsing unnecessary waste or gross excesses of consumption, even of things that are relatively benign.

Cloth Versus Disposable Diapers

When a couple is expecting a new child, curious friends are likely to ask them two anxiety-provoking questions: Have you selected a name for the baby, and will you be using cloth or disposable diapers? For many pending parents, the latter question seems to offer two unappealing alternatives: the inconvenience of cloth diapers versus the significant environmental damage of disposables. They may worry that choosing disposables will expose them to their friends and neighbors as environmentally irresponsible.

During the 1980s nothing seemed to symbolize America's wasteful throwaway society better than the disposable diaper. When writers tallied up the total production of disposable diapers, they came up with some truly dramatic and scary statistics: each year, disposables consumed 1,265,000 metric tons of wood pulp and 75,000 metric tons of plastic. As *50 Simple Things You Can Do to Save the Earth* observed, "Americans throw away 18 billion disposable diapers a year—enough to stretch to the moon and back seven times."[3]

Faced with such startling images, many parents—ourselves among them—concluded that a return to old-fashioned cloth diapers offered a straightforward, logical way to end this waste. Not only were cloth diapers made of natural materials and reusable many times, but when they wore out, diaper services recycled them into rags for industry. Surely here was a case where a traditional product was environmentally superior to a recent, wasteful technological innovation.

To counter this perception and show that their product was not so harmful after all, disposable diaper companies commissioned studies to directly compare the environmental impacts of paper and cloth diapers. A 1990 Arthur D. Little Company report, funded by Procter & Gamble, the largest manufacturer of disposables, claimed that the production, washing, and disposal of cloth diapers consumed over three times more energy than disposables. At the request of the industry-funded Council on Solid Waste Solutions, another consulting firm, Franklin Associates, produced results nearly as favorable to disposable diapers: compared with cloth, they consumed about half the energy, used one-quarter as much water, produced half as much air pollution, and generated about one-seventh the water pollution. This study did acknowledge, however, that disposable diapers sent four times as much garbage to landfills.[4]

In response, the National Association of Diaper Services produced its own study. It argued that cloth diapers actually used 70 percent less energy than disposables. In great part the differences between the studies came from their different starting assumptions. The Arthur D. Little report, for example, counted the burning of wastes from the manufacturing process to produce electricity as an energy credit, while the Diaper Services' report did not count this as a benefit, since the burning process produced air pollutants as well as energy.[5] Environmental groups and other researchers weighed in with their own critiques of the various studies.

A more sophisticated 1993 follow-up analysis by Franklin Associates—this time funded by the American Paper Institute—tried to end the debate by more thoroughly considering all the impacts of the two different types of diapers "from cradle to grave." For this assessment of diapers over their entire life cycle, the authors factored in the differing rates at which babies go through cloth versus paper diapers, the materials used in the packages for disposable diapers, and the plastic pants and pins used with the cloth variety. They also clearly distinguished between home laundering of cloth diapers and diaper services. They found that the differences between types of diapers were less dramatic than in the earlier studies. The authors concluded that commercially laundered cloth diapers required 13 percent more energy than disposable diapers. Because of the lower efficiency of home washers and dryers compared with commercial systems, home laundering of diapers used the most energy—27 percent more than disposables. In terms of water use, diaper services were the worst, requiring about 2.5 times more water than disposables, while home laundering required slightly more than twice as much. On the other hand, disposable diapers produced about twice as much solid waste as the other two alternatives. Air pollutant emissions were roughly comparable for disposable diapers and commercially laundered cloth ones.[6]

By the time this report appeared, hundreds of thousands of dollars had been spent studying the environmental impact of diapers. The numbing weight of all the statistics in the various studies had wrung much of the fury and emotional intensity out of the diaper debate. In the broader public, cloth diapers were no longer the same strong symbol of environmental purity they had been during the 1980s.

But this doesn't mean that there had been a definitive answer to the question of whether cloth or paper diapers are better for the environment. Despite all the money spent on life-cycle analyses, it remains difficult to conclusively decide the overall environmental merits of two different products, especially when it is clear that all the evidence does not point in the same direction. The public should assume that any life-cycle study contains some margin of error.

What we can conclude is that most people should not waste a lot of time or energy trying to decide which type of diapers to use based on environmental considerations. Even if it turns out that paper diapers are indeed marginally better than cloth or vice versa, it seems clear that the advantages of one over the other are nowhere near as dramatic as they had seemed back in the 1980s. Cloth and disposables will remain two relatively equally matched alternatives.

This means that other decisions described in this book are much more important than what type of diaper to use. If you live in one of the relatively few places where the cost of landfill disposal is very high and there are no sound alternatives to landfills, you might want to lean toward cloth diapers. If you live in a place where water is critically scarce, you might want to choose paper. But most people should choose whichever type of diaper makes the most sense in terms of cost, convenience, and the comfort of the child.

For society as a whole, there are ways to reduce the environmental impact of diapers no matter what type is used. In recent years, because disposable diapers have become thinner and lighter, their environmental impact has decreased. This trend should be encouraged to continue. Similarly, as commercial and home washers and dryers have become more efficient, the impact of cloth diapers has been reduced. This trend is also desirable.

Paper Versus Plastic Bags

In the 1980s many supermarkets tried to shift from using paper bags to plastic for packaging their customers' groceries, since the plastic (polyethylene) sacks were less expensive. Because so many customers complained—partly because the plastic bags were flimsier but also because they were not made of natural material like paper—most food stores ultimately backed down. They now generally give customers a choice between paper and plastic. Many shoppers choose paper because they assume it is the environmentally better alternative, while some others who find plastic to be more convenient feel guilty about their decision.

The plastic manufacturers were naturally unwilling to concede that their product was environmentally inferior, and they funded studies to show its advantages. In a thorough analysis of the two types of grocery bags, Franklin Associates—the same people who had conducted some of the diaper studies—concluded that the manufacture of plastic sacks actually produced considerably less air pollution, waterborne wastes, and industrial solid waste than the manufacture of paper. Because plastic bags are much lighter, they also produced much less postconsumer solid waste, taking up less space in landfills. The researchers found that plastic sacks continued to have these advantages even when one assumed that grocery store clerks packed less in each bag, thereby requiring 1.5 or 2 times as many bags to pack the same quantity of groceries as paper.[7]

It was less clear which type of sack was preferable in terms of energy use. Plastic bags required less overall energy to manufacture when the researchers assumed a use rate of 1.5 to 1, but about the same amount of energy at a use rate of 2 to 1, with relatively high recycling rates.[8] Moreover, much of the energy for making paper bags came from a renewable energy source—wood.

So what should we make of this study? On balance, plastic sacks seem to have come out as the environmentally superior choice. However, we should keep in mind that paper grocery bags are recycled at a higher rate and are probably also reused more frequently, since many home kitchen trash containers are designed with paper grocery sacks in mind. It is therefore unlikely that one choice is all that much better than the other. This means that there is no reason for consumers to feel obliged to use paper sacks or to feel guilty if they choose plastic.

When you go to the store, choose whichever type of bag you find most convenient. Personally, we find paper sacks work best since we can reuse them in our kitchen trash containers, thereby avoiding having to purchase plastic trash can liners. And it is certainly desirable to avoid waste by bringing your own cloth bags or asking store clerks to give you your purchases without bags when they are unnecessary. But no matter what you do, it's not all that big a deal.

Disposable Cups

The throwaway drinking cup has become a powerful symbol of America's wasteful, polluting society. Nevertheless, it is not a major sin against the environment to use an occasional paper or plastic cup. These lightweight products require relatively little energy to make and take up little space in landfills. Of course, you don't want to be wasteful, but a few dozen, or even a couple hundred, disposable cups a year will have relatively little environmental impact.

The popular demonization of disposable cups has caused some individuals and groups to spend too much time worrying about them. For example, the cup issue has often become an important one for religious congregations that want to make their church or synagogue more environmentally responsible. Their members have identified the use of throwaway cups as one of their major environmental failings. When they have then been able to reduce or eliminate the use of disposables easily, the end result is a desirable one.

Unfortunately, some congregations have squandered endless hours debating whether to ban disposables while other congregations have considered expensive, unnecessary measures. One minister told us that his congregants wanted to purchase ceramic coffee mugs and install a dishwasher in their social hall, so they could avoid using plastic cups at meetings. When we discovered that their total cup use was only about forty a week, we urged them to spend their budgeted $450 on other measures, such as weather-stripping for their old drafty building. They would not only do more for the environment but would end up saving money on heating.

Paper Plates, Plastic Utensils, and Paper Napkins

As with disposable cups, it all comes down to quantity. It is of course best to avoid wasting materials, but you should consider how much waste is involved. If you ate all your meals using one-time-use plastic utensils and paper plates, it would not only be unnecessarily wasteful but would cost more money than washing dishes. (However, we must remember that dishwashing also requires resources—water for cleaning and fossil fuels or some other energy source for heating the water.)

On the other hand, an occasional picnic or purchase from a fast-food restaurant will have little environmental impact and should not be a cause for concern. You do not need to make a fetish about always avoiding paper goods and plastic.

Spray Cans and Styrofoam Cups

Back in the 1970s spray cans of hair spray, deodorant, whipped cream, and other consumer products used ozone-depleting substances, so environmentally conscious consumers stopped using them. In response to consumer pressure, companies began in the late 1970s to switch away from using ozone-depleting substances as propellants for household aerosol products. Then later the Clean Air Act and EPA regulations mandated restrictions on environmentally harmful propellants. Nevertheless, many people still do not feel comfortable using spray cans.

Most spray cans currently rely on hydrocarbons such as methane, ethane, propane, cyclopropane, butane, and cyclopentane. They do not contribute to ozone depletion, have low toxicity, and have relatively little impact on global warming given the small quantities in a spray can. You should not feel embarrassed or guilty to spray away.

Like spray cans, polystyrene "styrofoam" cups previously damaged the ozone layer. They don't do this anymore, so you shouldn't feel guilty about using them in moderation.

Cotton Versus Synthetic Clothes

At various times, synthetic fabrics like polyester have made it onto environmentalists' enemies lists. Cotton, in contrast, has had a much more "green" image. After all, what could be more natural and pure than those fluffy little white balls growing on green plants in a farmer's field? It was because of cotton's wholesome reputation that President George Bush announced in 1992 that rejecting synthetics in favor of cotton would "restore America's moral fiber."[9]

Unfortunately, cotton farming causes considerable environmental damage. Cotton growers use large quantities of agricultural chemicals, much more than for most food crops. They may apply as many as ten pesticide treatments during a growing season, as well as fungicides, fumigants, fertilizers, and herbicides. The environmental damage doesn't end when the cotton is picked, since processing and dyeing also send dangerous chemicals into the environment.

Does this mean that we would make an important, if unfashionable, environmental statement by always wearing polyester and other synthetic fibers? Not really, since they are made from petroleum, whose extraction and refinement have severe effects on the environment, and toxic chemicals may be released in their dyeing. Even wool falls short on close inspection, since sheep can degrade grazing land and wool clothes generally require dry cleaning, which is more harmful than washing clothes in water.

All of the major fabrics have problems, although none of them rank all that high on our chart of impacts per dollar. Because the problems are different for each of them, it is hard to come up with a clear-cut answer to the question of which is best. If you can find clothes made from organic cotton or recycled materials, like the fleece sweaters that some "green" clothing companies offer, by all means give them special attention, but they are not going to be available for most of your clothing choices. In most cases, you should not dwell on whether one fabric choice is better or worse for the environment than another.

If you want to limit the environmental impact associated with the manufacture of clothing, you can purchase vintage clothes and avoid unnecessary clothing purchases rather than worry about whether you are dressing in cotton, rayon, wool, polyester, silk, or something else.

Crumpled-up Newspapers Versus Polystyrene "Peanuts" for Packing

Many people hesitate to use polystyrene "peanuts" (also sometimes called "ghost poops") or other similar packing products, because they are made from synthetic materials, require resources to manufacture, and will ultimately end up in landfills. It seems better to just take some old newspaper and crumple it up. In some cases this is indeed true, but we can't turn this into a general rule. Because the newspaper is heavier, it will take more energy to transport it to its destination. Depending upon whether and how you are going to be shipping a package, as well as on the exact weight difference between the packing alternatives and other factors, either newspaper or synthetic packing materials will be a marginally better choice for the environment. But we want to emphasize the word *marginally*. Neither choice does very much harm. Synthetic packing materials are intentionally designed to be light, so only small quantities of raw materials go into making the amount you will use for packing a box or two. Major businesses that ship hundreds of thousands of packages a year need to worry about the environmental implications of their packing and packaging choices; individual consumers do not.

LOOK FOR OPPORTUNITIES TO BE A LEADER

It is generally more effective to be an early adopter of a new technology or environmental practice than to be a later follower. We can illustrate this principle with the case of solar hot water heaters. The companies making these products are generally quite small and have relatively low sales. The purchase decisions of just several thousand people, or even several hundred in some cases, can mean the difference between the success and failure of these companies. A relatively few people across the country deciding to be early purchasers of the new generation of solar hot water systems can ensure the growth of the industry and lead to much wider later use of the technology.

Similarly, electric cars have recently gone on sale in several states. If just several thousand people choose to purchase or lease one of these cars, they will make electric cars a marketplace success and prod manufacturers to sell them in other parts of the country. The actions of these relatively few people will also encourage other companies to produce electric cars to appeal to the now-identified emerging niche market.

Being a leader also helps educate one's friends and neighbors. If you were to purchase a solar hot water system or an electric car, your neighbors would notice and would ask you about it and learn something about the promise of these technologies.

You don't need to purchase expensive items like cars and water heaters in order to be a leader, however. The first person in a neighborhood to ride a bicycle to work or adopt low-impact landscaping can have a powerful effect on those nearby. These sorts of publicly visible actions can have an impact on several levels. When you do something that your friends and neighbors can see, you go on record as being concerned about the environment and you act as a role model for them. Early recyclers in a community, for example, very publicly signaled their commitment to environment action. Gradually, as more people—whether in a neighborhood, office, or school—visibly demonstrated this commitment, others felt prodded or shamed into participating.

Ideally, your publicly visible leadership actions should be on the political as well as personal level. If government officials are to implement laws and regulations to reduce pollution, they need to feel that their constituents care about the environment. You can write letters to your local newspaper, contact your elected representatives, and join at least one environmental organization. By letting your elected representatives know that one of their constituents is active in a particular environmental

Changing an Institution

By changing a single institution, Walter Simpson, the energy officer at the State University of New York at Buffalo (UB), has made a big difference for the environment. Admittedly, he has a large institution to work with, but many people can multiply their impact by looking to change the institutions they are connected to.

With its 30,000 students, faculty, and staff, the university has a large environmental footprint. Simpson and a colleague calculated, for example, that the university was responsible for annually emitting 319,000 tons of the greenhouse gas carbon dioxide. That worked out to 10.5 tons per person per year!

Using a variety of energy-saving measures, Simpson has led an effort that reduced per-building energy use by over 25 percent. The payback has been economic as well as environmental—the university overall now spends $9 million less a year on its energy bills than would otherwise be the case.

Many of UB's measures have been decidedly low tech—installing low-flow showerheads, controlling lights with photocells, removing unnecessary lamps, and adding insulation. Just changing the target heating temperature from 72 to 68 degrees and the target cooling temperature from 74 to 76 or 80 degrees saved $600,000 a year.

Although some of the innovations at the university have been more complicated technically, Simpson does not believe the technical parts of his job are necessarily the most important. Instead, he realizes that, to change an institution, one needs to concentrate on motivating, changing, and organizing people.[10]

group, you will increase that organization's political clout. You can also think about which of your actions can serve as a model that will prompt your friends, colleagues, and neighbors to get involved in the political process.

A different way to be a leader is to work to change the various institutions and organizations you are a part of—

schools, businesses, community groups, and religious institutions. Part of your consumption takes place through these organizations—the paper you use at work, the food you eat at social club meetings, the energy that heats your child's school. If you want to reduce your overall environmental impact, you should think about ways to change your institutions so that you consume less through them.

Changing an institution will usually require you to play some sort of leadership role there. But because this will reduce other people's consumption at the same time it reduces yours, you can often have a much greater impact than by focusing just on your own household. If you can get your place of work to institute a paper recycling program, for example, you will obviously recycle much more material than you ever could around your own home. Similarly, insulating a building as large as a church will likely save more energy than insulating your house or apartment.

BUY MORE OF THOSE THINGS THAT HELP THE ENVIRONMENT

Perhaps it will seem ironic in a book about the problems associated with consumption for us to ask people to consume more. But there are instances where you can actually help the environment by buying more of certain products. In some cases, a purchase of one item can reduce your consumption of other, more environmentally damaging materials, especially fossil fuels. In other cases, you can be a leader who helps new environmentally beneficial products gain a foothold in the marketplace. We have already mentioned some of these products—energy-efficient appliances, solar hot water heaters, organic foods, electric cars, insulation and weather-stripping—but here are a few additional products that are good to buy.

Microwave Ovens

Many people concerned about overconsumption resist buying a microwave oven. After all, why do they need another appliance when they may already have a cook-top, full-size oven, and toaster oven? Moreover, something seems wrong about an appliance that doesn't cook food the "normal" way but instead uses high-frequency radio waves.

Microwaves are actually environment friendly devices compared with conventional ovens. Because a microwave only uses one-third of the energy of a conventional oven, it allows you to cut down on your consumption of electricity or natural gas. Because it throws off less heat into your kitchen, you will also keep your kitchen cooler and save on summer air-conditioning costs (if you have an air conditioner). The American Council for an Energy-Efficient Economy has estimated the relative costs and energy use of different methods for cooking the same casserole. What would take an hour in a 350-degree electric oven takes only one-quarter of that, or fifteen minutes, in a microwave. The difference in energy used and expense is even greater—2.0 kilowatt-hours and 16 cents versus 0.36 kilowatt-hours and 3 cents. Other options—a crockpot, a toaster oven, a frying pan, a gas oven, and an electric convection oven—are also better than the large electric oven, but they are all two to nearly four times worse than the microwave.[11]

We know that energy use in the form of either electricity or natural gas is responsible for considerable environmental damage. So don't feel guilty; if you can afford it, go out and buy yourself a microwave!

Recycled Products

Recycling fulfills its promise only when recycled products substitute for new ones. When people buy recycled rather than virgin paper, it saves trees and energy. When they choose clothes made from recycled plastics, they may avoid the pesticide use associated with cotton production or some of the fossil-fuel consumption associated with making synthetics. In addition, the more people buy recycled products, the more money local governments and businesses can get for the material they collect. When these prices are high, everyone has a greater incentive to recycle more of their trash.

Of course, you should never buy anything you don't need or want. But when you plan to buy something, it makes sense to go recycled. For the individual consumer, paper products are where you have the greatest opportunity to purchase recycled materials. For a wide range of uses, from toilet paper and paper towels to stationery, good-quality recycled products are available.

Office Equipment for Telecommuters

Telecommuting has been one of the most positive environmental trends of recent years, because it reduces the environmental damage associated with driving. It can also reduce traffic congestion. If the purchase of a computer, answering machine, or fax for your home is the obstacle preventing you from setting up a telecommuting relationship with your workplace, you should feel justified buying these things on environmental grounds. Of course, if you currently walk to work or ride a bicycle, telecommuting will not reduce your environmental impact in the same way.

Water-saving Faucets, Toilets, and Showerheads

Water-saving devices can reduce water use dramatically, often by half or more. Depending upon the water rates in your community, they can pay for themselves in lower water bills.

In addition to saving water, new showerheads and faucet attachments can reduce energy use and lower the amount of money you spend to heat water. If you have an older showerhead that uses 5 gallons per minute, you will find few easier or more cost-effective ways to help the environment than to buy a new 2.5-gallon-per-minute model. It will likely cost you less than $20 and take only a few minutes to install.

THINK ABOUT NONENVIRONMENTAL REASONS FOR REDUCING CONSUMPTION

This may seem like a peculiar way to become an environmentally responsible consumer, but it can actually make it easier to follow the previous seven rules.

Many Americans realize that there are reasons other than the environment for examining their personal consumption patterns. Deep down inside, and sometimes close to the surface, they feel that our society places too great an emphasis on money-making and material possessions. When, in 1995, the Harwood Group studied the public's views on consumption, materialism, and the environment, they found that most people expressed concern that "materialism, greed, and selfishness increasingly dominate American life, crowding out a more meaningful set of values centered on family, responsibility, and community." Although people want financial security and material comforts, they feel that materialism has thrown their lives out of balance. They sense that an overemphasis on making money to obtain more and more possessions does not lead to greater satisfaction but rather takes time away from such appealing and important activities as building a close-knit community, spending time with their family, teaching children sound values, and developing new skills and interests.[12]

Americans express especially strong concern about the impact of consumerism on the younger generation. The Harwood Group study found that 86 percent of adults believed that "today's youth are too focused on buying and consuming things."[13] Many parents feel pressed by their children to buy trendy toys, clothes, and electronic devices. Not only do parents have difficulty softening their children's acquisitiveness, but they also find it hard to change their own emphasis on material possessions. Daily, advertisers confront children and adults alike with hundreds of well-crafted messages designed to convince them to purchase additional items and lust after additional possessions. Many jobs are structured in a way that puts pressure on employees to work long hours to try to move up the corporate ladder to avoid being left behind. American culture makes it easy to fall into a pattern of spend and accumulate.

To counter the momentum to focus on material possessions, you can try to step back from your daily routine and think more reflectively about your goals and values. How do you want to live your life? What values would you like to pass on to your children? Are there important, enriching personal, family, or community activities that you wish you had more time for? Are there ways in which you can still have financial security and a reasonable level of material comfort while allowing more time for these activities? In recent years various religious organizations have shown an increasing interest in helping people address these sorts of questions, while secular books and community groups have also considered them.

Because of the considerable ambivalence about present-day materialism that most of us have, it is likely that, if you engage in the introspective exercise just described, you will end up deciding to at least modestly reduce the priority you have consciously or unconsciously been placing on accumulating material possessions. This will likely lead you to reduce your purchases, which will tend to have a beneficial environmental effect. You will probably also find it easier to resist the temptation to purchase heavily advertised products that you know are harmful to the environment. And you will more likely have the inclination and time for the sorts of political and community-oriented activities that are necessary to move the country as a whole in the right direction.

It is important, however, not to assume that a general avoidance of high consumption will be totally effective in reducing environmental damage. The basic premise of this book is that all consumption is not equally harmful. People who forgo purchasing a new energy-efficient refrigerator or low-polluting car, for example, because they want a more frugal lifestyle do not do a favor for the environment by continuing to use outmoded, more polluting models. The simultaneous application of the various recommendations in this chapter, and in the rest of the book, will therefore yield the best result.

7

What You Can Ask Government to Do

When faced with major problems, such as air pollution, global warming, habitat alteration, and water pollution, individuals can easily feel as if nothing they can do will make a meaningful difference. But as the previous chapters have shown, people can significantly reduce the environmental impacts associated with consumption if they consume wisely.

Nevertheless, by themselves, the personal actions we have recommended cannot solve all of these problems. Consumers are often severely limited in their choices, and the economic market is frequently structured in a way that makes environmentally sound options unattractive. In other cases, businesses and other institutions, rather than individual consumers, are the key decision-makers. Government can, and should, help expand the choices, make responsible behavior appealing, and influence the behavior of institutions. Good government policies are needed for action on the personal lifestyle level to succeed.

Anyone can take steps to improve the policies of local, state, and federal government. The methods you can use to accomplish this may not seem novel or exciting, but they have repeatedly been proven to work: keeping informed about what government and your elected representatives are doing for the environment; voting and working for candidates who will push for environmental improvement; contacting your elected officials to express your views; writing letters to newspapers to influence public understanding of environmental issues; supporting and working with environmental organizations that are working for sound government policies; and encouraging like-minded citizens to get involved in the political process.

Tens of millions of Americans care deeply about the environment. If just a small fraction of them were to spend just ten additional hours a year trying to influence government policy, it could make a dramatic difference. We hope you will commit to becoming more politically engaged.

If you do, what should you expect and ask of government? You might think of consumption as a game, with consumers as the players and government as developer and arbiter of many of the rules. We are reminded of our own childhood experiences, when we frequently altered game rules to suit our whims and meet our needs. In Monopoly, for example, we increased the amount of money players received when they landed on "free parking." In volleyball we gave the server two chances to get the ball over the net. And in baseball we prohibited hitting to right field when we didn't have enough players for full nine-person teams. Even though we didn't realize it at the time, each one of these rule changes affected how the games progressed, as well as who won and who lost.

In a similar way government's regulations, taxes, and spending priorities influence what gets produced by manufacturers and what gets consumed by the public. Over the years governments have instituted many sound policies for helping consumers act responsibly. However, because politicians and government officials think about multiple issues, many other policies have been set without consideration for how they will affect the environment. Either intentionally or unwittingly, policies have often ended up making it more difficult or less appealing for consumers to reduce environmental damage. So sometimes government has helped the environment, while other times it has hurt it.

In this chapter we will focus on four key strategies governments can use to ensure that the rules of the consumption game help consumers to act in an environmentally responsible manner.

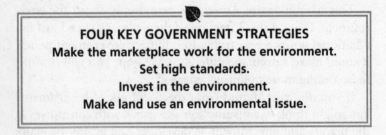

FOUR KEY GOVERNMENT STRATEGIES
Make the marketplace work for the environment.
Set high standards.
Invest in the environment.
Make land use an environmental issue.

MAKE THE MARKETPLACE WORK FOR THE ENVIRONMENT

When functioning properly, the free market provides people, businesses, and organizations with useful information about how to spend their money. But when the prices charged in the marketplace do not reflect the true cost of goods or services, consumers end up basing their decisions on incomplete information.

Some products have artificially low prices, because our economic system does not require manufacturers and distributors to pay for all the environmental and social costs of what they produce. When you fill up your car at a gas station, for example, the price of gasoline does not include what society will need to pay to address health problems caused by air pollution or clean-up costs from water pollution. Similarly, farmers who spray pesticides on their fields do not get charged for dealing with the chemicals that run off into streams or seep into groundwater.

Government policies that bring such "external" costs into the prices consumers pay make the marketplace work more effi-

---

Influencing Government Policy

Because Marjorie and Louis Davis of Decatur, Georgia, are model political activists, their actions illustrate many of the ways in which individuals can successfully influence their fellow citizens and the policymaking process.

For the Davises, the key to effectiveness is being well informed on those issues that they care most about, like renewable energy. They therefore belong to environmental organizations that provide useful information. Even more important, they rely on the Internet to keep up with developments. To inform others, they help staff environmental groups' literature tables at Earth Day and other community events.

With sound information as a starting point, they write frequent letters to the editor of the *Atlanta Journal Constitution.* Because that newspaper limits the number of times any individual's letters can appear, the Davises sometimes send their letters to other, smaller newspapers in the area. Every time one of their letters gets published, they reach many thousands of people and can influence their views.

The Davises have also made it a point to find out the names of the environmental aides to their senators in Washington. Through letters and phone calls, they have established first-name relationships with these individuals and feel comfortable contacting them to pass along information and ideas.

When an election is near, the Davises find out the environmental positions of the various candidates and then work for those candidates who will do the most to advance those issues. In addition, because of her political activism, Marjorie earned a seat on a state committee that interviews candidates for the Public Service Commission, which regulates the electricity industry.

ciently and reduce the consumption of environmentally damaging products. Policymakers can also use the free market in other ways to ensure that purchasing decisions take the environment into account. Here are key strategies for making the free market better reflect concern for the environment:

Stop subsidizing pollution and waste.

Because of decisions made long ago and the continued influence of powerful interests, the government subsidizes various environmentally harmful activities, thereby artificially lowering their cost. For the free market to work effectively, such subsidies should be eliminated, or at least reduced.

The federal tax code provides preferential treatment to the oil industry, for example. Because of special corporate income tax credits and deductions, oil companies pay an effective income tax rate of 11 percent, compared with an average of 18 percent for other companies. If they were taxed at the total industry average (including the oil industry) of 17 percent, they would have had to pay $2 billion extra in 1991. On top of these tax preferences, the Department of Energy spends more than $100 million a year to develop and improve oil production techniques, while the Army Corps of Engineers pays for infrastructure improvements related to the shipping of oil. These and other subsidies help keep the price of oil artificially cheap.[1]

Water is also often heavily subsidized, especially for agriculture, which consumes more water than all other uses combined. Nationwide, irrigation receives government subsidies totaling $2.5 billion.[2] Because the government does not charge the full price of the water it provides, farmers have not always had sufficient incentive to conserve or to install more efficient irrigation systems. And manufacturers have not had enough of a financial incentive to develop water-saving devices.

If farmers had to pay the full cost of the water they use, they would use less of it. Of course, the price of the products they sell would have to go up, but consumers are already paying, through the taxes that subsidize irrigation rather than at the grocery or clothing store. Especially in arid parts of the country like California and the Southwest, it is silly to have a subsidized price system that encourages inefficient use of such an important yet scarce resource as water. When farmers in parts of Texas and elsewhere have been forced to adopt water-efficiency measures because their water supply was running out, they have been able to reduce their use considerably, sometimes by more than half.[3] So there is much to be gained by eliminating subsidies and setting the price of water accurately.

The federal government undercharges users for taking valuable resources from government land. Ranchers in parts of the West pay much less to graze animals on government-owned lands than they would have to pay for the use of private lands. Similarly, some timber companies pay only part of the market price for logging on federal lands, with the National Forest Service picking up the rest of the tab—about $1 billion.[4] Not only does such undercharging encourage overuse, but it denies government agencies valuable income that could be devoted to resource conservation and environmental protection. Although a particular special interest may benefit from such subsidies, the environment and society as a whole suffer.

Germany has addressed a more subtle form of subsidy. In the United States manufacturers generally do not have to pay for the disposal of what they sell. Instead, consumers throw out or recycle any packaging or waste, and the costs of garbage pickup and disposal are covered by tax dollars or fees. A landmark 1991 German law makes producers responsible for the packaging they generate. They must either reuse it or pay for recycling it. Different packaging gets handled in different ways—it is either returned to the manufacturer, returned to retail stores, or handled through joint collection systems paid for by the manufacturers. Germany's complicated system has certainly had some difficulties, but it has also stimulated manufacturers to use much less packaging and to recycle much more. Inspired by the German example, several other countries have established systems for ensuring that producers take responsibility for the waste they produce.[5]

Tax pollution.

Taxes are such a politically charged subject in 1990s America that it is hard to have a calm, rational public discussion about them. For this reason, ever since President Clinton's ill-fated effort to introduce an energy tax in 1993, most environmentalists have avoided the topic. But when one asks economists about ways to improve environmental quality, they point to taxes on environmentally damaging products and activities as the most efficient and fair policy solution. Energy taxes get the most attention, but there are also other possibilities, such as taxes on harmful types of packaging.

From an economist's standpoint, a well-crafted tax is an easy and fair way to increase the price of a polluting activity so that it includes those external social costs that would otherwise be ignored. Economists also like the fact that even as taxes provide financial reasons to take better care of the environment, they ultimately leave the final decision on what to buy and do up to consumers acting through the free market. MIT economics professor Paul Krugman has observed that "virtually every card-carrying economist" believes pollution taxes are a good idea.[6]

Unsurprisingly, neither politicians nor the general public have embraced the concept of pollution taxes. Politicians know that they have little to gain politically from talking about new taxes. Many members of the public worry that somehow they will be left with less money, while the government gets more to squander.

To reduce the fears associated with environmental taxes, most proponents these days talk in terms of "tax shifting"—the idea that government should reduce other levies, such as the income tax, at the same time that it raises taxes on polluting activities. In this way, taxpayers would not have to pay more overall but would still receive marketplace price signals to get them to spend less on environmentally undesirable products. A few groups like Redefining Progress and the World Resources Institute have actively promoted the tax shifting concept and have even calculated that lower income taxes, offset by higher consumption taxes, would yield a net gain for the economy by increasing investment and reducing environmental restoration expenses.[7] Although some other economists have questioned whether tax shifting would yield such a windfall, they acknowledge that the environment would benefit and that taxpayers would not be seriously hurt. Of course, any tax shifting would need to be done carefully, and strategies would need to be instituted to compensate low-income Americans who do not pay income taxes but who would have to pay the new environmental taxes. Krugman concludes that "The Great Green Tax Shift . . . has everything going for it. It is supported by good science and good economics, as well as by good intentions."[8]

Unfortunately, even though tax shifting to benefit the environment is an unassailably logical idea, it has made little headway in the political arena. We only have to look at the fate of the President's Council on Sustainable Development to see how reluctant political leaders are to support a new tax, even one that would be offset by other tax reductions. This council, instituted in response to the 1992 Earth Summit's call for countries to move toward more environmentally responsible behavior, included a task force on the topics of population and consumption. When it came time in 1996 for the task force to make its recommendations, its first one on consumption was to shift taxes. The committee members recommended: "The federal government should reorient fiscal policy to shift the tax burden from labor and investment toward consumption, particularly consumption of natural resources, virgin materials, and goods and services that pose significant environmental risks."[9]

Although the task force was co-chaired by a prominent member of the Clinton administration, Undersecretary of State for Global Affairs Timothy Wirth, and included a cabinet member, Commerce Secretary Ron Brown, its recommendation on taxes was greeted by silence from the president and others in his administration. Those responsible for political strategy made it clear, then and in subsequent years, that the administration was not willing to be perceived as advocating taxes as a solution to environmental problems.

Despite the political obstacles, environmental taxes remain a sound policy solution. Perhaps they can become a part of efforts in Washington to generally overhaul the tax system.

Provide tax incentives.

Tax credits and tax breaks can be the flip side of higher environmental taxes, but they are certainly easier to sell to politicians and the public. Rather than provide discouragement for environmentally harmful behavior via taxes, the government encourages environmentally beneficial behavior via tax incentives.

Small tax credits are already in place, for example, to encourage development of wind power and biomass for electricity. In early 1998, President Clinton proposed tax credits of $2,000 or more for people who buy cars or vans that have at least double the fuel efficiency of the average vehicle in its class. Similarly, five energy and environmental groups, including the Union of Concerned Scientists, have called on the government to provide tax credits to encourage manufacturers to invest in new equipment. They argue that "as a rule, the more modern the plant technology, the more energy efficient and the lower the level of environmental emissions." Because society benefits when companies modernize, it makes sense to provide businesses with financial incentives to take this step.[10]

Combine rewards for good consumer decisions with penalties for bad ones.

Some of the features of taxes and tax incentives can be combined into a system of rebates and fees, or "feebates," that avoids mentioning the dreaded "t" word (taxes). Because the rebates and fees are designed to balance out, the government ends up with no more, or no less, money overall. Such a feebate system has been most frequently considered for the sale of cars. Several states have explored the idea of instituting feebates, and Maryland even passed a law, which the federal government overturned by claiming it unfairly took over federal responsibilities. It is quite likely that some state will soon develop a plan that can overcome federal objections.

Under a feebate system for vehicles, the purchaser of a car that has low emissions of air pollutants and high fuel efficiency (so therefore uses little gas) would receive a rebate of perhaps several hundred dollars. Purchasers of electric and nongasoline-powered vehicles would also receive rebates. The money would come from fees paid by purchasers of vehicles that guzzle lots of gasoline and emit large quantities of air pollutants. This transfer of payments can be justified on the grounds that the purchasers of the more polluting vehicles will be saddling society with higher costs for health care and environmental cleanup. The exact level of fees and rebates would have to be worked out carefully, but the general concept is not complicated.

Consumers would still be free to purchase any vehicle they wished, but a feebate program would provide them with a financial incentive for making a sound environmental choice. Feebates would also have a beneficial impact on manufacturers, who would have an incentive to produce more of the vehicles that qualified for rebates, since those vehicles would be especially appealing to consumers.

Set a limit on emissions and allow companies to trade pollution permits.

With this more complicated approach, usually called "tradable permits," "emission reduction credits," or a "cap-and-trade system," the government sets a limit for an industry on how much of a particular pollutant it can emit. Particular companies are then assigned individual quotas, generally either based on a percentage of their past emissions or as the result of an auction. Companies that emit less than their quota can sell the leftover "pollution rights" to someone else. Because this sort of system can work only if it is possible to accurately measure emissions and if good monitoring mechanisms can be put in place, emissions trading will not work for every environmental problem.

Economists find this approach efficient and cost-effective. Companies can decide for themselves whether it is cheaper to reduce their own emissions or pay to buy leftover pollution rights from another company that reduces its emissions more than the minimum. As environmental economics specialist Frances Cairncross notes, "Companies for whom cleaning up is relatively inexpensive thus have an incentive to be as clean as possible. But the dirty can also stay in business, though carrying the extra cost of buying more pollution credits."[11] The result is that total pollution is reduced at the lowest possible cost, as determined by the free market. Although it can seem odd for the government to give companies a right to pollute, the environment benefits and the industry in question pays the price for the cleanup.

Many U.S. policymakers have found cap-and-trade systems appealing, because they avoid taxes and do not impact average citizens directly, but only indirectly through higher prices on the products from affected companies. In addition, by including the market mechanism of trading, this approach seems philosophically virtuous during an era when politicans favor free market principles.

Cap-and-trade systems have been tried in several situations, but most notably as part of the 1990 Clean Air Act Amendments to reduce acid rain. The law set a limit on emissions of sulfur dioxide, a key factor in acid rain and air pollution, and then allowed trading between polluters, primarily fossil-fuel-based electricity-generating plants. As the advocates of this approach predicted, it worked with marvelous efficiency to reduce emissions at a low cost—less than one-tenth of what some in the electric utility industry had claimed it would cost.

Given the experience of the Clean Air Act, the Clinton administration has made a cap-and-trade system an important part of its proposals for cutting U.S. emissions of greenhouse gases. The administration persuaded the rest of the world to include a trading system between countries in the 1997 agreement on global warming in Kyoto, Japan.

Charge deposits on items that should be returned.

If consumers are charged a refundable deposit when purchasing a product, they will most likely return it in order to get their money back. And if they don't, someone else will probably take the item to claim the deposit for themselves. Deposits work best when it is important to ensure the proper disposal of a used product, either because it is hazardous or because it could otherwise end up as litter.

For this reason, a few states charge deposits on lead-acid batteries. Germany places deposits on paint cans. In Norway a refundable deposit on automobiles has ensured that over 90 percent of cars get brought to an approved site at the end of their life.[12]

In the United States ten states have deposits on beer and soda containers. They initially passed these laws to cut down on roadside litter, which then declined. From an environmental standpoint, beverage deposits are also useful because they increase the number of aluminum cans that get recycled, saving 90 percent of the energy required to make new aluminum cans and preventing other harmful environmental impacts of the aluminum production process. In the ten so-called "bottle bill" states, approximately 85 percent of aluminum cans get returned and recycled, while only about 50 percent are recycled in the other forty states. According to the Container Recycling Institute, 36 billion aluminum cans with a scrap value of $600 million ended up in landfills in 1996.[13] Deposit systems in all fifty states would certainly reduce this waste.

Ironically, beverage deposits have come under attack in recent years as community recycling programs have grown. The beverage deposit systems, which require consumers to keep their bottles and cans out of regular recycling containers, represent a duplicative and competing recycling program. Not only are they more expensive per recycled item than community recycling programs, but the community programs can suffer financially, in part because they cannot make money from selling high-value aluminum. On balance, however, bottle bills remain worthwhile because the extra cost is small and they do increase recycling rates and reduce litter. A study by the Tellus Institute found that the cost of container deposit plans can be reduced and the impact on community recycling systems can be minimized by using a streamlined version of California's system where the state, rather than individual bottlers, collects the returns.[14]

SET HIGH STANDARDS

Despite the advantages of market-based solutions like deposits, taxes, and cap-and-trade schemes, policymakers need other tools in their arsenal for changing environmentally damaging consumer behaviors. For one thing, it is hard to use the marketplace to protect resources that have little economic value or whose value is difficult to quantify. Making markets the sole vehicle for environmental protection is asking for endless arguments over the correct price of clean water or an endangered species or an especially inspiring scenic view.

Even when it is possible to address a problem through the free market, market-based solutions may not achieve the desired end. Sometimes a theoretically appropriate market mechanism can produce unintended and undesirable consequences. More than two hundred communities, for example, charge householders for each bag of garbage that gets picked up at the curbside or dropped off at a landfill. This, in effect, puts a tax on garbage, which gives people an incentive to send fewer bags of garbage to the landfill. However, if the fee is set too high, some people respond to the economic incentive not just by producing less garbage but by dumping garbage illegally. This can be at least as big an economic and environmental problem as the high quantities of garbage that the fees were designed to counteract.[15]

There is also another limitation to market-based solutions. In some cases, consumers may not understand the financial implications of a purchasing decision unless they have help. It has long been the case, for example, that consumers benefit from buying an energy-efficient refrigerator. If it costs an extra $180 for an efficient model and consumers then save $31 per year on their electric bills, the initial investment will pay back $310 over a ten-year period. This represents better than a 10.5 percent compounded annual rate of return, much more than they would earn by putting the $180 in the bank.[16]

But on their own, most consumers would not be able to make an informed decision, since it is hard for them to figure out how much their current refrigerator costs to operate and they cannot tell how much one new model will save compared with another just by looking at it. For this reason, the government wisely stepped in to require each refrigerator to carry a label indicating exactly how much electricity it uses in a year and how much that will cost. This means that potential refrigerator purchasers can get the information they need to choose wisely.

The federal government helped even more by requiring manufacturers to meet minimum standards for refrigerators. Over time the average refrigerator has become three times as efficient, and the worst models were taken off the market. Consumers have benefited by having a much better selection of products to choose from. This has not only helped the environment but has cut Americans' electricity bills.

Although some politicians like to attack the concept of government regulation and to argue that American society would be better off if current regulations were dismantled, policies like the refrigerator labels and refrigerator standards are popular with consumers. We don't hear many people complaining that the federal government should not have forced refrigerator manufacturers to improve their products and that they long for the older type of refrigerators so that they can squander money on electricity. Americans will willingly accept certain types of rules and regulations to reduce the environmental impacts of their consumption.

When using strategies other than market-based mechanisms, the government should focus on setting clear and high standards. It should then either require manufacturers to meet those standards or tell consumers about the standards so they can make their own decisions. There are plenty of successful examples of both approaches.

Require efficiency.

In 1987 amendments to the Energy Policy and Conservation Act established national efficiency standards for various home appliances, ranging from refrigerators, clothes washers, and ovens to pool heaters and fluorescent lamp ballasts. The law authorized the Department of Energy to periodically review and update these standards. Additional legislation in 1992 not only added other appliances but covered such commercial and industrial equipment as commercial air conditioners, electric motors, water heaters, and certain types of lamps. Most manufacturers, somewhat unexpectedly, supported these various national standards, since they seemed preferable to having to comply with a hodge-podge of divergent state regulations.[17] As in many similar situations, because companies want to be able to plan ahead, industry's greatest fear was not government regulation but rather uncertainty and unpredictability.

In 1996 the Department of Energy estimated that the various appliance standards would "save consumers $22 billion through the year 2000 and reduce emissions by more than 50 million tons of carbon dioxide and 750 thousand tons of nitrogen oxide through the year 2000."[18] The previous year the American Council for an Energy-Efficient Economy had estimated that the existing appliance and equipment efficiency standards will save consumers and businesses about $190 billion on their energy bills over the forty-year period from 1990 to 2030. This same study acknowledged that the standards will also cost consumers $59 billion in higher appliance and equipment prices, but on balance the net savings will be considerable.[19] And new, more rigorous standards that will go into effect in future years will only increase the savings to consumers and to the environment.

The refrigerator standards have often been held up as a special success, not only because they reduced substantially the energy requirements for a large household electricity user, but because they have had so little impact on the price of new models. Back in 1989, when the DOE issued a refrigerator standard requiring an average 25 percent reduction in energy use by 1993, no mass-produced models met the standard. But by 1993 all new refrigerators met the standard, and they did so at prices comparable to those of the inefficient 1989 models.[20] A new standard for refrigerators and freezers that will go into effect in

2001 will cut energy use another 30 percent.[21] We could easily tell similar success stories for most of the other appliances that consumers use daily.

Efficiency standards can work for water as well as energy. A 1992 federal law requires that new household toilets use only 1.6 gallons per flush. Given that toilets are the biggest water users in the home and that old toilets use up to six gallons per flush, this represents a tremendous reduction in water use. Unfortunately, some of the first of the new toilets on the market worked less than flawlessly and sometimes required two or three flushes. This certainly does not invalidate the concept of setting high but realistic standards for water efficiency. In the case of toilets, better models have already been developed, and most toilet manufacturers want to keep the toilet regulation, since they prefer to live with the certainty of a stable, long-term standard. The same 1992 law also established standards for showerheads and faucets.

Make renewable energy a standard.

Generating electricity from renewable energy sources, such as wind and sunlight, is usually much kinder to the environment than using fossil fuels—coal, oil, and natural gas. In recent years the cost of using renewable energy technologies has come down dramatically, but so has the cost of fossil fuels. This has made it difficult for renewables to capture a large share of the electricity market. Currently only 8 percent of the nation's energy is generated using them, and most of that comes from water power.

For America to make the needed transition away from fossil fuels, renewables will have to come on line at a much faster rate. Many public opinion surveys over the last decade have indicated that the public realizes this necessity and would like to get more of its electricity from renewables.[22] Various environmental groups and policymakers have consequently tried to find ways to speed their development. Initially they focused much of their attention on trying to eliminate subsidies for fossil fuels, as well as on other market-based approaches that would recognize the high environmental and social costs of these traditional energy sources. They also tried to secure and then retain tax credits for renewables.

But starting in 1995, when several states started to consider deregulating their electric utility systems and allowing consumers to buy power from competing suppliers, renewables advocates began working to ensure that deregulation would help rather than hinder renewables development. They worried that, in an unregulated market, environmental quality and other nonprice factors would be ignored. They looked for ways to ensure that the considerable advantages of renewable technologies would receive appropriate recognition.

One promising solution to this dilemma, most actively promoted by the Union of Concerned Scientists and the American Wind Energy Association, is the "renewables portfolio standard." It would require each competing electricity supplier or generator to get a certain percentage of its electricity from renewables. Over time the percentage would increase to encourage continued development of new renewable electricity facilities. The advocates of this approach stress the importance of the "portfolio" concept. They argue that, just as smart investors build a diversified portfolio rather than putting all their money into one stock, electric companies should rely upon a diversified portfolio of energy sources. This would protect consumers from sharp rate hikes if the price of any single energy source, like coal or nuclear power, were to go up quickly.[23]

Although a renewables portfolio standard would be a government-imposed regulation, it would use market mechanisms to achieve its objectives at the lowest cost. It would provide strong incentives for suppliers to find the most cost-effective renewables projects. Because the renewables portfolio standard holds the promise of helping the United States to switch to renewables economically, it is well worth instituting. By 1998 a renewables portfolio standard had been adopted in Arizona, Connecticut, Maine, Massachusetts, and Nevada. It was also being considered in many other states and at the national level.

Certify and label.

The government can have an important impact on consumer behavior without imposing required rules on companies. Instead, it can identify a standard for a particular product and then let the public know which companies' models meet that standard. The EPA, through its Energy Star program, certifies certain computers, TVs, and VCRs as meeting its standards for energy efficiency. The agency encourages manufacturers to produce models that can carry an Energy Star logo, but the incentive would increase if the EPA were to do a better job of publicizing the program. The most effective certification efforts combine prominently displayed logos with advertising to educate consumers about the reasons for the program.

Organic farmers have long understood that certification and labeling can help them market their agricultural products to consumers interested in food purity, and they have helped build state and local certification systems. They also supported the 1990 Organic Foods Production Act, which required the Department of Agriculture to work with the organic industry and other stakeholders in organic agriculture to set up procedures for inspecting and nationally certifying organic operations. Although the USDA is having difficulty coming up with standards that are strict enough for organic farmers and consumers, the usefulness of a third-party certification program for distinguishing organic foods from more conventional ones remains undisputed. Consumers, as well as organic farmers and processors, will benefit once labels tell consumers that a particular food has been certified by the government as meeting special requirements regarding pesticides, antibiotics, and animal confinement.

The government can also help consumers by labeling products, even without any formal certification process. The USDA-required nutrition labels on packaged foods have made consumers much more conscious of fat and sugar content. Although not an environmental measure, they demonstrate the ability of labels to change consumer buying patterns. Labels on appliances about electricity use also provide consumers with useful information and have increased sales of those appliances that use relatively little electricity. Fuel economy numbers for cars have served a similar purpose, although they would be much more effective if they included information about how much more it costs to operate an inefficient rather than an efficient model. And as states start to give consumers the ability to choose which electricity supplier they want to use, environmentalists have called for strong disclosure and labeling requirements. In that way consumers would know the air emissions, greenhouse gases, toxic metals, and other environmental impacts of the electricity each alternative supplier offers.

Private organizations rather than the government have sometimes carried out certification and labeling, but they don't always have the resources to do an effective job of evaluating products or informing the public of their conclusions. The Green Seals program had wanted to become an environmental version of the Good Housekeeping Seal of Approval, but they have had difficulty getting companies to cooperate. Certification and labeling of wood can tell consumers whether trees were grown in a sustainable fashion, either in this country or in a tropical country with endangered rain forests, but few people know that such certification exists. Over time, consumer awareness of wood certification should increase.

INVEST IN THE ENVIRONMENT

New, cleaner technologies can significantly reduce the environmental damage associated with consumption. Private entrepreneurs do not always have enough money to support research into such technologies, and they often cannot initially compete equally with more established products. A little assistance from the government can allow a company to get to the point where it can compete without further aid.

Fund research and development.

In recent years the federal government has provided funds for research and demonstration projects to perfect various renewable energy technologies like wind turbines and biomass gasifiers. Such assistance is certainly justified by society's interest in having a cleaner energy supply and by the many hidden and overt subsidies to traditional energy sources, such as coal, oil, and nuclear.

Similarly, the government has supported research and development of various environmental cleanup technologies, as well as more efficient cars and vehicles powered by fuels other than gasoline. Research funding to help farmers adopt systems that reduce the use of pesticides and chemical inputs has also been helpful, even though the USDA continues to spend much more on conventional high-input agriculture.

Buy green.

The government can use its own purchasing power to build a market for a new technology. A commitment by the federal government to purchase more recycled paper, for example, assured manufacturers that it would be worth their while to open recycled paper mills. Various solar power advocates have suggested that the federal government could jump-start the photovoltaic industry by agreeing to purchase large quantities of photovoltaic panels for use on government buildings. By being able to switch to low-cost mass-production techniques, manufacturers' costs would come way down. As part of the Clinton administration's "million solar roofs" program, the government plans to make at least some small purchases of solar technologies.

Government programs to help local transit agencies switch from dirty diesel buses to natural gas and fuel-cell ones not only clean the air but demonstrate new technologies and strengthen the companies that produce them. We could imagine lots of other ways in which the government could use its purchasing power to make consumption cleaner.

MAKE LAND USE AN ENVIRONMENTAL ISSUE

Here we get into the trickiest and probably most complicated area of environmental policy. As we have seen, scientists believe changes in land use rank among the most serious environmental problems (see chapter 3). The loss of wetlands, ancient forests, and other undeveloped land deservedly gets special attention from environmentalists, but the conversion of farmland to housing and business uses also deserves consideration.

Suburban development and other changes in land use not only directly threaten valuable natural resources but can also exacerbate other environmental problems. For example, the conversion of arid landscapes to green lawns puts added pressure on overstressed water supplies. Environmentally conscious transportation professionals bemoan suburban sprawl because it has been a major reason why people are driving more, thereby using more gasoline. In California, where the population increased 60 percent between 1970 and 1995, the number of miles vehicles travel increased by 162 percent.[24] This has made it harder to solve such problems as air pollution and

Helping Others to Reduce Their Environmental Impact

Ken Hughes's wide-ranging experiences illustrate some of the ways in which individuals can move beyond the personal realm to help their neighbors and influence their governments.

Ken has a special passion for bicycles and has long used one for recreation, errands, and commuting. Back in the 1980s, when he was living in Washington, D.C., a friend asked him to serve on the board of the Washington Area Bicyclists Association. In that role, he organized yearly bike-to-work days that stimulated hundreds of people to commute by bicycle for the first time. He also promoted a buddy system that matched experienced bicycle commuters with novices to help the newcomers overcome any fears they might have and to show them how to commute safely and easily.

When Ken moved to Santa Fe, he became active in local environmental groups and was asked to serve on a task force to help develop the city's bike plan. He was then asked to move into a yet wider sphere by serving as the chair of New Mexico's Bicycle Pedestrian Equestrian Advisory Committee. This group played a key role in getting the state to take such important steps as eliminating restrictions on bicycle traffic on highways and requiring new roads to be designed with wide enough shoulders to make biking feasible. Because of the work of people like Ken, New Mexico residents will have a much easier time using their bicycles, rather than their cars, for transportation.

global warming, not only because more driving means more emissions but because auto alternatives like mass transit are difficult and expensive to implement in dispersed suburbs.

Over the past several decades, communities, states, and the federal government have improved stewardship of the nation's public lands and have also taken some useful steps to encourage the environmentally sound use of private lands. Additional undeveloped natural areas have been protected as parks and refuges. The Endangered Species Act has saved plants and animals from extinction, by preserving the land they rely on. And millions of acres of highly erodable farmland have been protected by the Conservation Reserve Program. Yet these efforts ultimately represent small-scale holding actions that, by themselves, cannot counter the long-term trends threatening the nation's land-based resources.

Governments can most quickly and easily improve land-use policy by starting with those lands that are directly owned and controlled by government. In particular, the federal government, as the nation's largest landowner, has the opportunity to directly determine how a significant amount of land gets used. Moreover, when the government manages its own land wisely, it serves as a model of sound environmental stewardship for other landowners.

The U.S. Forest Service, for example, can restrict road-building in national forests and on Bureau of Land Management lands that threatens the loss of biodiversity. Similarly, federal agencies can prepare plans to restore lost or degraded habitats on lands they control, and Congress can provide them with sufficient funding to implement such recovery plans.

Although activities aimed at improving public lands are clearly essential, we want to focus here on those land-use problems that are caused most directly by individual consumers' decisions and on those land-use policies that intersect with individual consumers' choices and options. When we do this, we can quickly see that the traditional ways of approaching environmental problems do not work especially well for land use. As land conservationists John Turner and Jason Rylander have pointed out, from the 1970s to the 1990s "the nation's many environmental laws addressed one problem at a time—air or water pollution, endangered species, waste disposal"—whereas truly effective policy would look at land use holistically, considering the interaction between these and other environmental, social, and economic factors.[25] Otherwise one problem—say, traffic congestion—may be solved at the cost of making another problem, like water pollution, worse.

In general, policymakers and the public have an insufficient appreciation of the ways various government activities—from constructing highways to imposing zoning regulations to assisting selected businesses—affect both land use and environmental quality. And in truth it would be a major task for policymakers to try to consider all the likely land-use implications of even a seemingly straightforward decision about whether to widen a road.

The daunting challenge of addressing land use in a comprehensive way is not the only reason that it is hard to institute land-use policies that effectively protect the environment. Another considerable obstacle is the large number of people and institutions responsible for problems and involved in their solution. When environmentalists and policymakers wanted to end the production of ozone-depleting chemicals, they could concentrate on the relatively few manufacturers who made those chemicals. In contrast, most harmful changes on private land are caused by the cumulative actions of a large number of individuals and businesses making separate decisions. Policymakers wanting to slow the annual conversion of tens of thousands of acres of farmland in California's Central Valley to housing and industry cannot hold just a few, or even a few hundred, corporations responsible. And then for the Central Valley to effectively tackle the job of preserving agricultural land, many different local governments, as well as state agencies, would need to be involved.

Environmental problems associated with changes in private land will therefore never be solved by just passing a few federal laws. On the other hand, because so many important decisions are made in local settings, individual citizens have considerable opportunity to make their views heard. Particular communities and regions can move ahead with solutions without having to wait for the rest of the country to join in. And indeed, this has already been happening.

Unfortunately, policymakers seeking to change harmful land-use patterns face an even bigger challenge to effective action because of Americans' very strong belief in individual property rights and emotional attachment to any land they own. As former EPA administrator William Reilly has observed, "The sense of pride in the ownership of a piece of real estate is indeed fierce, and public officials trifle with it at considerable risk."[26]

In recent years, government officials who have appeared to be triflers have felt considerable wrath from angered citizens. They have been accused of caring more about snail darters and socialistic theories than about people's livelihoods or fundamental rights. Aggrieved individuals have combined with self-interested business interests to build the so-called "wise use" movement and a wide range of property rights organizations. These groups have persistently and forcefully advocated for "takings" legislation, to make it more difficult for governments to take private property and to require governments to reimburse property owners whenever they impose regulations restricting what property owners can do with their land.

The principle of reimbursing property owners for government actions that reduce property values initially sounds logical, but the concept tends to fall apart under closer scrutiny. Since, as we have seen, an unusually large number of government policies influence land use, would property owners be eligible for compensation anytime they are adversely affected? Where would society draw the line? If a county were to build a new road that diverts traffic from an older road, would businesses along the deserted road be entitled to compensation? Would a town have to pay a landowner who wants to build a factory on his or her property but is prevented from doing so by a zoning ordinance that prohibits industry in the neighborhood? What if a city allows construction of an office building that makes a condominium owner's dwelling less valuable by blocking a harbor view? And what about government actions designed to protect some people's property, but at the expense of others—for example, forcing an individual to close a hazardous waste dump that threatens a neighborhood's water supply? Taken to its logical conclusion, the concept behind takings legislation would open a veritable Pandora's box of disputes and would paralyze government. Admittedly, most advocates of these sorts of laws do not want to go this far, but it would be harder than many of them acknowledge to draw a clear line once the concept was institutionalized.

Nevertheless, the property rights movement is not likely to go away, and many people will continue to believe fervently that they should be able to do whatever they want on their land. Any attempts to protect and improve the environment through land-use planning or growth management are therefore bound to remain controversial. As Reilly notes, "The continuing lack of consensus about the proper reach of government and public authority in constraining the behavior of private landowners" has made and will continue to make it difficult to manage land rationally.[27] But that does not mean the attempt to regulate and improve land use should be abandoned. Environmentalists and policymakers should emphasize strategies that cannot be easily criticized for restricting property owners and reducing the value of their land:

Help people who want to preserve land.

Some people who own undeveloped land would like to see it stay that way. Many farmers would like to keep their land from being built upon. Groups of conservationists would like to buy up natural ecosystems to keep them in their current state. Policymakers should take steps to make it easier for all these people to do what they want.

Various states have passed laws to help preserve farmland. In Massachusetts, for example, through the Agricultural Preservation Restriction Act, farmers can apply for payments from the state in exchange for agreeing to continue to use their land for agriculture. They retain ownership of the property, but neither they nor any subsequent owners can develop it for nonagricultural purposes. The amount of money available for this program is unfortunately quite limited, but it is a step in the right direction. These sorts of programs protect the nation's future food supply, since 86 percent of the nation's fruits and vegetables, 80 percent of dairy products, and 45 percent of meat and poultry are grown on farms near urban areas.[28]

Governments can help people who want to permanently preserve undeveloped land by increasing tax benefits to individuals who donate their land to conservation organizations. Policies can also provide more favorable tax treatment for those who establish conservation easements preventing certain types of future development on their land.

In recent years "land trust" organizations have proliferated across the country. There are now eleven hundred of these groups dedicated to managing undeveloped land that they have either been given or purchased. These groups deserve government assistance, which can include grants, loans, and the elimination of cumbersome red-tape procedures. Land trusts already protect more than 4 million acres, but they could do much more with greater government support.[29]

Some developers and homebuyers also want to preserve natural land, but they are too often thwarted by insufficiently flexible government regulations, such as zoning ordinances requiring certain lot sizes. Cluster developments, where houses are placed close together, so that most of a tract of land can be kept as open space, should be promoted rather than impeded by public officials.

Look for popular actions.

Policymakers and environmentalists should be on the lookout for sprawl-preventing actions that will win wide popular support. If people in a community are fed up with traffic congestion or worry that further development will destroy appealing aspects of life in their town, they will be receptive to regulations to slow sprawl. Even actions that restrict property owners' freedom, like zoning regulations, can be quite popular if residents believe they enhance property values and their own quality of life. Of course, it is important to avoid having antigrowth measures turn into vehicles for preventing racial, ethnic, or income diversity in a community.

The public will often be receptive to protecting open space, as long as it does not increase tax rates too much. As evidence of the potential appeal of land preservation, we can point to a 1995 survey sponsored by a home-builders group, in which 77 percent of those questioned selected "natural open space" as the most desirable feature for a new home development.[30] There is also evidence that local residents will support measures, like bike paths and pesticide-use restrictions, that reduce a community's environmental impact.

Stop encouraging sprawl.

Governments do many things that speed the land-development process and make it artificially cheap to convert farms and natural ecosystems to dispersed house lots and business facilities. Obviously, housing and business are desirable, but governments can encourage relatively compact developments that preserve land in a natural state.

Road-building is perhaps the most obvious government activity speeding development. A more cautious approach emphasizing good transportation within an existing metropolitan area rather than constructing new and wider roads to undeveloped areas would clearly discourage sprawl. Governments should also much more clearly acknowledge the considerable expense of providing services to new developments. In most cases, developers and home-builders do not have to pay the full cost of providing water, utilities, sewers, and roads to the new homes they build. In Loudon County, Virginia, for example, the average house in 1994 sold for $200,000. Yet the real estate tax rate was set at a level where only owners of new houses costing more than $400,000 paid tax that equaled the average cost of the services the county provided to them.[31] This meant that the county generously subsidized development and new home construction.

In many places the hidden local government subsidy for new development is so great that it actually pays for a community to buy up land to keep it out of development. In Acton, Massachusetts, where one of us lives, the town recently bought 33 acres of land for $1.3 million. The price was steep, but if the land were to be converted to twenty-two house lots, the town would have lost $92,000 each year because tax payments would not cover the total cost of services to the new residents.

Another approach communities can use is to charge so-called "impact fees" to recover more of the cost of servicing new developments. A 1990 study of thirty-three places that charge such fees found that they averaged $9,425 for single-family houses. The fees have not always been effective or popular, however. If they are to work well, public officials cannot view them greedily as just a new pot of tax revenues but must instead link them to a conscious strategy for managing and controlling growth. They also need to make sure that fees are not structured in a way that unfairly burdens less affluent residents of their community.[32]

Not only local communities but states also encourage suburban sprawl, sometimes unwittingly. For example, they often provide state aid to growing communities to build new schools and libraries, but do not give equivalent money to older communities for the maintenance of existing public buildings.

Make existing communities and older housing attractive.

Some people choose to move to new suburban communities because of dissatisfaction with their existing living situation. Not only center cities but many inner suburbs have been losing residents turned off by crime, declining public services, and lousy schools. By tackling such problems and building on the advantages of life in a compactly settled community, public officials can slow migration to new developments in far-flung suburbs. Policies that reward property owners for preserving and upgrading old homes and historic buildings have a similar effect.

Where possible, be more ambitious.

So far we have focused on land-use policies that do not directly challenge the ideology of property rights groups, but there are circumstances where it is possible to do this. In some states and cities, public support for environmental protection has been strong enough or concern over the impact of rapid development great enough to forge a political consensus around limiting development and preserving agriculture and natural ecosystems. In such circumstances it makes sense to try to implement a comprehensive approach to controlling growth and protecting land.

In Oregon concern over the environment and unmanaged growth has long run high, so the state was able to pass a comprehensive land-use law in 1973. Every town in the state is required to have zoning laws and land-use plans that meet statewide goals. Most significantly, all cities have had to create an "urban growth boundary," an area encompassing the existing built-up land plus enough vacant land for twenty years of growth. Compact development on small lots is encouraged within the boundary, while farming and forestry are protected outside of it. This approach has had a significant impact on slowing land conversion, and it retains widespread support in the state, even though it can be difficult to implement and clearly limits property owners' ability to do whatever they want with their land. Like Oregon, Vermont has been relatively successful in looking at land use in a comprehensive way.

Boulder, Colorado, has been one of the communities where

residents have shown an admirable willingness to spend their own money to protect open space. In 1967 they voted in favor of a one-cent sales tax, 40 percent of which went for purchasing land that would otherwise be developed. This made Boulder the first city to pass a tax for preserving open space. Twenty-two years later they agreed to increase the open-space component of the tax by a third of a cent. In 1976 the city adopted a growth limit reducing the rate of growth "substantially below" that of the 1960s when the city expanded rapidly. Various popular regulations have helped ensure that Boulder remains surrounded by a 27,000-acre greenbelt, nearby mountains remain off limits to developers, and large houses on oversize lots are discouraged.[33]

Focus on ecosystem protection.

Scientists have become increasingly disillusioned with the piecemeal, one-problem-at-a-time approach to land-related environmental problems. They have, for example, called on the federal government to transcend the strategy of the original Endangered Species Act, which looked at each species in isolation. A better approach, they argue, would be to identify and conserve those threatened ecosystems that would protect the maximum amount of biological diversity. This would be beneficial for reasons beyond species preservation, since as scientists have become increasingly aware, properly functioning natural ecosystems perform valuable services for human society—for example, forests that ensure a dependable water supply, marine ecosystems that detoxify wastes, wetlands that purify water and mitigate flooding.[34]

Secretary of the Interior Bruce Babbitt embraced the ecosystem protection approach early in his tenure. Unfortunately, his initial efforts met fierce opposition from property rights organizations and the wise use movement. Nevertheless, bipartisan proposals for reauthorizing the Endangered Species Act have moved in the direction of ecosystem protection.

Not just the federal government but states and local communities can take this more holistic approach. They can find out which are the most important ecosystems to protect and then develop comprehensive strategies for doing so. For example, five fast-growing southern California counties have worked together to preserve biological diversity by preserving a threatened habitat—coastal sagescrub.[35]

Educate the public.

Because so many individuals, businesses, and local governments influence American society's use of land, education and grassroots activism must be essential elements of any effort to reduce the harmful environmental impacts of land-use practices. It will inevitably be a lengthy, gradual process to help these many people and institutions to view land use as an environmental issue.

Nature centers and other traditional environmental education programs can help, as can policy initiatives that include a significant public awareness component. Quite a few cities and towns have affiliated with the "sustainable communities" movement and have attempted to put into place various policies to make their communities sensitive to environmental needs, including the use of land. Even though they have often had limited success in actually redirecting land practices, they have helped teach local residents about the need to be sustainable. This should pay back over the long run.

EPILOGUE

From Walden to Wal-Mart: Consumers and Their Critics
by Susan Strasser

When Henry David Thoreau renounced the comforts of modern life in 1845, moving to a cabin near Walden Pond to live "deliberately," he did not give up much by our standards. "Most of the luxuries, and many of the so-called comforts of life," he wrote, "are not only not indispensable, but positive hindrances to the elevation of mankind. With respect to luxuries and comforts, the wisest have ever lived a more simple and meagre life than the poor."[1] But Thoreau did not leave behind a house with electric lights, central heating, or a telephone. In his time luxury meant brightening dark nights with a whale oil lamp instead of a tallow candle or a flaming rag in a pool of grease. Comfort meant heating and cooking with a cast iron stove instead of a fireplace—but in either case there was wood to chop and haul. Thoreau and his friends in Concord dressed in clothes sewn and laundered entirely by hand; the sewing machine and the earliest mechanical clothes washers were first patented during the two years he was in the woods. The overwhelming majority of Americans had no running water. Not even the White House yet had a full bathroom.

Although it sold only a few hundred copies when it was

published, *Walden* has in recent decades served as an inspiration for Americans discontented with a much more complex consumer society. In 1971 *Whole Earth Catalog* editor Stewart Brand described it as "the prime document" of the revolution he saw himself building, which proposed using ingenuity and appropriate technology to reclaim people's lives from a system of governmental and corporate control.[2] Another quarter of a century later, *Walden* is a staple of college courses on American attitudes toward wilderness and the environment. Although veterans of hippie communes remember what didn't work, and while younger generations seem tied to their phone lines and battery packs, Thoreau's back-to-the-land vision still has appeal. The story of the couple who chucks it all to live in the country—"appropriate technology" now including a computer and modem to help with making money—has become a staple of contemporary magazines.

The central thread of Thoreau's critique—that we not only don't need all the stuff we have but that it actually gets in the way of living the good life—has an appeal beyond the rural vision. At the same time that victims of corporate layoffs find themselves "downshifting" involuntarily, other people are choosing self-employment or cutting back their working hours, in order to reduce stress or reshape their days, even though it means scaling back their income.

This current interest in Thoreau and other advocates of simple living reflects one side of a longstanding American ambivalence toward consumer culture. On the one hand, Americans have eagerly embraced consumer products. Most people have been willing to pay for innovations that save time and labor, from the cast iron stove to the microwave, and they have regarded those purchases as positive contributions to an ever-increasing standard of material well-being. Many have also been willing to pay for novelty and variety: frozen strawberries in the wintertime, a new pair of earrings, a radio. Some have eagerly spent their money to obtain the status conferred by an expensive automobile or the latest wide-screen TV.

At the same time that they have clamored for new products and filled their houses with them, many Americans have been uneasy with rampant consumerism. They have responded with interest to writers who question the imperative to shop and spend. It has therefore not been surprising that in the 1990s books like Joe Dominguez and Vicki Robin's *Your Money or Your Life* and Juliet Schor's *The Overworked American* have climbed onto the best-seller lists.

Why do Americans have mixed feelings about something that they perceive to be "the American way"? How do current attitudes toward consumption compare with those expressed by earlier generations of Americans? More fundamentally, how and why did a consumption-oriented culture develop in the United States? To answer these questions, we need to look at how the economy has been transformed since Thoreau's era, and at how Americans have responded to that transformation.

The Triumph of Factory-made Goods

Thoreau's friends in town may have enjoyed few of the conveniences we associate with a modern lifestyle, but the rise of the factory system in the late eighteenth and early nineteenth centuries had already transformed their economy and made store-bought goods much more common. American families had never been entirely self-sufficient. Even the poorest "subsistence" farmer in colonial America purchased such necessities as salt and ironware, while tradespeople and professionals bought tea, silk, and china from abroad as well as local food and crafts. But as factories began to develop in the new nation, they dramatically increased the supply of manufactured goods, and prices declined. Soap, candles, and cloth—once produced arduously at home or available as imported luxuries—became widely available. Glassware and metal items, previously purchased from individual craftsmen, now were sold by ped-dlers and general stores at prices that farmers and working people could afford. To earn the cash to buy manufactured products, farm families devoted more of their time to produc-ing crops and other goods they could sell. With less time to make things other than money, they had no choice but to purchase more factory-made products.

Few people minded becoming more dependent on store-bought goods, since the new products eased many burdens. By the time of the Civil War, the first manufactured goods had tri-umphed decisively: hardly any women still spun their own thread or wove their own cloth. But life remained hard by today's standards. Food, clothing, and shelter required about 95 percent of most Americans' income. The other 5 percent went for everything else, including medical care, local transporta-tion, education, recreation, entertainment, and church contri-butions.

The transformation of an agricultural workforce to an industrial one entailed radical change, as people abandoned traditional values and assumptions about daily life and work. Farm people had to readjust their lives to work in factories. Now the clock regulated their day, not the weather or the light in the sky. The boss told them what to do.

This was the life of "quiet desperation" that Thoreau said most men lived. In shops, offices, and fields as well as in facto-ries, he wrote, people "have appeared to me to be doing penance in a thousand remarkable ways." The laboring man "has no time to be anything but a machine."[3] Thoreau was explicitly criticizing the Industrial Revolution and capitalism itself. "I cannot believe that our factory system is the best mode by which men get clothing," he contended. "The principal object is, not that mankind may be well and honestly clad, but, unquestionably, that the corporations may be enriched."[4]

Thoreau challenged his contemporaries to question how

they spent time and money. He maintained that people should have time to read, write, think lofty thoughts, or ramble in the woods. Speaking as a senior at Harvard's 1837 Class Day, he suggested that the "order of things should be somewhat reversed," with one day of toil and a six-day "Sabbath of the affections and the soul."[5] Nor should people install conveniences and luxuries just to emulate their neighbors. "Shall we always study to obtain more of these things, and not sometimes to be content with less?" he wrote in *Walden*.[6]

Although Thoreau was, in historian David Shi's words, "the most conspicuous and persuasive exponent of simple living in the American experience,"[7] his was not the only critique of luxurious consumption that emerged during the early decades of American industrialization. Clergyman and educator Francis Wayland (1796–1865), president of Brown University for more than twenty-five years and author of many books, offered a conservative view, grounded in a moral stance. Wayland opposed the "insatiate striving for more" fostered by the newly available industrial products. Instead he promoted industry and frugality, hard work, and sober living. French travel writer and social theorist Alexis de Tocqueville saw Americans grasping for a standard of living beyond their reach, "restless in the midst of abundance," thanks to democracy itself.[8] In an aristocracy everybody's lot was predestined, he explained; the rich were comfortable, while the poor looked to the next world. Democracy encouraged the wealthy to worry about what they had and the poor to want what they did not have.

Such critics of consumption were drowned out by its fans. Senator Daniel Webster (1782–1852) reflected the majority opinion when he extolled commercial growth and spoke about the benefits of an abundance of consumer goods, the "vastly increased comforts" that had come to be enjoyed by working people.[9] Yet even this promotor of industrial capitalism remained somewhat ambivalent toward luxury. Like Abraham

Lincoln, Webster spoke sentimentally about the rustic simplicity of "log cabin days," even though many Americans' personal lifestyles had moved far from the rustic.

On the other hand, Thoreau, the quintessential critic of luxury, couldn't resist it completely. He built his Walden fireplace of local stone, with his own hands, but he purchased lamp oil and paid the cobbler to repair his shoes. At other points in his life, he succumbed to the attraction of certain consumer comforts, as in 1841 when he admitted to a friend that he was "living with Mr. Emerson in very dangerous prosperity."[10]

MASS CONSUMPTION AND ITS CRITICS

When Thoreau died in 1862, the Civil War was launching the next stage in the development of a mass consumption society. The war promoted business in both the North and the South: uniforms, guns, and railroad ties had to be produced, and factories and businesses were set up to manufacture them. This economic expansion continued during the following decades, at least in the North and the West. Basic industries such as railroads, oil refineries, steel mills, and coal mines prospered.

At first the lifestyles of industrial workers were hardly affected by economic growth. According to the first systematic study of workers' consumption, published in Massachusetts in 1875, most had little to spend. They lived in simple houses and dressed modestly, accumulating few possessions beyond a bit of furniture and their cooking and eating utensils. The most highly paid skilled workers, often older, might own a sewing machine or a piano or light their homes with gas; they had a bit of money to spend on better clothes or on leisure in the form of books, magazines, newspapers, and memberships in fraternal lodges and other organizations. But most children of workers needed to start work well before they were fifteen.[11]

By the 1880s new production and distribution systems

were developing that would generate a profound transformation in the daily lives of all classes of Americans. The luxuries of 1875—newspapers and magazines, sewing machines, gas lighting—became commonplace among working people over the next four decades. Innovative manufacturing techniques made possible not only mass production, but also efficient production of products like clothes, made in many styles and sizes. Big corporations combined these production techniques with mass distribution, selling to a national market. Singer and McCormick, for example, sold sewing machines and harvesters to seamstresses and farmers respectively, offering installment plans through their networks of retail stores and franchises. Swift and Armor built packing houses and refrigerated warehouses all across the country, revolutionizing meat production. Gigantic wholesaling firms coordinated huge regional distribution systems. Sears and Montgomery Ward sold farmers nearly every kind of manufactured product, while city dwellers shopped in department stores that created desire by displaying goods in fantastic settings. Chains—Woolworth's five-and-tens, the A&P groceries, the United cigar stores, Child's restaurants—began to unite Main Streets in towns all over the country.

The bureaucracies that did the paperwork and the planning for all of these big companies supported a new class of accountants and clerks, engineers and chemists, salesmen and advertising executives. Unlike impoverished immigrant laborers and cash-starved farmers, these people had money to spend. In the newly developing suburbs served by streetcar lines, their households were literally connected to economic life with the wires and pipes that delivered water, natural gas, electricity, and telephone service. They became the consumers of a broad variety of new products. Some of these—canned and packaged foods and cleaning products, cigarettes and chewing gum, and ready-made clothing—were even cheap enough for industrial workers.

Such goods were sold in new ways. Manufacturers used advertisements to convince Americans of the desirability of new and unfamiliar products. Thus, when the National Biscuit Company advertised Uneeda Biscuits and Nabisco Sugar Wafers, it promoted the concept of crackers in cardboard boxes to people accustomed to dipping into the cracker barrel. In general, the manufacturers of the new mass-produced goods had to convert people accustomed to homemade things and unbranded merchandise to buying standardized, uniform, advertised, packaged products. They used brands to create new kinds of relationships between corporations and consumers, relationships built on trust in Nabisco or Quaker Oats. They promoted those brands using free samples and market research, and with billboards, streetcar placards, and whole pages of magazine and newspaper advertisements. Not all new products succeeded, but most of the leading brands of the early twentieth century are still familiar, such as Ivory, Campbell's, Kodak, Wrigley's, Ford, Colgate, and Gillette.[12]

A transition of this magnitude naturally spawned considerable comment and critique. Few individuals expressed ambivalence about the revolution of mass production and mass marketing, but the range of reactions suggests that the cultural ambivalence was as strong as it had been about the Industrial Revolution itself. The principal celebrants, of course, were the manufacturing companies and their advertising agencies. They publicized the benefits of mass production and distribution of consumer goods—cleanliness, convenience, style, and technological progress.

Other celebrants of consumption included George Gunton (1845–1919), a labor radical and leader of the eight-hour-day movement, who theorized that more leisure would create both new desires and more opportunities for workers, therefore increasing consumption, comfort, refinement and democracy. Simon Patten (1852–1922), an economist at the Wharton School, called industrialization "a new basis of civilization," leading to a new economy of abundance. "The new morality," Patten wrote, "does not consist in saving, but in expanding consumption."[13] Probably the most widely read champion of consumption was Edward Bellamy, whose best-selling utopian novel *Looking Backward* (1888) prompted the formation of clubs all over the country devoted to bringing about the future it described. Set in the year 2000, the book depicted a benevolent state socialism that fostered an effortless, abundant and orderly consumer society, with stores no more than ten minutes from wherever one might be.

Some women writers also celebrated the transfer of production from home to factory, because they assumed the new products would liberate women from endless toil. Charlotte Perkins Gilman (1860–1935), a popular writer and lecturer, suggested that the new principles of production could now be applied to housework, freeing women from what she saw as the primitive conditions of solitary labor in their homes. At the other extreme, Christine Frederick (1883–1970) spent the early part of her career telling housewives how to run their homes as if they were the purchasing agents of businesses, while the latter advised businessmen on how to sell to "Mrs. Consumer." In the middle the activists, writers, and educators of the home economics movement insisted that people needed to be educated for their new roles as consumers. Like Gilman and Frederick, the home economists emphasized the importance of the historical transition that had made everybody in the modern world into a consumer.[14]

Even people without much money to spend were urged to be careful how they spent it. Studies of workers' consumption habits ranged from photographic essays such as Jacob Riis's *How the Other Half Lives* (1890) to detailed statistical investigations of workers' budgets. Poor families, they asserted, could achieve a minimally acceptable standard of living if they learned to budget their money. Such studies provided intellectual ammunition for the many social workers who taught new immigrants from peasant backgrounds—many of whom had little experience with a cash economy—how to budget and buy.

Many reformers connected to the wide-ranging network of organizations, movements, and ideas that have been described using the single word *Progressivism* responded more cautiously to the new mass consumption. Activists and journalists demanding state and federal regulation denounced the claims of patent medicine manufacturers as fraudulent. These reformers helped pass the federal Pure Food and Drug Act, only months after Upton Sinclair's sensational novel *The Jungle* (1906) exposed the horrific conditions in Chicago's meat packing plants. Although we now regard them as early advocates of consumer protection, these activists did not focus on the roles or the rights of consumers. Despite its name, even the National Consumers' League mobilized consumers in campaigns against sweatshops, child labor, and other abuses of women workers, not on consumer rights. The League urged consumers to learn about the conditions under which the products they bought were made, and to choose only goods produced under non-exploitative conditions.

There were, as historian William Leach points out, "leaders in every religious community who understood and resisted" the developing consumer culture. "Competitive commerce," wrote social gospel preacher Walter Rauschenbusch in 1907, "spreads things before us and beseeches and persuades us to buy what we do not want. Men try to break down the foresight and self-restraint which were the slow product of moral education, and reduce us to the moral habits of savages who gorge today and fast tomorrow."[15] Various influential priests and ministers from other denominations likewise sermonized that modern Americans should pay less attention to money and things and more to social justice, community, and their relationships to God. But on the whole, mainstream religion accommodated itself to the new ways.

The most prominent critic of the new consumption was

economist Thorstein Veblen, who coined the phrase *conspicuous consumption* in his 1899 *Theory of the Leisure Class*. Veblen was famous for his asceticism and bohemian appearance, reflecting his rejection of display and artifice. Despite his eccentricities and scandals regarding his sexual behavior, he had substantial influence on other progressives and on later critics of consumption. Veblen formulated ideas that became fundamental to the consumer movement, offering an institutional analysis, a challenge to the idea that more is better, and an antipathy toward waste. He used anthropology to put the "captains of industry" and their Newport mansions in their place, comparing their habits and routines to activities that served similar functions in "primitive" tribes. He claimed that the consumption patterns of the wealthy set standards for the rest of society; the middle and working classes became caught up in a competition for prestige, to be achieved through buying. Although he appreciated mass production, he also argued that the market does not operate perfectly but is instead influenced by institutions and power relationships, and that economic growth is not necessarily good.

A CULTURE OF CONSUMPTION

By the 1920s the economic transition of the previous fifty years had produced a new kind of consumer society. The new economy was oriented to consumers, and the culture was based more on buying things than on making them. The United States had shifted from an agricultural to an industrial society, while modern organizational systems and advanced production and distribution technologies had transformed industry itself. Marketing concerns came to dominate corporate decision-making about production, while economists gave increased attention to the role of consumption. In addition to wearing more ready-made clothes and buying more factory-made furniture, Americans of all classes were using products that nobody had ever made at home or in craft shops. Products like toothpaste, corn flakes, safety razors, and cameras were the material basis for new habits and the physical expression of a genuine break from earlier times. Even poor urban workers, with little land for gardens and insufficient time for handcrafts, joined the expanding market for manufactured goods.

Wealthy people got new things before poor ones, city people before country ones, young people before old. But all over the country, new technologies—electricity, gas, indoor plumbing, telephones, radios—transformed both the work and the diversions of private life, saving household labor and bringing paid entertainments into homes. New products made old ones obsolete, as, for example, electric lights had replaced oil lamps in American cities. Wholly new classes of human activity joined the realm of commodities, as leisure-time experiences became something even the masses could buy. Working people could now spend their money and their leisure time at movies, vaudeville shows, baseball games, dance halls, and the amusement parks located at the end of trolley lines in every city.

As factory-made goods and commercially provided services continued to supplant household production, shopping and planning for consumption became ever more essential parts of housework. These were tasks of a new kind, shaped by advertising and by shopping environments designed to stimulate desire and to associate buying with pleasure and fantasy. New products and the new media—movies and radio—changed people's expectations, desires, and needs, in turn influencing the development of later products. There was always another shopping trip, always some new thing to buy.

Although most Americans applauded consumer society in the 1920s, the popularity of critics, such as novelist Sinclair Lewis, suggests some continued ambivalence. Lewis's *Babbitt* (1922) begins with real estate man and town booster George Babbitt waking up to "the best of nationally advertised and quantitatively produced alarm-clocks, with all modern attachments, including cathedral chime, intermittent alarm, and a phosphorescent dial." Babbitt was proud of the clock. "Socially it was almost as creditable as buying expensive cord tires." But for Lewis, George Babbitt's very soul was impoverished by "the large national advertisers," who "fixed . . . what he believed to be his individuality. These standard advertised wares—toothpastes, socks, tires, cameras, instantaneous hot-water heaters—were his symbols and proofs of excellence; at first the signs, then the substitutes, for joy and passion and wisdom."[16]

Middletown: A Study in Contemporary American Culture (1929), Robert Lynd and Helen Merrell Lynd's sociological investigation of Muncie, Indiana, supported the notion that George Babbitt was becoming the middle-class norm. The Lynds worried that the desire to consume was undermining traditional allegiances and values, and that "more and more of the activities of living are coming to be strained through the bars of the dollar sign."[17] There were many "new urgent occasions for spending money in every sector of living."[18] The people of Muncie learned to want new things from magazines, "a ceaseless torrent of printed matter."[19]

According to *Middletown,* automobiles and movies were "re-making leisure," threatening family solidarity and reducing attendance at churches, lodges, and union halls. Cars "unsettled the habit of careful saving,"[20] while movies exposed people to the products and lifestyles of higher classes. The Lynds admitted that Muncie's main recreations were, in fact, still cards and dancing, lectures, reading, and music, but they warned that the moral effects of the new entertainments were profound. Motion pictures lifted the taboo against boys and girls sitting together in the dark; high school students argued with their parents about using the family car, and, when they got it, they drove to dances twenty miles away without asking anybody's permission.

Stuart Chase, an accountant who turned to popular writing,

offered a different critique of consumerism and provided the intellectual basis for a growing consumer movement. In *The Challenge of Waste* (1922) and *The Tragedy of Waste* (1925), he declared that many new products were detrimental, inefficient, or just worthless, not genuine responses to human needs. With F. J. Schlink, he wrote *Your Money's Worth: A Study in the Waste of the Consumer's Dollar* (1927), which advocated sophisticated testing labs to provide technical advice to consumers. Schlink followed up by forming Consumers' Research, Inc., the progenitor of Consumers Union and *Consumer Reports*.

DEPRESSION, WAR, AND POSTWAR AFFLUENCE

The Great Depression put American ambivalence about luxurious consumption temporarily on hold. People bought less, did without, and practiced countless small economies in their daily lives. But some kinds of consumption actually rose. Sales remained constant in food stores and went down in restaurants and jewelry stores, but consumption of gasoline and residential electricity continued to go up despite hard times. Purchases of new cars declined, but overall car registrations continued to rise. At the beginning of the Depression, only about 10 percent of American homes had electric refrigerators; 10 million were sold during the 1930s, thanks to aggressive advertising, and by 1940, 56 percent of American households owned them.[21] Likewise, many Americans began the Depression with no radio, but by 1940 only one out of five households was left without one.[22]

World War II propaganda assigned an important place to consumer sacrifice. After 1942, when the government established rationing and banned the production of civilian motor vehicles, radios, and electrical appliances, consumers had grounds for believing that they had money but nowhere to spend it. Clothing was not rationed, but its production was regulated: the government outlawed double-breasted suits and full skirts, to conserve fabric. Americans were encouraged to conserve razor blades, turn in old toothpaste tubes when they bought new ones, and bring waste fat back to the butcher for use in nitroglycerin manufacture. "Use it up, wear it out, make it do, or do without," went the slogan. Still, consumption of many products rose steadily throughout the war. Per capita consumption of food went up, as did clothing, cosmetics, toys, jewelry, paper products, alcohol and tobacco, and electricity.

After the war, virtually all categories of personal consumption increased yearly. As factories returned to civilian production and wartime shortages ended, encouragement of consumption became the essence of economic policy. Once again Americans could buy automobiles, radios, and washing machines. Fifty-eight percent of American families owned automobiles in 1942; by 1960 the figure was 75 percent.[23] And there were new products and materials—clothes dryers, detergents, transistors, polyester, frozen orange juice—some of them the result of wartime research. Total per capita personal consumption increased 20 percent between 1948 and 1960.[24]

Real estate development was the most striking aspect of postwar recovery. Because residential construction had been dormant during the Depression and the war, millions of Americans were living with relatives or friends, or in temporary housing. After the war new federal legislation favored residential construction and financing, and the Veterans Administration offered mortgages with no down payment. The government programs of the late 1940s and 1950s made it profitable for developers to virtually mass-produce housing, creating large suburban subdivisions full of almost identical houses. Levittown, Long Island, was the most famous: 4,000 acres of curved streets with 17,450 homes for 82,000 people, built between 1947 and 1951. Such developments contributed to the creation of the child- and family-centered and consumption-oriented suburban lifestyle.

The shopping mall was as fundamental to postwar economic

development and to suburban living as the subdivision. Throughout the country, especially in California, developers had planned clusters of stores as early as the 1920s, but the Depression and the war halted construction. Postwar developers had grander plans, grouping small stores with large ones to attract shoppers from far away. The first regional complex, Northgate Shopping Center near Seattle, opened in 1947 with two department stores "anchoring" a pedestrian walkway lined with forty smaller retailers. Next came the fully enclosed, climate-controlled mall, beginning with Southdale Center in Minnesota (1956), a protected, self-contained environment with two levels of stores and a tree-filled garden court. In surroundings such as this, as in the spectacular department stores of the late nineteenth century, consumption merged with leisure. Although most shoppers arrived at the mall with limited time and limited budgets, shopping there was advertised as an experience, a pleasurable activity, a way to pass the time.

No matter how many malls got built and appliances got sold, and however attractive postwar consumerism might have seemed, it again drew critics. Their popularity suggests many Americans' continuing discomfort with fast-changing ways of life; their concerns about the power of corporations and the degradation of American culture are reminiscent of previous generations of critics. Vance Packard's *The Hidden Persuaders* (1957) asserted that consumers were being manipulated by the psychological techniques used in advertising and warned about the extension of these techniques into political life and corporate management. His book *The Waste Makers* (1960) warned about planned obsolescence and, more generally, American overabundance; here consumers were at fault as well as manipulative advertisers.

Economist John Kenneth Galbraith published *The Affluent Society* (1958), which challenged "the wisdom of our preoccupation with more and more consumer goods as a goal."[25] Galbraith raised fundamental questions about the nature of needs as opposed to wants, luxuries as opposed to necessities. "One cannot defend production as satisfying wants," he wrote, "if that production creates the wants."[26] He suggested that the quest for fulfillment through private consumption was overwhelming public life, prompting Americans to undervalue and underfund public goods like schools, museums, and hospitals.

Seven years later Ralph Nader's *Unsafe at Any Speed* provided an exposé of the automobile industry that launched the author's career as the modern leader of the consumer movement. During the 1960s Nader's Center for the Study of Responsive Law played a central role in the passage of a string of consumer legislation, such as the National Traffic and Motor Vehicle Safety Act.

NEW CRITIQUES

In the late 1960s and early 1970s, many younger Americans participated in a very different sort of critique of consumer culture, seeking to develop and live a "countercultural" lifestyle. It was a time of unprecedented increase in the range of products available and in general income levels; total personal consumption rose another 31 percent between 1960 and 1970.[27] But these young people eschewed material success and voluntarily minimized their purchasing or bought secondhand goods. They argued that corporations and the government were too big to provide properly for people's needs, and that those institutions were devoted to the private enrichment and empowerment of the few people in control, "the establishment."

Believing that people who lived a high-consumption lifestyle were inevitably corrupted by doing so, some in the counterculture worked for money as little as possible and pooled what money they had with partners in communal living situations. Others accepted low wages for devoting their time to "anti-establishment" social causes or collective alternatives to large-scale institutions. Food coops in particular came from a long political tradition that explicitly offered alternatives to capitalist economic forms. Recycling collectives reflected a growing environmental consciousness and offered an outlet for the consumer culture's trash. Like intentional communities, experimental schools, and the underground press, these alternative institutions offered ways to fill universal and traditional needs outside the system.

Others in the counterculture espoused using capitalist forms for new ends. *The Whole Earth Catalog* served as the consumer bible of the movement, promoting an ethic of local self-sufficiency and giving attention both to traditional methods and high-tech products. If you were out in the middle of nowhere building a new society, the *Catalog* asked, what would you want to have purchased in preparation? Books and tools, the answer went, information about how to provide for yourself, and the wherewithal to do it.

Although the counterculture attacked large corporations and rejected the prevailing high-consumption lifestyle, entrepreneurs and corporations eventually adopted and transformed certain aspects of the countercultural identity to sell products. Blue jeans, the emblematic countercultural clothing for both genders, were restyled and sold for high prices, emblazoned with fashion designers' names. But other aspects of the counterculture entered and altered the mainstream in more profound ways. The environmental consciousness embodied in recycling, for example, became commonplace, as the actual work of recycling moved from hippie collectives to municipal solid waste departments.

As the war in Vietnam wound down during the early 1970s,

environmentalism became increasingly central to the network of intertwined political and social organizations and ideas that composed the counterculture in its largest sense. And as Americans became aware of environmental problems, that understanding became central to the critique of consumerism and reinforced the longstanding ambivalence about luxury and abundance. Environmentalism itself came out of a conservation tradition going back to the Progressives, but it was also fed by a growing awareness of new forms of pollution. In agriculture, for example, postwar technologies had generated new chemical pesticides and fertilizers, the result of a revolution in industrial chemistry that had been advanced by war research. That revolution also produced detergents, synthetic fibers, plastics, and antibiotics.

Biologist Barry Commoner's best-selling *The Closing Circle* (1971) convinced many people of the negative impact of these changes. Commoner insisted that environmental deterioration suggested "something seriously wrong with the way in which human beings have occupied their habitat, the earth."[28] Economic activity withdraws resources from ecosystems, he explained, while adding back waste, fertilizers, and other pollutants. Commoner specifically targeted new technologies—fertilizers and pesticides, synthetic fibers and detergents, plastics, air conditioning, the concrete and aluminum construction methods that were replacing steel and lumber, and the triumph of shipping by truck rather than rail. He attacked high-tech agribusiness, which produced more food in less space but did not return nutrients to the soil. "The environmental crisis," Commoner wrote, "is somber evidence of an insidious fraud hidden in the vaunted productivity and wealth of modern, technology-based society."[29]

Environmental activists were further alarmed by *The Limits to Growth*, a report issued in 1972 by the Club of Rome. The report insisted on the interconnections of world resources, population, and environment, and it forecast the depletion of resources if current growth rates continued. E.F. Schumacher's *Small Is Beautiful: Economics as if People Mattered* (1973) brought these concerns about world resources and the lives of people in the Third World together with the counterculture critique of large institutions. Schumacher argued against mechanization as a goal of economic development, instead insisting on "appropriate technology."

Poet and farmer Wendell Berry offered yet another version of the environmental critique of consumption in *The Unsettling of America* (1977). Echoing Commoner, Berry attacked high-tech agriculture, calling the ecological crisis a crisis of character, of agriculture, and of culture. "I cannot think of any American whom I know or have heard of, who is not contributing in some way to destruction," he wrote.[30] Berry argued that consumers had responsibilities as well as rights, insisting that responsible consumption was moderate consumption and that the responsible consumer (and citizen of the planet) would purchase only what was needed and would indeed reduce needs. "These things, of course, have been often said," Berry wrote, "though in our time they have not been said very loudly and have not been much heeded. In our time the rule among consumers has been to spend money recklessly."[31]

Indeed, reckless spending was the order of the day. Per capita expenditures on women's clothing, toiletries, housing, furniture, kitchen appliances, china, cleaning supplies, stationery, electricity, water, and motor vehicles doubled between 1960 and 1990. Expenditures on telephone service and jewelry quadrupled.[32] Americans lived in larger houses, bought more of everything to put in them, and when they ran out of room, rented storage facilities for their stuff. People who grew up in the 1950s and 1960s in homes with three bedrooms, one bath, one TV, one car, no air conditioning, and no dishwasher aspired to larger houses with more bathrooms and appliances, including items like VCRs and computers that had been unknown when they were children.

Products for recreation and leisure are a particular case in point. Personal consumption expenditures for recreation in the United States, totaling $91 billion in 1970, skyrocketed to $149 billion in 1980 and $304 billion in 1993, in constant dollars. Even the oldest kinds of recreation industries enjoyed the boom, but the biggest increases by far came in products based on new technologies. Video games advanced in sophistication conceptually and technically, from Pong (the electronic tennis game of the 1970s) to PacMan (the arcade hit of the early 1980s) to Super Mario Brothers (Nintendo's successful home TV game at the end of that decade) to Myst (the personal computer star of the mid-1990s). Technological change similarly powered growth in the sales of sports equipment, stereos, and computers. Commercial amusements like theme parks and casinos boomed, as did film processing, gardening supplies, and videocassette rentals.

An expansion in leisure industries did not, however, indicate an expansion in leisure time. In fact, it took ever more wage earners per capita and per household to pay for all the compact discs and snowmobiles. Women had entered the labor force in record numbers throughout the 1950s, but their labor force participation rate rose from 38 percent in 1960 to 57 percent in 1988. Most of the increase came among married women: 32 percent had worked for pay in 1960, 61 percent by 1994. In order to attain middle-class lifestyles, many of the children worked, too, staffing McDonald's and Kentucky Fried Chicken franchises rather than baby-sitting or raking leaves.

One result was a demand for even more new products, as employed women used consumer goods to make their double day easier. Fast-food outlets blossomed. By the end of the 1970s, a third of the nation's food dollars were spent on restaurant meals; by 1985, about a third of the population ate out on any given day; and by 1988 restaurants accounted for 41 cents of every food dollar. Many of those who ate at home relied on packaged convenience foods, especially products designed to be heated in microwave ovens. Child care products and services likewise eased the double burdens of women in the labor force.

In the 1990s a new group of writers advocating a "simple life" began to ask what the point was. Echoing Thoreau, they described the harried lifestyle of typical working people as quiet desperation, only this time they included women as well as men. Economist Juliet Schor stated the argument powerfully in *The Overworked American* (1992). After a forty-year shopping spree, "the American standard of living embodies a level of material comfort unprecedented in human history," Schor wrote.[33] But to achieve that comfort, she asserted, Americans were trapped in "an insidious cycle of 'work-and-spend.'"[34] They experienced consumption as a treadmill—going around and around, but going nowhere—and they had to work long hours just to stay on it. Indeed, they were working harder than ever, putting in more hours at work every year since the 1960s. They suffered from stress and sleep deprivation and were losing contact with their families. The basic problem, Schor reiterated in the preface to the paperback edition, was "an economy and society that are demanding too much from people."[35]

Joe Dominguez and Vicki Robin's *Your Money or Your Life* (1992) proposed a self-help program to help individuals get off the treadmill, outlining concrete steps for keeping track of money, minimizing spending and maximizing income. "Money," the authors insisted, "is something we choose to trade our life energy for."[36] Those who understood this, they claimed, could transform their relationships with money and with work. They too echoed Thoreau, who 150 years earlier had phrased as philosophy what Dominguez and Robin prescribed as self-help. "The cost of a thing is the amount of what I will call life which is required to be exchanged for it, immediately or in the long run," Thoreau explained in *Walden*.[37] But *Your Money or Your*

Life made a global environmental argument. The authors maintained that in postwar America people had gone from using material goods for needs, through comfort and luxury, to excess. "The planet itself began showing signs of nearing its capacity to handle the results of our economic growth and consumerism," they wrote, citing numerous environmental issues involving soil, air, and water.[38]

Alan Thein Durning's *How Much Is Enough?* (1992) offered an extended treatment of that argument. Durning, a researcher at the Worldwatch Institute, asserted that overconsumption by the world's fortunate constitutes an environmental problem that rivals population growth. The pursuit of unlimited consumption, he maintained, is propelling the planet beyond its ability to sustain itself.

OUR CONTINUING CONFUSION

As the United States approaches the end of the twentieth century, continued rising consumption levels mix with awareness of environmental problems to leave Americans conflicted and confused about the real relationship between consumption and the environment. Public opinion surveys reveal this confusion. The poll results are not conclusive, at least in part because most pollsters have not connected the questions they ask about environmental attitudes with the ones they ask about the American Dream and the American way of life. Still, a few results are suggestive:

• In a 1995 study funded by the Merck Family Fund, 88 percent of those interviewed believed that protecting the environment "will require most of us to make major changes in the way we live," but only 51 percent believed that their own buying habits had a negative effect on the environment.

- A 1993 poll taken by the Roper Center for Public Opinion Research found that 31 percent were willing or very willing "to accept cuts in your standard of living in order to protect the environment," while 38 percent were not very willing or not at all willing. The other 31 percent said they were "neither willing nor unwilling," were unable to choose, or gave no answer.
- On the other hand, a 1991 poll of Floridians asked, "If you had to choose between the two, which of the following would you choose? A worse quality of your own material life but a higher quality environment, or a worse quality environment but a higher quality of your own material life?" Seventy-four percent chose a worse material life, 18 percent a worse environment, 9 percent didn't know.

Maybe people in Florida are just different. But more likely the differences in the poll results reflect Americans' confusion about what they understand to be complex issues. The Roper poll suggests that we do not expect miracles. Only 18 percent agreed with the statement: "Modern science will solve our environmental problems with little change to our way of life." Fifty-three percent disagreed.

In part, our confusion is just the latest manifestation of a historical tradition of ambivalence and moralism toward consumption that reaches back to Thoreau and even to the initial British settlement of the colonies. But it stems as well from something new: a consciousness of global ecology as well as of global economics. On the one hand, the conclusion to be drawn from the vast differences between lifestyles on the planet seems obvious: We of the developed nations must scale back our consumption and change our wasteful ways. On the other, planting trees and carrying bags to the supermarket seem like mere drops in a bucket—or an ocean—inconsequential practices that can hardly make a difference to the fate of the planet. We know that every economic activity has environmental costs, but where do we draw the line between good and bad activities? We may be willing to change our lifestyles, but how do we do so, and what can we do that will really make a difference?

APPENDIX A
RESEARCH METHODS
AND RESULTS

THE MOST SERIOUS ENVIRONMENTAL ISSUES

The task of ranking environmental problems obviously raises some difficult issues. It is easy to name a host of environmental problems; it is much harder to decide which of these are the most important to deal with. Should we care more about oil spills than the paving over of wetlands for shopping malls? Is air pollution of greater concern than toxic wastes?

Environmental scientists have tackled this problem using an analytical technique known as comparative risk assessment.[1] Despite its limitations—which we will get to later—this is a valuable method for measuring and comparing the dangers posed by various human activities. The word *risk* denotes the statistical character of many environmental problems. Not all hazards inevitably cause harm or cause harm equally to all people, so scientists try to assign probabilities to different outcomes and calculate an expected, or average, outcome. To take a familiar example, there is no guarantee that a heavy smoker will die at an earlier age than he would if he did not smoke, but he certainly faces a higher *risk* of early death.

The process of comparative risk assessment starts by developing a list of environmental problems to analyze. The list may be based on expert judgment, topics of existing environmental protection efforts, public perceptions, or other information. Then the risks are categorized according to whether they affect human health, other aspects of social welfare (such as income or quality of life), or ecological communities (plants and animals). Usually no attempt is made to rank environmental problems across these overarching categories.[2] Instead, the process focuses on ranking risks within each category.

Once environmental hazards are identified and categorized in this fashion, then scientists begin to pull together all of the available information leading to an estimate of the risks they pose. Health specialists examine data relating human exposure to toxic chemicals and pollutants to rates of death and disease, then derive a predicted number or range of numbers of illnesses from each type of pollutant. Economists calculate the lost economic productivity that could result from a declining natural resource base, such as the lost income for commercial fisheries if oil pollution damages spawning grounds. Ecologists consider evidence of declining animal and plant populations and degraded or disappearing habitat linked to a variety of human activities. The end result is—or should be—a comprehensive ranking of problems from the most to the least severe.

In reality, the process is much messier and less precise than this brief description makes it appear. One of the biggest difficulties is a lack of reliable and comprehensive data on the effects and sources of many environmental problems. One might think that there would be an abundance of data on the human health effects of various chemical pollutants, for example, but many of the hundreds of chemicals used in our society have not been adequately studied. Moreover, much of the evidence of health effects comes from animal experiments, which are difficult to extrapolate accurately to humans. Good data on the extent and causes of various problems affecting ecological communities are even more difficult to obtain, since there are few widely accepted, easily measured indicators of ecosystem health. Much analysis must in the end rely on subjective judgments.

Some critics also raise theoretical problems with comparative risk assessment, although recent studies have addressed at least some of these issues.[3] One complaint is that the analyses often ignore the distribution of risks, such as whether a problem presents a low-level risk for a large group of people or an acute risk for a small group. Instead, they focus on a single number, the average risk. Plenty of evidence shows that people do not really weigh risks with such very different characteristics in the same fashion. For example, some people express an aversion to living near a nuclear power plant and yet show little fear of driving, despite the fact that the risk of dying in a car accident is far higher than that of being killed in a nuclear plant accident. Factors that affect risk perceptions include whether the risk is within the control of people affected and whether it endangers entire communities rather than individuals.[4]

Comparative risk assessment studies also sometimes ignore questions of justice or equity. If the people most exposed to a risk are not causing the problem, then simple fairness may dictate some corrective action, even if the overall risk is relatively small. If you dump your trash on your neighbor's lawn, it is no defense to say that the trash poses no threat to your neighbor's health! There is also the question of whether exposure is voluntary or not. Sports fishermen may choose to catch and eat fish contaminated with mercury, but children do not choose to be exposed to lead in paint dust.

All of this is by way of saying that any conclusions reached through comparative risk assessment must be interpreted with caution. The method is not a precision tool that can distinguish accurately between problems of comparable magnitude, and we should not get so carried away with the technique that it becomes the last word in setting environmental priorities.[5] But it does help place problems in broad perspective. And because it relies on the best available scientific data, it is the best place to start in trying to decide which environmental issues require the most attention.

In the following sections we will take a look at the findings of two comparative risk assessments that greatly influenced our choice of the top four environmental problems. In 1987 the Environmental Protection Agency released the first national comparative risk assessment, *Unfinished Business: A Comparative Assessment of Environmental Problems*. Its purpose was to survey thirty-one types of environmental problems within the EPA's jurisdiction and to evaluate how much risk to the public or to plants and animals was posed by each. A few years later, the EPA's Scientific Advisory Board endorsed the report's main conclusions while revising and updating some of the rankings of specific environmental problems.[6]

The other, in some ways superior, study is *Toward the 21st Century: Planning for the Protection of California's Environment*, an assessment of environmental risks in California performed by the Comparative Risk Project for the California EPA in 1994.[7] Although limited only to one state, the study was done in a more systematic and quantitative fashion than the first-of-a-kind *Unfinished Business*, and it took some pains to address criticisms of the technique that have been advanced since the national report was released. Where possible, for example, the report deals with the uneven distribution of environmental risks by identifying population subgroups (such as children or sports fishermen) facing the greatest threats.

Risks to Human Health

In the late 1980s researchers at Wayne State University conducted a study of babies born to women who were in the habit of eating Lake Michigan fish. Thanks to the polluting practices of decades past, which left a residue of pollutants in lake sediments, many of the fish found in the lake are contaminated with chemicals known as polychlorinated biphenyls, or PCBs. The researchers found that at birth babies born to these women weighed an average of five to seven ounces less than babies born to mothers who had not eaten contaminated fish. Other signs of infant difficulty included weak reflexes, sluggish movements, smaller head circumference, and reduced short-term memory.[8]

Such research illustrates a typical way in which environmental problems can affect human health. Most of the significant health risks that have been identified involve chemicals of one sort or another. Chemicals, of course, are ubiquitous in the environment, and as toxicologists love to point out, no chemical is entirely benign or entirely harmful: it all depends on how much is absorbed and in what manner. A few sips of wine will not induce noticeable signs of intoxication in a typical adult. But several glasses of wine can cause slurred speech, blurred vision, and slowed reaction times, while much more may induce unconsciousness, coma, and even death. When a chemical is released into the environment in sufficient quantity to cause measurable harm to humans, plants, or animals, we call it a pollutant.

Industrial societies like ours spew many different pollutants into the environment, each of which has its own unique characteristics. Some, such as the common air pollutants nitrogen oxide, carbon monoxide, and volatile organic compounds, are extremely widespread because they are produced in large quantities by many different activities. Fortunately, none of these are acutely toxic in the moderate concentrations observed in the United States, but because so many people are exposed to them over long periods, they represent a significant health concern and have become the subject of strict monitoring and regulation.

Many other pollutants are released into the environment in

much smaller quantities. Although some are known to be highly toxic, many have not been the subject of detailed toxicological study, so their true risks are unknown.

Ranking the risks to human health from these many chemicals usually involves taking several steps:[9]

- *Identifying the hazards.* This means listing the specific substances to be examined. Usually the list is restricted to unintentional environmental hazards, so wine and cigarettes are excluded, as are the *intended* effects of pesticides on weeds and insects.
- *Modeling the dose-response relationship.* This step involves examining all available scientific evidence to determine the health effects of different levels of exposure to each chemical.
- *Estimating exposures.* On a separate track, scientists estimate how much of each chemical people are normally exposed to. This step, too, can become complicated, since the degree of exposure may depend on where people live, how they behave, what they eat, their size, and other factors.
- *Characterizing risks.* Combining the dose-response relationships and exposure assessments, scientists then determine the overall health impact. How many cases of cancer or noncancer illness are produced in a given population? Which subgroups in the population are more affected than others?
- *Risk ranking.* Lastly, scientists compare their conclusions about different hazards to come up with a ranking of environmental problems. Considering the uncertainties involved, the rankings are usually cast in very broad terms, such as high, medium, and low.

Some health threats, such as the "hole" in the stratospheric ozone layer, do not result from direct exposure to chemicals, but they can be analyzed in a similar manner.

Table A.1 compares the public health risk rankings of the EPA's *Unfinished Business* and the California Comparative Risk Project's *Toward the 21st Century*. There are a lot of inconsistencies in the way environmental problems are named and categorized between the two studies, but we have done our best to make the findings comparable.

The table reveals some important similarities as well as significant differences. Among the similarities, both indoor and outdoor air pollution rank high on these lists of human health risks, as does exposure to chemicals in consumer products (such as paints, solvents, and cleaners). Likewise, both the national and California reports put hazardous waste sites in the medium-risk category and genetically engineered organisms and global warming in the low-risk or indeterminate category.

Other problems are ranked somewhat differently, however. For instance, occupational exposure to chemicals is a ranked a high health risk in the national study but a medium health risk in the California study. Some of these differences may be merely the result of different thresholds for the high, medium, and low classifications. The upper and lower bounds of these categories are not very clearly defined in either report. In addition, *Unfinished Business* provided separate rankings for cancer and noncancer health risks, which we combined to yield a single ranking.

Lastly, a few problem categories appear in only one of the reports. This doesn't mean that these problems are not considered in both reports, but in one report they may be incorporated into another category. (For example, asbestos is counted in consumer exposure to chemicals in *Unfinished Business*.)

Risks to Ecological Communities

The kinds of risks affecting ecological communities are often difficult to quantify. The ecological risk rankings consequently tend to be more subjective than the health risk rankings. Rather than modeling dose-response relationships, estimating expo-

Table A.1. Human Health Risk Rankings*

	National Report**	California Report***
High-ranked risks	Outdoor air pollutants	Outdoor air pollutants
	Indoor air pollutants	Indoor air pollutants
	Pollutants in drinking water	Chemical contamination of fish
	Occupational exposure to chemicals	Consumer exposure to chemicals
	Consumer exposure to chemicals	
	Pesticides on food	
Medium-ranked risks	Depletion of stratospheric ozone	Lead in homes
		Pollutants in drinking water
	Hazardous waste sites	Hazardous waste sites
	Nonhazardous waste sites	Occupational exposure to chemicals
	New chemicals	
	Radiation (other than radon)	Pesticides on food
	Chemical spills and leaks	
Low- or unranked risk	Genetically engineered organisms	Genetically engineered organisms
	Global warming	Global warming
	Pollutants in estuaries and coastal waters	Depletion of stratospheric ozone
		Non-hazardous waste sites
		New chemicals
		Radiation (other than radon)

*Environmental problems have been grouped as far as possible in common categories to aid in comparison. Listings in the referenced reports consequently differ in some cases.

**U.S. Environmental Protection Agency, *Unfinished Business, Vol. 1: Overview* (February 1987), tables 2–2 and 2–4.

***California Comparative Risk Project, *Toward the 21st Century: Report of the Human Health Committee* (May 1994), table 2.

sures, and all the rest, ecological risk assessment studies more often rely on field surveys that attempt, first, to characterize the state of well-being of a particular species or ecological community, and second, to identify the principal sources of harm to them. In some cases such surveys are quite accurate and the sources of harm easy to identify—for instance, there is no doubt that the numbers of cod and other commercial fish in the Georges Bank have greatly declined and that the cause is overfishing. In other cases, though, the task is more challenging. Bird surveys are notoriously inaccurate, for example, and as we saw with neotropical migratory birds in chapter 3, even when a decline in numbers is definitely observed, it is not always easy to figure out what is causing it.

The rankings from the national and California studies are shown in the table below. (The national rankings are from the Science Advisory Board's update of *Unfinished Business,* not from the original report.) Once again we had to rename and regroup some of the categories in the two studies to ease comparisons between them.[10]

There are significant differences between the two lists. For example, stratospheric ozone depletion was not ranked in the California report but was given a high risk ranking in the national report; introduced species—nonnative invaders

Table A.2. Ecological Risk Rankings

	National Report	California Report
High-ranked risks	Habitat alteration	Habitat alteration
	Global warming	Water pollution
	Stratospheric ozone depletion	Air pollution
		Introduced species
Medium-ranked risks	Pesticides	Global warming
	Water pollution	Pesticides
	Air pollution	
	Acid deposition	
Low-ranked risks	Oil spills	Wildfires
	Groundwater contamination	Acid deposition
	Radiation	Pathogenic microorganisms
	Thermal pollution	

brought by humans—is given a high rank in California but was not listed in *Unfinished Business*; and global warming and acid deposition are given less weight, and water and air pollution more weight, in the California report than in the national report.

The differing rankings of some environmental problems may partly reflect differences between studies in the definition of high-, medium-, and low-risk categories. The national report, for example, assigned six ranks from high to low.

We assigned category 1 risks to the high-risk group, categories 2 to 4 to the medium-risk group, and categories 5 and 6 to the low-risk group. Other methods of grouping the categories would yield somewhat different results.

Nevertheless, when viewed as a whole, the two reports appear to be quite consistent with each other. In particular, water and air pollution, global warming, and habitat alteration are regarded as significant problems in both lists.

Consolidating the Risks

In trying to trace the environmental impacts of consumer habits, we need not consider all of the problems listed in the two comparative risk reports. For one thing, we are interested only in those problems that have the most serious human health or ecological impacts, which we take to mean problems that rank as of either medium or high risk on either the EPA or California list. There is no point in worrying about the consumer contribution to wildfires or thermal pollution, for example, since they pose little overall ecological or health risk. It may be a bit more controversial to exclude oil spills and similar chemical accidents (as distinct from more routine chemical releases from manufacturing and storage facilities, which are considered in our study), but severe accidents of this type are quite rare, and the studies suggest they are not a major source of danger to public health or wildlife.

We were able to subsume many of the specific risks noted by the two reports under our four broad environmental problems of air pollution, global warming, habitat alteration, and water pollution. For example, we were able to account for acid deposition under our category of air pollution. Pesticide releases and emissions from waste sites were tracked partly under air pollution and partly under water pollution.

Furthermore, since our aim is to help consumers decide what they can do to protect the environment, we considered only problems that are linked to current consumer activities or expenditures. As we mentioned in chapter 3, this meant ignoring the impacts of inactive waste sites and mines, as well as chemicals that have already been banned or whose use has been greatly curtailed, such as PCBs, lead in paint, and chlorofluorocarbons (which deplete the stratospheric ozone layer). Some of these problems pose serious environmental hazards, but consumer actions today have little to do with them.

Lastly, we excluded problems that fall in the categories of occupational and household health and safety. Again, we don't mean to dismiss or minimize the importance of these health threats, but we have chosen not to treat them as distinct environmental problems in this book. In the former case, we believe worker exposure to chemicals should generally be addressed directly in the workplace, rather than through the indirect means of everyday consumer decisions. In the case of household health and safety issues, our examination of air and water pollution partially addresses some of these concerns, such as indoor air pollution and pesticides on food. We must acknowledge, however, that we are not able to differentiate between consumers' exposure to chemicals outside the home and their exposure to chemicals in items, such as paints and cleaning products, that are used in the home.

CALCULATING THE IMPACTS OF CONSUMER ACTIVITIES

What share of global warming results from, say, the purchase of household appliances? To what degree do our purchases of clothing contribute to water pollution?

The answers to such basic questions are surprisingly hard to come by. Although the federal government and many states collect large amounts of data on different kinds of environmental harm, the coverage is incomplete in many respects. There is plenty of data on sources of air pollution, for example, but surprisingly little on sources of water pollution, toxic chemicals, threats to biodiversity, and other serious problems. What is more, even where the information is theoretically available, few attempts have been made to trace the sources back to the consumer. "Agriculture" and "industry" often get blamed, but the damage they do almost always occurs in the process of making things people buy. What things?

The task of pinpointing the responsibility of the consumer is made especially challenging by the fact that we live in a complex society where products are manufactured in many different places from many different materials. Take the case of the family car. The federal government produces estimates of how much air pollution is generated by the nearly 140 million cars on the road today. That part is easy. But manufacturing cars takes an enormous investment of materials and energy, and in that process much more pollution may be generated. The average domestic automobile contains 2,170 pounds of steel and iron, 200 pounds of aluminum, 140 pounds of rubber, 245 pounds of plastics and composites, 200 pounds of fluids and lubricants, and 280 pounds of assorted other materials.[11] That is a lot of stuff, some of it made with quite toxic chemicals— and there is no easy place to look up how much pollution is generated in producing it, or in producing numerous other consumer products.

We are hardly the first to recognize this problem. Environmental scientists have long sought ways to calculate the impacts of producing various products and services. The main research tool that has been developed so far is a method called life-cycle analysis, or LCA.[12] This technique attempts to trace the impacts of products throughout their life cycle from the extraction of the raw materials to their final disposal. It is much like a financial audit, except that what is being tracked is the flow of materials and pollution rather than of dollars. The best-known life-cycle analyses have compared cloth and disposable diapers, but similar studies have been done on paper and plastic bags, packaging, batteries, and other products.[13]

Life-cycle analysis can be very valuable, especially for analyzing ways to improve product designs, but it was not well suited to our purpose, which was to paint a comprehensive picture of the impacts of consumer decisions. It simply takes too much effort to trace the impacts of every product consumers buy in such a painstaking fashion. Even in analyses that focus on just one or two products, LCA practitioners usually do not trace the impacts more than a few links up the production chain. The study may consider the pollution generated in making a car's steel panels, for example, but not in making the machinery that makes the panels.

The approach we took allowed us to analyze the impacts of large numbers of different products in a systematic fashion, through the use of an input-output model, a standard tool of economic analysis.[14] Unlike life-cycle analysis, our method considered all inputs to the production process. As a trade-off, we gave up a lot of the detail provided by life-cycle analysis, such as the exact environmental implications of recycled versus virgin paper, or plastic versus glass containers.

The Environmental Indicators
The first step in the analysis was to develop a set of environmental indicators that would define and quantify the problems

we are most concerned about. The indicators we developed follow closely from the four major environmental problems we had concluded were most relevant:

Global warming.

Our indicator of global warming was annual emissions of greenhouse gases from human activities, expressed in tons of carbon in carbon dioxide. Emissions of methane were included after adjustment for their greater ability to trap heat.[15]

Air pollution.

In the category of common air pollutants, we selected the four that appear to pose the greatest risk to human health: nitrogen oxides (NO_x), volatile organic compounds (VOCs, also known as hydrocarbons), sulfur dioxide (SO_2), and particulate matter below 2.5 microns in size ($PM_{2.5}$).[16] The indicator gives equal weight to the *total* emissions of each type of pollutant, so for example, the approximately 6.9 million tons of particulate matter emitted into the air in 1995 count as much as the 21.5 million tons of NO_x.[17]

For toxic air pollutants, we chose total annual emissions of the 188 hazardous air pollutants defined by Congress in the Clean Air Act Amendments of 1990.[18] In this case, each pollutant was assumed to have the same impact per unit of weight on human health, although in fact the toxicity of the chemicals varies greatly. Much more research would be needed to come up with an indicator that fully reflects toxicity, persistence, human exposure, and other factors that determine health impact.[19]

Water pollution.

It surprised us to learn that the federal government keeps little comprehensive data on the sources and quantities of common water pollutants such as nutrients, suspended solids, sediments, and biological oxygen demand. Major industries and municipal waste facilities (known as point sources) are covered in the *Permit Compliance System*, a database maintained by the EPA. But industrial and municipal point sources represent only a small fraction (10–20 percent) of all sources of water pollution. The runoff of fertilizers and pesticides from agriculture, animal wastes from livestock, and urban sources are far more important.

Nevertheless we were able to piece together a complete set of data by drawing on the EPA's *National Water Quality Inventory* for 1994. This report links observed water quality problems to specific sources, such as agriculture, urban runoff, mining, dams, and industrial and municipal facilities. Although no quantities of pollution are given in the survey, it tells us roughly how important the industrial and municipal point sources are compared with the others. Through extrapolation, we were able to estimate the quantities of pollution entering water from all sources in tons per year.[20]

There is likewise no comprehensive database of toxic water pollution, so we relied on the EPA's *Toxic Release Inventory*, which covers pollutant discharges from major factories and other industrial point sources.[21] To this we added one more very important class of chemical, pesticides. Drawing on research on the transport of pesticides from land to water in the Midwest,[22] we assumed that 0.5 percent of pesticide applications to land would wind up in water. Because of the uncertainty in the land-water transport fraction and the absence of information on other potential source of toxic chemicals not covered in the EPA inventory (such as consumer solvents), this indicator is probably not as reliable as the other pollution indicators we developed.

Habitat alteration.

Human appropriation of land for various purposes is closely linked to threats to terrestrial plant and animal habitats. Different kinds of land use can have very different impacts on wildlife, however. Forest that is cleared every ten or fifteen years for timber can still support much natural wildlife, but forest that is paved over for a shopping mall cannot. Also, some types of land development tend to encroach on areas of greater biological diversity (such as wetlands) more than others.

To account for the wide disparity in land use impacts on wildlife, we relied on data collected by the U.S. Forest Service that associate the numbers of endangered plant and animal species with agriculture, livestock grazing, urban development, highways and roads, forestry, and other land uses.[23] By combining this information with government data on the number of acres of land devoted to each use,[24] we concluded that an acre of urban land has about the same negative impact on biodiversity as using 17 acres of range to graze livestock, 10 acres of forest to produce forest products, 6 acres of land to grow crops, and 0.6 acre of land for highways. We applied these adjustment factors to create an index of "urban-equivalent" land use in acres.[25]

Water use provides only a rough measure of threats to aquatic habitats. (Water pollution and, for marine habitats, overfishing are probably at least as important.) Nevertheless, we decided it was worth including since many consumers are conscious of water consumption as an environmental problem and the indicator captures at least one significant aspect of the problem.

Water consumption is reported by the government in two ways: as water withdrawals (the total amount withdrawn from streams, lakes, or groundwater, regardless of how much is ultimately returned to the source), and consumptive use (the amount that evaporates or is otherwise not returned).[26] Of the two indicators, water withdrawals put more emphasis on electric power generation, which uses enormous amounts of water to provide cooling but returns almost all of it in usable form (just somewhat warmer). Consumptive use, on the other hand, places more emphasis on agriculture, since most of the water used for irrigation evaporates (and what is returned is frequently highly polluted with minerals, pesticides, and nutrients). Our indicator relies on consumptive use (expressed in gallons per day).

BUILDING THE MODEL

Once the indicators were in hand, we proceeded to construct a model that would allow us to link consumer purchases and activities to specific environmental problems. Here are the basic steps we followed.

1. First, we classified each type of pollution or environmental damage according to whether it was due directly to households or indirectly to agriculture or industry. (A direct impact, for example, is the water pollution generated when you spread pesticides on your lawn; an indirect impact is the water pollution generated by the industries that manufacture pesticides.)

2. Second, we distributed the indirect sources of pollution among some five hundred industry and commodity sectors. In some cases, the original data provided the breakdown for us (usually in terms of standard industrial classifications, or SICs, a common way of classifying industries and commodities). For instance, two air pollution databases, the *National Emissions Trends* database and the *National Toxics Inventory*, provide estimates of emissions for several hundred source categories, including, as a subset, the SICs. In other cases, we had to infer the distribution based on surveys of such things as industry fuel expenditures, fertilizers and pesticides applied to different crop types, and water use in mining and manufacturing.

3. Third, we combined the data on how much pollution (or other environmental damage) is generated by each sector with the value of goods or services produced by that sector to create a coefficient that expresses the quantity of damage per dollar of economic output. For example, if our data showed that meat packing plants emit eighty-two tons of toxic air pollutants per year, and the total value of products sold annually by that sector is $53 billion, then the toxic air pollution coefficient for that sector is 1.55 kilograms per million dollars.

4. Fourth, we used an input-output model to estimate the amount of economic output (in dollars) generated in each industry sector by any given set of consumer purchases. In effect, rather than having to track the pollution generated at each stage of the manufacture of every product we wanted to study, we simply tracked the dollars. Not only is there a lot more information about the flow of money in the economy than about the flow of materials and effluents, the input-output model provides a ready-made method for calculating the economywide effects of individual consumer expenditures. (See box.)

5. Last, we multiplied the environmental impact coefficients calculated in step 3 by the estimated industry output for different types of consumer expenditures calculated in step 4. This resulted in an estimate of the indirect environmental impacts for each type of purchase. To this we added the direct impacts (from step 1), yielding an estimate of the total impacts.

To impose some order on things, we grouped household expenditures into several broad categories:

• Transportation, including personal cars and trucks, air, rail, and water travel, recreational boats and aircraft, and off-road vehicles
• Food, alcohol, and tobacco products
• Household operations such as electricity and gas, appliances, paints, cleaning chemicals, and the like

Input-Output Analysis

An input-output model provides a framework for tracking the payments made by industries to other industries, and by consumers to industries, in the production of commodities and services. The framework consists of a transactions matrix describing cash flows among different economic sectors. The economist Wassily Leontief developed a method of inverting the transaction matrix so that the effect of any given set of consumer purchases on industry expenditures throughout the economy could be calculated.[27] He won a Nobel prize for this work in 1973.

The input-output approach assumes that the complicated interactions within an economy can be represented by proportional relationships. For example, if $10 million worth of steel is purchased to make 10,000 cars, then the model assumes that $100 million of steel will be purchased to make 100,000 cars. This assumption creates problems for some types of economic modeling, but it is actually an advantage in our study, since we are interested in assigning responsibility for environmental impacts among different consumer products in a proportionate manner.

The input-output model we used, called IMPLAN, was developed by the U.S. Forest Service and is now marketed by an independent company, the Minnesota IMPLAN Group. It has 528 industry and commodity sectors, most of which are identical to the standard industrial classifications (SICs). The model uses national industry output and expenditure data for 1995, which have been extrapolated and adapted from 1992 benchmark data tables published by the U.S. Bureau of Economic Analysis.[28]

- Housing (new homes, mobile homes, home maintenance)
- Personal items, such as reading materials, clothing, jewelry, and services
- Yard care, including pesticides and fertilizers and yard equipment

Case Study: The Family Car

For those who want to understand a little more about how our model works, we will show you by looking at the case of the family car. One of the questions we wanted to answer was: How much does owning and driving a typical car contribute to global warming? The model first had to consider the direct household impacts. According to government data, personal use of cars and light trucks (including minivans, pickups, and so forth) generated about 289 million metric tons of carbon in 1995.[29] In the same year cars and light trucks were driven for personal use a total of about 2 trillion miles (ten thousand round trips between the earth and the sun!).[30] The average emissions rate is therefore 0.145 metric ton per thousand vehicle miles. So if we assume that a typical family car is driven 12,000 miles a year, then it produces on average about 1.7 metric tons of carbon a year.

Our analysis also had to carry out the more complicated task of determining the impacts from the car's manufacture. The average purchase price of a new car is about $18,000. According to the IMPLAN model, when a consumer spends this amount, on average the car manufacturer receives $13,892. Of the rest of the purchase price, $2,916 goes to the retail automotive dealer, with smaller amounts going to wholesale automotive dealers, and trucking and rail services (for transporting the cars from the factory to the dealers.)[31]

The money these various industry sectors receive does not stop there, however. We need to look at how they in turn spend the money they earn on the sale. We call such expenditures the *upstream* impacts of the sale because they occur up the production chain from the point of final manufacture and delivery. The upstream expenditures are spread out over a great many more industries, as shown in table A.3. Here we've listed only the more important materials components, leaving out many other factors such as real estate and banking services (included in the very large "other" category). The total comes to more than the original cost of the car because the money goes through many cycles of spending and respending.[32]

Table A.3. Upstream Expenditures for a Typical $18,000 Car

Item	Expense
Motor vehicle parts and accessories	$3,550
Automotive stampings	1,140
Miscellaneous plastics products	754
Blast furnaces and steel mills	670
Electric services	331
Car manufacturers[33]	299
Refrigeration and heating equipment	275
Cyclic crudes and intermediates, and industrial organic chemicals	273
Natural gas and crude petroleum	256
Engine electrical equipment	248
Plastics materials and resins	221
Internal combusion engines (not elsewhere classified)	214
Automotive apparel and trimmings	209
Other	17,061
Total	$25,501

Let's look at one row of the table: blast furnaces and steel mills.

According to the model, they will receive $670 in payments from the purchase of the car. From our environmental impacts data, we know that blast furnaces and steel mills produce 693 metric tons of carbon for every million dollars of value shipped. Therefore that component of the car purchase alone is responsible for about 464 kilograms of carbon emitted into the atmosphere. After applying the appropriate carbon emissions factors to all of the industry sectors, we find that manufacturing the car and delivering it to the consumer produces 3.8 metric tons of carbon. If that sounds like a lot, you're right—it's nearly three times the weight of the car itself![34]

Now, how do we combine the impacts of manufacture and the impacts of use? One way to do this is to suppose that the average car lasts a certain period, maybe 15 years, before it is scrapped. Then we can divide the impacts of manufacturing by the car's life to get an average impact per year. If you do this for our car example, you get an average annual greenhouse gas impact of 0.25 metric ton/year. That figure is added to the annual driving impacts (1.7 metric tons/year) to get a total of 1.95 metric tons of carbon per year.

However, this method of spreading the manufacturing impacts over time would quickly become unwieldy if applied to the many hundreds of products consumers purchase every year. (Quick: What is the average life of a refrigerator? Of a lawn mower?) Instead, to produce the results presented in this book, we relied on the average annual household expenditures for various products as determined by government consumer expenditure surveys. Such data contain information about both the average lifetime and price of products. If a particular product has a short life, for example, it will be replaced often, and that will boost annual average expenditures for that item.[35]

We also tossed in education, financial and legal expenses, and medical expenses for good measure.

Then, after comparing the impacts across these broad categories, we started looking at important items within each category, such as automobiles (under transportation) and home appliances (under household operations). We continued breaking things down in this fashion until we had results for 134 different types of consumer expenditure in all.

REPORTING THE RESULTS

From our analysis, we generated two different sets of results. The first set shows the total environmental impacts of a particular category of household expenditures. For example, we can see how the damage automobiles do compares with the harm caused by eating meat, purchasing clothes, or buying newspapers. This is the information we used to reach our central conclusions in chapter 3. Our full results for all 134 household spending categories are shown in table A.4, at the end of this appendix.

We also derived a second set of results to show the relative environmental impact of spending a dollar on the various types of household expenditure. We obtained these results by dividing the entries in table A.4 by the average amount of money a household spends on that category. For example, the average household emits 3.5 tons of greenhouse gases as a result of automobiles and light trucks and they spend an average of $2,700 per year on these vehicles. The impact per dollar is therefore 3.5 tons divided by $2,700, which equals 1.3 tons per thousand dollars.

The significance of the impact per dollar is that it can help steer expenditures away from high-impact activities. For example, spending a dollar on recreational boating produces fifteen times as much common air pollution as spending the same amount on jewelry, toys, and instruments. Similarly, a dollar spent on heating and hot water is responsible for much higher levels of greenhouse gases than a dollar spent on furnishings or clothing. Of course, the environmental impact per dollar is only one factor you need to consider when making consumer decisions. At the end of this appendix, in table A.5, we have placed our impacts-per-dollar results for all 134 categories. We think you will find it interesting to compare the implications of the various ways you can spend your money.

SOME QUALIFICATIONS

As we have been quick to point out, our approach has limitations, even though it provides a good broad-brush picture of consumers' relationship to the environment. We therefore want to make a few qualifications and point out some subtleties in the analysis.

First, the qualifications. We must stress above all that in any given case our results will not be perfectly accurate by any means. It is probably already clear that several of our environmental indicators give only a rough measure of impact (although we believe firmly that using such flawed measures is better than ignoring the problems altogether). There are, in addition, substantial variations among regions both in the severity of environmental problems and in the sources of those problems. Overconsumption of water is a much more serious problem in the Southwest than in the Northeast; air pollution is generally worse in big cities than in small towns; most electricity in the Northwest comes from hydropower, which generates no pollution, but in the industrial Midwest most of it comes from highly polluting coal.

Furthermore, even within the same region there are wide variations in the impacts of individual households. Some of the variations result from differences in income and expenditure patterns. Low-income households, in particular, spend less on most things than do high-income households and so can be expected to have a lower environmental impact overall. Households may also *choose* to spend their money in ways that have less, or more, of an impact. Indeed, one of the main goals of this book is to encourage people to deliberately reduce their burden on the environment, whether by driving less, buying organic produce, or (something that is only now becoming possible in some states) buying electricity from clean sources such as wind energy.

Last, the input-output model itself is not a perfect representation of the economy. Some of the industries and commodities in the model are defined rather too broadly for our purposes; the raw materials for plastics, for instance, are lumped into one sector, even though some kinds of plastics manufacturing (such as polyvinyl chlorides, or PVCs) pose a much greater threat to the environment than others. Also, even the government does not have hard data on purchases by every industry from every other industry. Wherever blanks existed, analysts at the U.S. Bureau of Economic Analysis and the Minnesota IMPLAN Group had to fill them in with approximate figures.

So to be absolutely clear, we do not claim that our findings represent the final word or that our analysis has no room for improvement. In fact, we hope that our work will stimulate others to collect and publish more data that will enable us to improve and refine our model. What we do claim is that the findings provide a much clearer overall picture of the impacts of household spending than has been put forward in the past.

Now to some of the subtleties. First, there is the question of whether household consumption of goods and services explains all environmental damage, and if not, what fraction it does account for. In the input-output model we use, agricultural and industrial output is driven by several types of what is called final demand. The biggest component of this by far (about 60 percent) is household demand, but there is also considerable demand by federal and state government and for exports to consumers in other countries. Now, you could argue that all government activities are merely responding to a different sort of household demand (for military or police protection, for example), and so they should be included in evaluating the environmental impacts of household decisions. But we think that this takes us too far afield from the ordinary consumer, which is where we want to focus our attention.

As for exports, we see no reason why environmental impacts incurred in the production of goods for consumption in other countries should be counted against American consumers, and we do not do so in our model. By the same token, however, we cannot let American consumers off the hook when it comes to imported goods. Pollution, for example, is generated in pumping oil out of the Middle Eastern deserts and shipping it to the United States to supply gasoline for cars. How can impacts such as these be accounted for in a systematic fashion?

We knew from the start that it would be impossible for us to analyze imports in any detail, since the data on environmental problems in many countries are extremely spotty. Instead, we employed a trick: We modified our input-output model so that all products, whether imported or not, are assumed to be produced in the United States. In effect, this means that imported items are assumed to be produced with the same technology, and the same environmental impacts, as if they were produced here.

This is, admittedly, a heroic assumption. Some countries have more stringent environmental standards than the United States; many have much weaker standards. But absent the data we need to do a truly global analysis, we thought this approach would be much better than ignoring imports altogether. Although most of the items Americans consume are manufactured or grown domestically, in some cases imports are a significant factor. With the modified model, for example, we are able to count at least some of the methane produced from oil and gas wells in other countries, an important factor when you consider that roughly half of the oil we use in the United States is imported. Of course, when countries have significantly weaker environmental standards than the United States, our research model does not allow us to show the extent to which American consumers' purchases—such as carnations from Colombia, oil from Nigeria, and certain types of wood from tropical rain forests—cause significant local environmental damage in those countries.[36]

THE DETAILED RESULTS

The following two large tables present the detailed results of our analysis of the environmental impacts of consumer activity. We analyzed the impacts of 134 separate categories of activity ranging from distilled liquors to shoes. These were then aggregated into 50 larger categories, such as alcoholic beverages and clothing, and then once again into 10 broad activity areas, such as food and household operations. Although the resulting tables may initially seem daunting, we believe you can find lots of interesting and surprising information in them.

The first table gives the impacts per household. The row labeled *Total* shows the sum total of an average household's yearly impacts. The other rows give the impacts as a percentage of the total. Note that the impact of any particular category equals the sum of the impacts of any subcategories below it. For instance, the impacts from dairy products equal the sum of the impacts from butter, cheese, condensed and evaporated milk, ice cream, and milk.

In most cases, the figures in the table include the impacts of both manufacturing and use of the products. The category of cars and trucks, for example, includes the impacts of driving the vehicles. We made an exception for the categories of appliances and lighting, computers, and heating, hot water, and air conditioning. We did this to avoid combining the impacts of different fuels for the same types of appliances, such as gas and electric stoves, and because of limited data on the fuel use of minor appliances.

The impacts of the disposal of any product are included in the solid waste category, not under the individual items.

It should be stressed that, in general, the more finely differentiated the categories, the less accurate the results. For instance, we have a good sense of the overall impacts of transportation. The impacts of automobile maintenance, however, are less well known, and the uncertainties are still greater for the impacts of batteries (a subcategory of maintenance). We estimate that, for the smaller subcategories, the actual impacts may be greater or smaller than indicated by a factor of two or more.

The second table, showing environmental impacts per dollar, is derived from the first by dividing the impact per household by the amount consumers spend for each category. The data provide a measure of the relative impact of spending the same amount of money on different things. To make the table easier to read we have indexed the results to the average for all expenditure categories (denoted by 100). Any activity with a score over 100 has a higher-than-average impact per dollar of spending, while those with scores under 100 have relatively low impacts.

One way to use this table is to estimate the impacts of your own household's expenditures. For instance, you may be curious about the common air pollution associated with the ice cream you eat. On the table, you would find that ice cream scores a 115, or 115% of the average. So, for every dollar you spend on ice cream, you are responsible for the average amount of common air pollution (10.4 grams) x 1.15, which equals 12 grams of common air pollution. You could then further multiply this number by the number of dollars you spend on ice cream in a month or year. Keep in mind, though, that the figures represent national averages. The impacts in your local area or for the particular product you're buying may be different.

The figures in the table should also be used with some caution when comparing the impacts of similar items with different prices. Why should malt beverages (beer) have greater impacts per dollar than distilled liquors? It could be because of differences in the way these products are made; but it also could be because the price of distilled liquors is generally higher, per-unit of volume sold, than that of the others. If the volume of liquor produced is the main determinant of the environmental impact, then a higher price per unit volume will cause the impact per dollar to appear lower. That doesn't mean that distilled liquors are to be preferred over beer and wine—just that they are more expensive. Similarly, when comparing the per dollar impact of vegetables with those of chips and snacks, you have to consider how much food by weight and nutrition you actually get for each dollar you spend.

In many cases, however, the figures contain an unambiguous message about the relative impacts of different consumer activities and purchases. For instance, the table shows that off-road vehicles have a tremendously high air pollution impact (both toxic and common) per dollar spent on them. That is a good indication that one should avoid owning and riding jet skis, snowmobiles, and similar vehicles. Similarly, yard chemicals are responsible for relatively large emissions of toxic air and water pollution (from pesticide evaporation and runoff) and common water pollution (from fertilizer runoff). If you reduce expenditures on these items, the benefit for the environment will be that much greater than if you reduce expenditures on a moderate-impact item, such as clothing.

This appendix ends with a final table (table A.6) that summarizes our results for the seven most harmful consumer activities. In this case, we included the impacts of fuel use for home appliances, lighting, heating, hot water, and air conditioning so that you could easily see consumers' total environmental impact from these activities.

Table A.4. Environmental Impacts per Household (% of total)

IMPACT	Global Warming	Air Pollution		Water Pollution		Habitat Alteration	
CATEGORY	GREENHOUSE GASES	COMMON	TOXIC	COMMON	TOXIC	WATER USE	LAND USE
TOTAL	12,893 kg/yr	507.8 kg/yr	28.95 kg/yr	631.0 kg/yr	571.8 grams/yr	767.2 gallons/day	88,920 sq. ft.
Financial and legal	1.2%	1.1%	1.0%	0.6%	1.2%	0.3%	1.0%
Banking, credit, investment	0.6	0.6	0.5	0.3	0.6	0.2	0.5
Insurance	0.3	0.3	0.3	0.2	0.4	0.1	0.4
Legal	0.1	0.1	0.1	0.1	0.2	0.0	0.1
Other	0.1	0.1	0.1	0.0	0.1	0.0	0.0
Food	11.7	16.7	8.8	37.9	22.3	73.4	45.1
Alcohol	0.5	0.7	0.4	0.4	0.9	1.1	0.4
Distilled liquors	0.1	0.2	0.1	0.1	0.1	0.1	0.0
Malt beverages	0.4	0.5	0.3	0.3	0.7	0.9	0.3
Wines & brandy	0.1	0.1	0.1	0.0	0.1	0.1	0.1
Dairy products	0.8	1.2	0.6	4.1	1.8	7.2	2.2
Butter	0.0	0.0	0.0	0.1	0.0	0.1	0.0
Cheese	0.2	0.4	0.2	1.0	0.5	2.2	0.7
Condensed & evaporated milk	0.1	0.1	0.1	1.0	0.2	0.7	0.2
Ice cream	0.1	0.1	0.1	0.2	0.1	0.3	0.1
Milk	0.4	0.6	0.3	1.8	0.9	3.8	1.2
Fruit, vegetables, & grains	2.4	5.2	2.5	3.5	5.0	29.6	5.6
Baked goods	0.2	0.4	0.2	0.4	0.4	2.3	0.8
Breakfast cereals	0.2	0.4	0.2	0.4	0.4	2.3	0.8
Canned	0.3	0.4	0.2	0.3	0.5	1.0	0.3
Chips & snacks	0.1	0.3	0.2	0.3	0.3	1.2	0.3
Chocolate & candy	0.2	0.4	0.2	0.3	0.4	1.0	0.3
Coffee	0.1	0.1	0.1	0.0	0.1	0.3	0.0
Dried	0.0	0.0	0.0	0.0	0.0	0.1	0.0
Flour	0.1	0.2	0.1	0.3	0.2	1.6	0.5
Frozen	0.2	0.2	0.1	0.1	0.2	0.7	0.1

Table A.4. Environmental Impacts per Household (% of total) *(cont.)*

IMPACT	Global Warming	Air Pollution		Water Pollution		Habitat Alteration	
CATEGORY	GREENHOUSE GASES	COMMON	TOXIC	COMMON	TOXIC	WATER USE	LAND USE
Fruits	0.2%	1.0%	0.5%	0.3%	0.8%	7.3%	0.4%
Nuts	0.0	0.2	0.1	0.1	0.1	1.7	0.2
Oils	0.1	0.3	0.1	0.3	0.4	1.0	0.6
Pasta	0.0	0.0	0.0	0.0	0.1	0.2	0.1
Rice	0.0	0.0	0.0	0.0	0.1	0.3	0.1
Sauces & dressings	0.1	0.2	0.1	0.1	0.2	0.5	0.2
Sugar	0.1	0.2	0.1	0.1	0.1	0.9	0.1
Vegetables	0.3	1.1	0.4	0.4	0.6	7.4	0.6
Meat	2.8	2.8	1.5	19.8	6.0	18.2	25.8
Beef & pork	1.6	1.5	0.8	10.5	3.7	11.7	19.2
Poultry & eggs	0.6	0.8	0.4	6.4	1.2	3.3	1.4
Prepared	0.5	0.5	0.3	3.0	1.1	3.3	5.2
Other	1.7	2.5	1.5	3.4	3.9	8.4	4.5
Bottled & canned drinks	0.6	0.7	0.5	0.5	1.4	1.1	0.5
Canned specialties	0.2	0.2	0.1	0.2	0.3	0.3	0.2
Frozen specialties	0.2	0.3	0.1	0.5	0.3	0.8	0.6
Greenhouse & nursery	0.1	0.1	0.1	0.3	0.2	0.6	0.1
Misc	0.4	0.8	0.5	1.5	1.2	3.8	2.4
Pet	0.2	0.3	0.2	0.5	0.5	1.7	0.8
Out of home	3.1	3.5	1.8	5.9	3.8	8.7	6.2
Seafood	0.1	0.1	0.1	0.5	0.1	0.1	0.1
Canned	0.0	0.0	0.0	0.1	0.1	0.0	0.0
Fresh	0.0	0.0	0.0	0.0	0.0	0.0	0.0
Prepared	0.0	0.0	0.0	0.3	0.1	0.1	0.0
Tobacco products	0.4	0.6	0.4	0.3	0.7	0.2	0.3
Household Operations	35.4	32.2	19.9	21.4	13.9	10.5	4.1
Appliance Manufacturing	0.9	0.9	0.8	0.4	2.9	0.2	0.4
Cooktops & stoves	0.1	0.1	0.1	0.0	0.3	0.0	0.0
Lighting	0.1	0.1	0.1	0.0	0.1	0.0	0.0

Table A.4. Environmental Impacts per Household (% of total) *(cont.)*

IMPACT	Global Warming	Air Pollution		Water Pollution		Habitat Alteration	
CATEGORY	GREENHOUSE GASES	COMMON	TOXIC	COMMON	TOXIC	WATER USE	LAND USE
Other	0.2%	0.2%	0.1%	0.1%	0.5%	0.0%	0.1%
Radios & TVs	0.4%	0.4	0.4	0.2	1.4	0.1	0.2
Refrigerators & freezers	0.1	0.1	0.1	0.0	0.3	0.0	0.0
Stereos	0.0	0.0	0.0	0.0	0.0	0.0	0.0
Telephones	0.0	0.0	0.0	0.0	0.0	0.0	0.0
Washers & driers	0.1	0.1	0.1	0.0	0.3	0.0	0.0
Heating & A/C unit manufacturing	0.0	0.0	0.0	0.0	0.1	0.0	0.0
Air conditioners & electric heaters	0.0	0.0	0.0	0.0	0.1	0.0	0.0
Nonelectric furnaces	0.0	0.0	0.0	0.0	0.0	0.0	0.0
Chemicals	0.1	0.3	0.1	0.1	0.5	0.1	0.1
Adhesives & sealants	0.1	0.2	0.0	0.0	0.1	0.0	0.0
Other	0.1	0.1	0.1	0.0	0.3	0.1	0.0
Paints & preservatives	0.0	0.1	0.0	0.0	0.2	0.0	0.0
Cleaning products & services	1.1	3.0	9.0	0.4	1.9	0.3	0.4
Brooms, brushes, sponges	0.0	0.0	0.0	0.0	0.0	0.0	0.0
Dry cleaning	0.1	0.3	2.1	0.1	0.1	0.1	0.0
Services	0.0	0.0	0.2	0.0	0.1	0.0	0.0
Soaps, polishes, cleaners	0.9	2.6	6.6	0.3	1.7	0.3	0.4
Computers	0.1	0.1	0.1	0.1	0.3	0.0	0.0
Hardware	0.1	0.1	0.1	0.0	0.3	0.0	0.0
Software & services	0.0	0.0	0.0	0.0	0.0	0.0	0.0
Electrical equipment	0.1	0.1	0.1	0.1	0.6	0.1	0.0

Table A.4. Environmental Impacts per Household (% of total) (cont.)

IMPACT	Global Warming	Air Pollution		Water Pollution		Habitat Alteration	
CATEGORY	GREENHOUSE GASES	COMMON	TOXIC	COMMON	TOXIC	WATER USE	LAND USE
Furnishings	1.3%	1.8%	1.7%	1.5%	2.6%	1.5%	1.8%
Carpets & rugs	0.2	0.2	0.2	0.2	0.6	0.4	0.1
Fabric	0.4	0.5	0.4	0.4	0.7	0.8	0.2
Furniture	0.7	1.1	1.1	0.9	1.3	0.3	1.5
Glassware & ceramics	0.1	0.1	0.1	0.0	0.1	0.0	0.1
Metalware	0.2	0.2	0.2	0.1	1.1	0.1	0.1
Cutlery	0.0	0.0	0.0	0.0	0.2	0.0	0.0
Other	0.1	0.1	0.1	0.0	0.5	0.0	0.0
Plumbing fixtures	0.0	0.0	0.0	0.0	0.1	0.0	0.0
Tools	0.1	0.1	0.1	0.0	0.3	0.0	0.0
Other	0.2	0.2	0.2	0.1	0.4	0.1	0.1
Paper products	0.1	0.1	0.1	0.1	0.3	0.0	0.1
Bags	0.0	0.0	0.0	0.0	0.0	0.0	0.0
Containers	0.0	0.0	0.0	0.0	0.0	0.0	0.0
Other	0.1	0.1	0.1	0.1	0.2	0.0	0.1
Plastic products	0.4	0.4	0.5	0.1	1.0	0.1	0.2
Bags	0.0	0.0	0.0	0.0	0.1	0.0	0.0
Other	0.3	0.4	0.4	0.1	0.9	0.1	0.1
Solid waste	0.7	1.8	0.4	0.0	0.1	0.0	0.1
Utilities	30.1	23.0	6.7	18.5	1.9	8.0	0.7
Coal	0.1	0.0	0.0	0.0	0.0	0.0	0.0
Electricity	20.8	18.0	0.7	6.5	0.6	2.5	0.3
Fuel oil	2.2	0.7	0.3	0.1	0.3	0.0	0.0
Natural gas	6.3	1.1	1.3	0.7	0.2	0.2	0.1
Telephone & cable service	0.2	0.2	0.1	0.1	0.4	0.1	0.2
Water & sewage	0.4	0.3	0.7	10.9	0.4	5.2	0.1
Wood fuel	0.0	2.7	3.5	0.0	0.0	0.0	0.0

Table A.4. Environmental Impacts per Household (% of total) *(cont.)*

IMPACT	Global Warming	Air Pollution		Water Pollution		Habitat Alteration	
CATEGORY	GREENHOUSE GASES	COMMON	TOXIC	COMMON	TOXIC	WATER USE	LAND USE
Housing	**6.0%**	**7.0%**	**4.1%**	**9.6%**	**10.0%**	**2.1%**	**25.7%**
Maintenance	0.7	0.9	0.5	0.5	1.6	0.3	1.5
Mobile homes	0.1	0.2	0.2	0.1	0.4	0.0	0.3
New home construction	2.9	3.7	2.0	6.4	6.2	1.2	23.1
Real estate & rental lodging	2.2	2.3	1.4	2.6	1.8	0.5	0.9
Medical	**5.8**	**5.6**	**6.5**	**3.9**	**13.2**	**2.7**	**3.2**
Drugs	0.7	0.8	0.8	0.5	5.4	0.3	0.4
Other	0.2	0.2	0.1	0.1	0.4	0.1	0.1
Services	4.9	4.6	5.5	3.3	7.5	2.3	2.8
Other	**0.8**	**1.0**	**0.5**	**2.1**	**0.8**	**0.2**	**0.3**
Personal Items and Services	**6.1**	**6.5**	**5.6**	**7.2**	**11.9**	**5.9**	**5.1**
Clothing	2.7	2.8	2.3	2.1	4.6	4.1	2.4
Apparel	2.1	2.1	1.6	1.3	3.2	3.2	1.4
Hosiery	0.1	0.1	0.1	0.1	0.2	0.2	0.1
Leather goods	0.1	0.1	0.1	0.1	0.2	0.1	0.2
Shoes	0.4	0.4	0.6	0.6	0.9	0.5	0.8
Entertainment	1.0	1.0	0.8	3.7	1.4	1.2	0.8
Jewelry, toys, & instruments	0.8	0.9	1.1	0.5	3.1	0.3	0.5
Dolls & toys	0.2	0.3	0.2	0.1	0.6	0.1	0.2
Jewelry	0.3	0.3	0.6	0.2	1.8	0.1	0.1
Markers, pens, & pencils	0.0	0.0	0.0	0.0	0.1	0.0	0.0
Other	0.1	0.1	0.1	0.1	0.2	0.1	0.1
Sporting goods	0.2	0.2	0.2	0.1	0.4	0.1	0.1
Watches & clocks	0.0	0.0	0.0	0.0	0.1	0.0	0.0
Paper products	1.0	1.2	0.9	0.7	2.2	0.3	1.2
Books	0.2	0.2	0.2	0.1	0.3	0.1	0.2
Cards	0.1	0.1	0.1	0.0	0.1	0.0	0.1

Table A.4. Environmental Impacts per Household (% of total) *(cont.)*

IMPACT	Global Warming	Air Pollution		Water Pollution		Habitat Alteration	
CATEGORY	GREENHOUSE GASES	COMMON	TOXIC	COMMON	TOXIC	WATER USE	LAND USE
Newspapers & magazines	0.3%	0.3%	0.3%	0.2%	0.5%	0.1%	0.3%
Sanitary	0.4	0.5	0.4	0.3	1.2	0.1	0.5
Stationery	0.0	0.0	0.0	0.0	0.1	0.0	0.0
Services	0.5	0.6	0.4	0.3	0.5	0.1	0.2
Small arms & ammunition	0.0	0.0	0.0	0.0	0.2	0.0	0.0
Private education	**0.6**	**0.7**	**0.5**	**0.4**	**0.9**	**0.2**	**0.4**
Transportation	**32.3**	**28.3**	**51.2**	**7.4**	**23.2**	**1.9**	**15.1**
Auto rental	0.3	0.1	0.1	0.0	0.1	0.0	0.0
Cars & trucks	26.8	22.2	46.2	5.6	12.6	1.2	12.6
Ground freight	0.8	1.0	0.8	0.1	0.1	0.0	0.4
Maintenance	1.8	2.1	1.9	0.9	8.6	0.5	0.8
Batteries	0.1	0.1	0.1	0.0	4.3	0.0	0.0
Other	0.3	0.3	0.2	0.2	1.1	0.1	0.1
Services	1.1	1.2	1.2	0.5	2.8	0.2	0.3
Tires	0.3	0.5	0.4	0.2	0.5	0.1	0.3
Motorcycles	0.1	0.2	0.5	0.1	0.3	0.0	0.1
Off-road vehicles	0.0	0.3	0.5	0.0	0.1	0.0	0.0
Other	0.0	0.0	0.0	0.0	0.1	0.0	0.0
Campers & trailers	0.0	0.0	0.0	0.0	0.1	0.0	0.0
Miscellaneous	0.0	0.0	0.0	0.0	0.0	0.0	0.0
Passenger air	1.2	0.7	0.5	0.2	0.4	0.1	0.8
Passenger intercity	0.4	0.5	0.4	0.1	0.3	0.0	0.1
Passenger other	0.0	0.0	0.0	0.0	0.0	0.0	0.0
Passenger rail	0.0	0.0	0.0	0.0	0.0	0.0	0.0
Passenger water	0.2	0.1	0.0	0.0	0.1	0.0	0.0
Personal aircraft	0.1	0.0	0.0	0.0	0.0	0.0	0.0
Personal boats	0.5	0.9	0.3	0.4	0.4	0.0	0.1

Table A.4. Environmental Impacts per Household (% of total) *(cont.)*

IMPACT	Global Warming	Air Pollution		Water Pollution		Habitat Alteration	
CATEGORY	GREENHOUSE GASES	COMMON	TOXIC	COMMON	TOXIC	WATER USE	LAND USE
Yard care	**0.1%**	**0.9%**	**2.0%**	**9.3%**	**2.6%**	**2.8%**	**0.0%**
Chemicals	0.1	0.2	0.5	9.3	2.4	0.0	0.0
Lawn & garden equipment	0.0	0.4	0.9	0.0	0.1	0.0	0.0
Materials	0.0	0.0	0.0	0.0	0.0	0.0	0.0
Services	0.0	0.3	0.6	0.0	0.1	0.0	0.0

Table A.5. Environmental Impacts per Dollar of Expenditure

	Global Warming	Air Pollution		Water Pollution		Habitat Alteration	
	GREENHOUSE GASES	COMMON	TOXIC	COMMON	TOXIC	WATER USE	LAND USE
RAW AVERAGE	264 grams	10.4 grams	.59 grams	12.9 grams	11.7 grams	2.05 ounces	1.8 sq. ft
INDEXED AVERAGE	100	100	100	100	100	100	100
Financial and Legal	11	11	9	6	11	3	9
Banking, Credit, Investment	12	12	9	6	10	3	9
Insurance	9	8	8	5	10	2	9
Legal	12	11	11	7	14	3	9
Other	33	36	31	19	53	8	23
Food	71	101	53	229	135	444	273
Alcohol	56	75	45	45	95	112	41
Distilled liquors	36	79	48	34	69	28	23
Malt beverages	63	78	46	55	117	153	50
Wines & brandy	52	62	35	23	51	72	29
Dairy products	83	132	69	444	201	783	244
Butter	88	115	64	455	174	602	193
Cheese	78	127	66	363	187	778	246
Condensed & evaporated milk	89	121	64	886	176	625	201
Ice cream	83	115	65	231	186	424	148
Milk	85	142	74	423	220	904	275
Fruit, vegetables, & grains	64	141	68	93	135	796	149
Baked goods	30	51	26	59	57	318	117
Breakfast cereals	62	106	54	122	119	659	242
Canned	82	101	58	79	123	264	76
Chips & snacks	61	116	61	105	131	506	129
Chocolate & candy	66	95	54	68	117	278	93
Coffee	63	97	61	34	97	270	42
Dried	79	95	51	59	105	233	76
Flour	79	154	70	207	165	1,138	387
Frozen	97	144	76	64	153	419	81

Table A.5. Environmental Impacts per Dollar of Expenditure *(cont.)*

	Global Warming	Air Pollution		Water Pollution		Habitat Alteration	
	GREENHOUSE GASES	COMMON	TOXIC	COMMON	TOXIC	WATER USE	LAND USE
Fruits	55	276	137	93	235	2,118	129
Nuts	62	234	94	78	200	2,396	304
Oils	107	239	112	217	305	842	488
Pasta	75	105	63	91	125	366	147
Rice	105	174	76	208	237	1,269	421
Sauces & dressings	71	104	56	90	120	330	103
Sugar	149	227	100	123	217	1,250	119
Vegetables	64	274	100	108	149	1,841	143
Meat	134	138	73	965	293	888	1,259
Beef & pork	166	151	80	1,058	373	1,180	1,939
Poultry & eggs	87	126	64	941	181	486	212
Prepared	137	128	68	769	280	841	1,348
Other	69	99	60	138	157	337	181
Bottled & canned drinks	76	94	66	61	176	134	62
Canned specialties	75	87	56	89	136	168	99
Frozen specialties	68	90	51	168	119	283	193
Greenhouse & nursery	55	51	30	115	83	255	27
Miscellaneous	64	116	65	219	177	548	345
Pet	75	135	74	184	182	668	307
Out of home	59	67	34	113	72	167	119
Seafood	45	54	31	260	76	49	32
Canned	53	55	32	179	75	47	33
Fresh	34	49	32	16	53	9	14
Prepared	43	57	30	451	88	69	38
Tobacco products	41	63	41	29	70	20	30

Table A.5. Environmental Impacts per Dollar of Expenditure *(cont.)*

	Global Warming	Air Pollution		Water Pollution		Habitat Alteration	
	GREENHOUSE GASES	COMMON	TOXIC	COMMON	TOXIC	WATER USE	LAND USE
Household operations	271	246	152	163	106	80	31
Appliance manufacturing	50	51	46	21	164	11	22
Cooktops & stoves	72	70	70	28	252	17	26
Lighting	48	48	49	19	136	14	18
Other	66	65	56	24	194	14	24
Radios & TVs	42	43	40	20	142	9	23
Refrigerators & freezers	75	88	71	28	272	18	25
Stereos	23	23	17	8	28	4	10
Telephones	28	29	22	13	89	6	11
Washers & driers	78	70	64	26	264	16	22
Heating & A/C unit manufacturing	61	59	52	24	223	13	19
Air conditioners & electric heaters	60	62	52	25	230	13	20
Nonelectric furnaces	65	51	51	22	200	13	17
Chemicals	128	250	120	44	458	67	45
Adhesives & sealants	149	453	90	27	266	24	29
Other	112	145	120	52	450	105	41
Paints & preservatives	136	216	164	46	751	36	80
Cleaning products & services	63	176	524	25	113	20	25
Brooms, brushes, sponges	53	60	48	30	108	59	42
Dry cleaning	47	114	702	26	37	17	14
Services	31	51	267	18	89	8	15
Soaps, polishes, cleaners	70	202	510	25	133	21	28

Table A.5. Environmental Impacts per Dollar of Expenditure *(cont.)*

	Global Warming	Air Pollution		Water Pollution		Habitat Alteration	
	GREENHOUSE GASES	COMMON	TOXIC	COMMON	TOXIC	WATER USE	LAND USE
Computers	29	28	22	14	76	7	12
Hardware	32	31	24	15	88	7	12
Software & services	18	18	14	10	34	4	9
Electrical equipment manufacturing	49	48	43	23	212	21	18
Furnishings	66	92	85	74	131	78	92
Carpets & rugs	85	92	72	84	234	153	35
Fabric	63	74	62	59	124	135	34
Furniture	64	102	101	80	113	31	135
Glassware & ceramics	82	73	40	26	87	18	36
Metalware	66	58	53	25	311	14	20
Cutlery	52	48	51	20	262	10	18
Other	84	73	64	30	386	17	23
Plumbing fixtures	86	93	69	41	1,526	18	22
Tools	56	48	43	21	211	12	17
Other	51	52	53	27	127	16	28
Paper products	104	115	95	62	254	36	117
Bags	108	128	105	52	253	30	89
Containers	128	141	114	82	283	39	178
Other	99	108	90	61	249	37	112
Plastic products	83	93	105	32	220	23	37
Bags	106	128	111	52	253	29	88
Other	81	90	104	31	217	23	32
Solid waste	528	1,463	283	31	65	10	72
Utilities	563	431	126	346	36	150	13
Coal	3,863	720	374	490	87	18	62
Electricity	1,058	912	38	332	29	126	14
Fuel oil	1,362	456	196	92	161	26	14

Table A.5. Environmental Impacts per Dollar of Expenditure *(cont.)*

	Global Warming	Air Pollution		Water Pollution		Habitat Alteration	
	GREENHOUSE GASES	COMMON	TOXIC	COMMON	TOXIC	WATER USE	LAND USE
Natural gas	861	145	172	100	34	26	11
Telephone & cable service	10	10	7	6	18	2	8
Water & sewage	93	85	189	2,864	113	1,368	32
Wood fuel	174	21,436	27,979	85	265	31	243
Housing	**55**	**65**	**38**	**89**	**92**	**19**	**237**
Maintenance	67	86	49	50	147	32	134
Mobile homes	41	46	47	39	112	11	70
New home construction	81	102	56	179	172	33	644
Real estate & rental lodging	38	39	24	44	31	9	16
Medical	**31**	**30**	**35**	**21**	**71**	**14**	**17**
Drugs	38	42	45	29	287	17	19
Other	54	49	37	25	91	17	24
Services	30	28	34	20	46	14	17
Other	**31**	**38**	**19**	**84**	**32**	**7**	**11**
Personal items and services	40	44	37	48	80	40	34
Clothing	56	57	48	43	94	84	50
Apparel	57	58	43	37	87	89	37
Hosiery	70	72	50	38	127	110	34
Leather goods	39	39	34	46	92	52	69
Shoes	53	56	73	72	119	67	106
Entertainment	44	48	36	170	63	54	36
Jewelry, toys, & instruments	46	50	62	28	170	14	27
Dolls & toys	44	49	40	23	107	13	28
Jewelry	48	52	93	27	298	9	15
Markers, pens, & pencils	45	36	34	19	77	9	20
Other	56	65	99	118	163	72	121

Table A.5. Environmental Impacts per Dollar of Expenditure (cont.)

	Global Warming	Air Pollution		Water Pollution		Habitat Alteration	
	GREENHOUSE GASES	COMMON	TOXIC	COMMON	TOXIC	WATER USE	LAND USE
Sporting goods	44	53	46	20	96	13	25
Watches & clocks	44	41	44	20	100	10	17
Paper products	62	69	54	39	130	18	70
Books	53	57	43	33	82	15	52
Cards	36	36	27	21	45	9	27
Newspapers & magazines	59	61	47	34	92	15	60
Sanitary	87	107	89	60	270	31	120
Stationery	61	68	53	40	116	19	74
Services	11	13	9	6	12	2	5
Small arms & ammunition	36	45	35	16	217	7	17
Private education	**23**	**30**	**20**	**18**	**36**	**6**	**17**
Transportation	**316**	**276**	**500**	**72**	**227**	**18**	**147**
Auto rental	97	28	26	14	40	8	15
Cars & trucks	504	416	866	105	237	22	237
Ground freight	271	328	258	28	47	8	136
Maintenance	72	86	78	35	354	19	32
Batteries	74	93	97	30	4,673	13	20
Other	72	84	62	37	266	29	31
Services	65	73	74	32	169	14	20
Tires	108	156	113	51	154	29	99
Motorcycles	80	132	271	41	197	14	45
Off-road vehicles	90	708	1,222	28	189	14	26
Other	58	62	72	39	186	16	78
Campers & trailers	55	60	73	40	176	16	85
Miscellaneous	79	80	58	28	275	15	20
Passenger air	131	78	52	22	45	8	90
Passenger intercity	117	169	136	33	87	12	39
Passenger other	14	14	7	7	13	3	8
Passenger rail	108	297	25	17	102	7	241

Table A.5. Environmental Impacts per Dollar of Expenditure *(cont.)*

	Global Warming	Air Pollution		Water Pollution		Habitat Alteration	
	Greenhouse Gases	Common	Toxic	Common	Toxic	Water Use	Land Use
Passenger water	269	165	32	23	79	11	16
Personal aircraft	332	155	133	36	143	14	15
Personal boats	350	584	166	273	248	19	50
Yard Care	**55**	**347**	**768**	**3,570**	**982**	**1,082**	**16**
Pesticides & fertilizers	123	215	678	13,110	3,361	51	31
Lawn & garden equipment	61	1,231	2,662	20	221	11	20
Materials	82	90	51	25	129	14	28
Services	4	253	507	7	47	15	2

More than twice the average impact.
More than five times the average impact.

Table A.6 The Seven Most Harmful Consumer Activities: Share of Total Impact

Type of Consumption	Global Warming	Air Pollution		Water Pollution		Habitat Alteration	
	GREENHOUSE GASES	COMMON	TOXIC	COMMON	TOXIC	WATER USE	LAND USE
Cars and light trucks	27%	22%	46%	6%	13%	1%	13%
Meat and poultry	3	3	1	20	6	18	26
Fruit, vegetables, and grains	2	5	3	3	5	30	6
Home heating, hot water, A/C	16	11	5	3	1	1	0
Household appliances and lighting	15	13	2	5	4	2	1
Home construction	3	4	2	6	6	1	23
Household water and sewage	0	0	1	11	0	5	0
Total	66%	58%	60%	54%	36%	58%	68%

More than 5% of total

More than 10% of total

APPENDIX B
RESOURCES FOR ENVIRONMENTALLY CONCERNED CONSUMERS

BOOKS AND REPORTS

Consumption and the Environment

Many books are available on environmental problems. Here we mention a few that are especially relevant to understanding the relationship between American consumerism and the environment.

Ackerman, Frank. *Why Do We Recycle? Markets, Values, and Public Policy.* Washington, D.C.: Island Press, 1997. A fair-minded assessment of the pros and cons of recycling, with interesting discussions of related topics like packaging and municipal composting. Ackerman concludes that recycling is generally desirable, even when its direct costs are slightly higher than those of disposal.

Alexander, Judd H. *In Defense of Garbage.* Westport, CT: Praeger, 1993. Its tone is cranky and the author overstates his case, but this spirited defense of garbage, packaging, and throwaway products includes interesting information and serves as a useful counterbalance to some of the attacks on packaging and disposable items.

Barnet, Richard J., and John Cavanagh. *Global Dreams: Imperial Corporations and the New World Order.* New York: Simon & Schuster, 1994. A fascinating study of the way in which large corporations are spreading American consumer culture worldwide.

Chestow, Marian R., and Daniel C. Esty. *Thinking Ecologically: The Next Generation of Environmental Policy.* New Haven: Yale University Press, 1997. A broad-ranging collection of scholarly essays examining the ways in which policy should be shaped to best benefit the environment.

Daily, Gretchen C., ed. *Nature's Services: Societal Dependence on Natural Ecosystems.* Washington, D.C.: Island Press, 1997. How society benefits from natural habitats, and suggestions for how decision-makers can consider those benefits.

Durning, Alan Thein. *How Much Is Enough? The Consumer Society and the Future of the Earth.* New York: Norton, 1992. An introduction to the connection between consumer behavior and environmental problems.

Feldman, Andrew J. *The Sierra Club Green Guide: Everybody's Desk Reference to Environmental Information.* San Francisco: Sierra Club Books, 1996. A useful reference work with descriptions of twelve hundred organizations, books, government clearinghouses, and magazines on various environmental topics.

Gardner, Gerald T., and Paul C. Stern. *Environmental Problems and Human Behavior.* Needham Heights, MA: Allyn & Bacon, 1996. A textbook analyzing why humans act in the ways they do toward the environment, explaining why some strategies for environmental improvement fail, and suggesting ways in which the insights of behavioral scientists can be applied to solve environmental problems.

Goodwin, Neva, et al., eds. *The Consumer Society.* Washington, D.C.: Island Press, 1997. Brief summaries of eighty-seven articles and books on the economic, environmental, ethical, and social implications of a consumer society and consumer lifestyles. A way to sample the varied ways in which scholars have looked at consumerism.

Gordon, Deborah. *Steering a New Course: Transportation, Energy, and the Environment.* Washington, D.C.: Island Press, 1991. Overview of the environmental implications of cars and other transportation technologies, along with a discussion of various policy strategies for reducing environmental harm.

Jacobson, Michael F., and Laurie Ann Mazur. *Marketing Madness: A Survival Guide for a Consumer Society.* Boulder: Westview Press, 1995. A fascinating examination of the impact of advertising on American consumer behavior and how it can affect the environment, as well as consumers' pocketbooks.

Ryan, John C. and Alan Thein Durning. *Stuff: The Secret Life of Everyday Things.* Seattle: Northwest Environment Watch, 1997. A fascinating look at the objects a typical American uses in an average day—what they are made of, how they are made, and what their environmental impact is.

Schor, Juliet B. *The Overspent American: Upscaling, Downshifting, and the New Consumer.* New York: Basic Books, 1998. After looking at spending patterns and the forces in the United States that encourage an overemphasis on consumerism, the author argues that Americans should transform their relationship to spending.

Stern, Paul C., et al., eds. *Environmentally Significant Consumption: Research Directions.* Washington, D.C.: National Research Council, 1997. Discussion of the research needed to better understand the relationship between consumption and the environment, along with examples of the ways scholars are already studying this subject.

U.S. EPA, Office of Solid Waste. *Characterization of Municipal Solid Waste in the United States: 1997 Update.* Washington,

D.C.: U.S. EPA, 1998. The latest statistics on a range of solid waste issues, including amounts of different types of municipal solid waste produced in the United States; relative amounts and types of materials disposed, recycled, and incinerated; and the number and types of recycling programs. Updated annually.

Wackernagel, Mathis, and William Rees. *Our Ecological Footprint: Reducing Human Impact on the Earth.* Philadelphia: New Society Publishers, 1996. Helps readers visualize the resources required to sustain typical North Americans in their current lifestyle.

World Resources Institute. *World Resources 1998–99.* New York: Oxford University Press, 1998. A biennial survey of global environmental conditions and trends, with detailed statistical tables organized by country.

Practical Advice

Cole, Nancy, and P. J. Skerrett. *Renewables Are Ready: People Creating Renewable Energy Solutions.* White River Junction, VT: Chelsea Green Press, 1995. Case studies of efforts to implement renewable energy at the local level, along with advice on how to implement a project in your own community.

DeCicco, John, and Martin Thomas. *The Green Guide to Cars and Trucks: Model Year 1999.* Washington, D.C.: The American Council for an Energy-Efficient Economy, 1999. This annual consumer guide provides comprehensive environmental ratings for cars, vans, pickups, and sport utility vehicles, enabling consumers to comparison-shop with the environment in mind.

Dominguez, Joe and Vicki Robin. *Your Money or Your Life: Transforming Your Relationship with Money and Achieving Financial Independence.* New York: Viking Penguin, 1992. A detailed plan for people who want to get off the earn-and-spend treadmill.

Gershon, David, and Robert Gilman. *Household Ecoteam Workbook: A Six-month Program to Bring Your Household Into Environmental Balance.* Woodstock, NY: Global Action Plan for the Earth, 1992. A step-by-step guide to help a group of households work together to evaluate their consumption and reduce environmental damage.

Harland, Edward. *Eco-Renovation: The Ecological Home Improvement Guide.* White River Junction, VT: Chelsea Green Press, 1993. How to make your home more environmentally sound, with information on such topics as design, energy use, toxic materials, and radon.

Harte, John, et al. *Toxics A to Z: A Guide to Everyday Pollution Hazards.* Berkeley: University of California Press, 1991. A solid overview of the nature and impact of toxic substances. The book's second half is a listing of commonly encountered toxics, with information on their properties, how people get exposed to them, and their health and environmental effects.

Heede, Richard, et al. *Homemade Money: How to Save Energy and Dollars in Your Home.* Snowmass, CO: Rocky Mountain Institute, 1995. Information on which energy-saving measures make economic and environmental sense and advice on how to get started.

Keniry, Julian. *Ecodemia: Campus Environmental Stewardship at the Turn of the 21st Century.* Washington, D.C.: National Wildlife Federation, 1995. Much of the advice for responsibly handling landscaping, transportation, solid waste, energy, and other aspects of college management is applicable to other large institutions, including schools, local governments, and businesses.

Needleman, Herbert L., and Philip J. Landrigan. *Raising Children Toxic Free: How to Keep Your Child Safe from Lead, Asbestos, Pesticides, and Other Environmental Hazards.* New York: Farrar, Straus & Giroux, 1994. Information on key environmental health risks for children, along with advice on how to evaluate risks and reduce exposure to hazards.

Schaeffer, John, and the Real Goods Staff. *Solar Living Sourcebook: The Complete Guide to Renewable Energy Technologies and Sustainable Living.* 9th ed. White River Junction, VT: Chelsea Green Press, 1997. The distributors of a mail-order catalog have compiled technical information, product listings, and general advice on solar panels, composting toilets, and other products for people who want to live independently and sustainably.

Wilson, Alex, and John Morrill. *Consumer Guide to Home Energy Savings.* Rev. ed. Washington, D.C.: American Council for an Energy-Efficient Economy, 1998. An indispensible handbook for consumers who want to reduce their home energy use. It lists the most efficient appliances and heating systems and also provides useful general advice on such topics as insulation, windows, and lighting.

Lawns and Gardening

Many recent books can help you to reduce environmental hazards associated with pesticides and chemicals. Good representatives of this genre include:

Carr, Anna, and Fern Marshall Bradley, eds. *Rodale's Chemical-Free Yard and Garden: The Ultimate Authority on Successful Organic Gardening.* Rev. ed. Emmaus, PA: Rodale Press, 1995.

Cutler, Karen Davis, et al. *Burpee: The Complete Vegetable and Herb Gardener: A Guide to Growing Your Garden Organically.* New York: Macmillan General, 1997.

Ellis, Barbara, and Frances Tenenbaum, eds. *Safe and Easy Lawn Care: The Complete Guide to Organic, Low-Maintenance Lawns.* Boston: Houghton Mifflin, 1997.

Sombke, Laurence. *Beautiful Easy Lawns and Landscapes: A Year-Round Guide to a Low-Maintenance Environmentally Safe Yard.* Chester, CT: Globe Pequot Press, 1994.

PERIODICALS

Consumer Reports. Includes useful information about the relative environmental benefits of particular products, as well as occasional general stories about the environmental implications of certain classes of products.

Environmental Building News. Useful information for individuals and groups designing or constructing new homes or office buildings, or interested in "greening" existing buildings.

Green Guide. A newsletter, published by Mothers and Others for a Livable Planet, that focuses on environmental health risks people face at home and what they can do about them. Although its emphasis on individual consumer actions tends to deemphasize the need for policy solutions to problems and it sometimes overemphasizes relatively minor risks, it includes useful information.

Organic Gardening. Practical tips and general information for the individual who wants to reduce chemicals and pesticides in landscaping and gardening.

WEB SITES

Agency for Toxic Substances and Disease Registry
(http://astdr1.atsdr.cdc.gov:8080/atsdrhome.html)
This agency of the U.S. Department of Health and Human Services provides useful fact sheets on a wide range of hazardous substances as well as general information on toxics and public health.

Center for a New American Dream
(www.newdream.org)
This web site from an organization dedicated to reducing and shifting American consumption has wide-ranging infor-

mation on such topics as sound environmental practices, simple living, commercialism, and building strong families and communities.

Center for Renewable Energy and Sustainable Technology
(www.crest.org)
Rich, layered information on energy efficiency, renewable energy, and transportation technologies.

Children's Environmental Health Network
(www.cehn.org)
A national project organized by public health professionals and physicians to improve pediatric environmental health. Its site includes a comprehensive collection of links to government sites and nonprofit organizations, organized alphabetically by such topics as air pollution, aluminum, arsenic, and asbestos.

Cornell Composting
(www.cals.cornell.edu/dept/compost)
Online and print resources for the compost amateur or professional. It provides an excellent tutorial and links to other useful sites on the subject.

Earthshare
(www.earthshare.org)
This federation of environmental and conservation charities provides everyday tips to improve the earth. A wide range of topics includes green gifts, camping, recycling appliances, and paper reduction.

EcoNet Home Page
(www.igc.apc.org/igc/econet)
To keep abreast of headline environmental news stories, use this searchable news page and links to other important sites that deal with environmental issues.

Energy Efficiency and Renewable Energy Network (EREN)
(www.eren.doe.gov)
This site is part of the U.S. Department of Energy's customer service center and contains numerous fact sheets on all aspects of energy-efficient building materials and technologies as well as energy-efficicient landscaping tips. You can also ask a question of an energy expert.

Environment Canada
(www.ec.gc.ca)
Lots of advice for what you can do around the home, as well as what you can do for wildlife. Also sustainability toolkits for communities.

Internet Consumer Recycling Guide
(www.obviously.com/recycle/)
This site offers simple guidance for the household consumer on recycling everything from newspapers to car batteries and motor oil.

Partners for Environmental Progress
(www.cygnus-group.com)
This site, developed by a group originally established by Dow Plastics, focuses on waste reduction. Its motto is ULS ("use less stuff") and includes an online version of the *ULS Report*, a bimonthly newsletter whose technical adviser is the garbage expert William Rathje.

Sprawl Resource Guide
(www.webcom.com/pcj/sprawl/sprawl6.html)
For reports on sprawl and related activities, by state. It is a good way to learn about groups working on these issues in your area.

Union of Concerned Scientists
(www.ucsusa.org)
This national advocacy organization maintains up-to-date information on many of the topics covered in this book and offers suggestions for what individuals can do to influence policy at the community, state, and national levels.

U.S. Department of Energy Community Education Site
(www.sandia.gov/ESTEEM/House.html)
This site links to DOE's home energy saver site, an interactive site where you can analyze your home for energy savings. It has an online version of *Home Energy Magazine,* as well as information on solar, wind, and other renewable energy technologies.

U.S. Environmental Protection Agency
(www.epa.gov)
Besides information on news events, laws, regulations, current publications, programs, and available support, EPA offers useful information for the home or office. For kids there is the Explorer's Club, with interactive storybooks and activities related to ozone depletion, garbage, and recycling. There are also aids and environmental fact sheets for students and teachers as well as links to other sites. Here are some of the especially useful parts of the EPA's site:

- *At Home* (www.epa.gov/epahome/home.htm). Tips on preventing pollution by recycling and conserving water and energy, as well as information on indoor air quality issues and reducing environmental risks at home.
- *Your Lawn and the Environment* (www.epa.gov/OMSWWW/lg-emiss.htm). How to reduce emissions from lawn and garden equipment.
- *Energy Star Programs and Products* (www.epa.gov/energystar.html). Information on energy-saving lighting, heating

and cooling equipment, computers, printers, fax machines, and copiers for the home and office, as well as financing information for building a new energy-efficient home. This site also links to the EPA's Green Lights Program (www.epa.gov/greenlights.html), a voluntary partnership program that promotes energy-efficient lighting in the workplace.

• *Office of Pollution Prevention and Toxics* (www.epa.gov/p2). Promotes practices that reduce or eliminate pollutants through increasing efficiency of raw material use, energy, water, and land. It features a pollution prevention clearinghouse with information on reducing industrial pollutants through technology transfer, education, and public awareness. Numerous publications are available as well as conference proceedings and training materials.

Waste Prevention World
(www.ciwmb.ca.gov/mrt/wpw)
A site of the California Integrated Waste Management Board, it focuses on ways to generate less waste and provides practical information for businesses and institutions, as well as individuals, on topics as diverse as composting and how to create an office paper-reduction campaign.

WaterWiser: The Water Efficiency Clearinghouse
(www.waterwiser.org/)
For publications, events, conferences, a company directory, and water conservation links. A joint project of the American Water Works Association, the U.S. EPA, and the U.S. Bureau of Reclamation, this site links to more than fifty sites with specific information on programs and tips for your state or region.

NOTES

Introduction
1. Union of Concerned Scientists, "World Scientists Call for Action at the Kyoto Climate Summit" (September 1997).

Chapter 1
1. Leslie Rubinkowski, "Want a Better Life? Way to Achieve It Is Simplicity Itself," *Pittsburgh Post-Gazette,* December 24, 1995, G10; Jura Koncius, "The Frugal Road to Family Values," *Washington Post,* September 24, 1992, T14.
2. Koncius, "The Frugal Road," T14.
3. World Resources Institute et al., *World Resources: A Guide to the Global Environment, 1996–97* (New York: Oxford University Press, 1996), 287.
4. British Petroleum, *Statistical Review of World Energy '97* (London: British Petroleum Company, 1997), 42; World Resources Institute, *World Resources,* 290.
5. U.S. Energy Information Administration at www.eia.doe.gov.; Alan B. Durning and Holly B. Brough, "Taking Stock: Animal Farming and the Environment," *Worldwatch Paper 103,* July 1991, 10.
6. Harwood Group, *Yearning for Balance: Views of Americans on Consumption, Materialism, and the Environment* (Takoma Park, MD: Merck Family Fund, 1995).
7. EarthWorks Group, *50 Simple Things You Can Do to Save the Earth* (Berkeley, CA: Earthworks Press, 1989).
8. See, for example, Michael Viner, *365 Ways for You and Your Children to Save the Earth One Day at a Time* (New York: Warner Books, 1991); Diane MacEachern, *Save Our Planet: 750 Ways You Can Help Clean Up*

the Earth (New York: Dell, 1990); Bernadette Vallely, 1,001 Ways to Save the Planet (New York: Ballantine Books, 1990); Jeremy Rifkin, ed., The Green Lifestyle Handbook: 1001 Ways You Can Heal the Earth (New York: Henry Holt & Co., 1990).

9. Anil Agarwal and Sunita Narain, "View from the South: We Can No Longer Subsidize the North," Development Forum (May/June 1992), 15.

10. "Sustainable Development: Ten Points to Clarify the Concept," Third World Resurgence (August/September 1992), 33.

11. Social scientist Paul Stern has often made this point. See, for example, "Toward a Working Definition of Consumption," in Paul C. Stern et al., Environmentally Significant Consumption: Research Directions (Washington, D.C.: National Academy Press, 1997), 18.

12. Richard Elliot Benedick, Ozone Diplomacy: New Directions in Safeguarding the Planet (Cambridge: Harvard University Press, 1991), 45.

13. Lydia Dotto and Harold Schiff, The Ozone War (Garden City, NY: Doubleday & Co., 1978), 174.

14. Dotto and Schiff, Ozone War, 169.

15. Alan Durning, How Much Is Enough? The Consumer Society and the Future of the Earth (New York: Norton, 1992), 118; Richard J. Barnet and John Cavanagh, Global Dreams: Imperial Corporations and the New World Order (New York: Simon & Schuster, 1994), 171.

Chapter 2

1. "Curbside Recycling Comforts the Soul, but Benefits Are Scant," Wall Street Journal, January 19, 1995, 1.

2. Nora Goldstein, "The State of Garbage," BioCycle (April 1997), 61.

3. U.S. Environmental Protection Agency, Characterization of Municipal Solid Waste in the United States: 1996 Update (Washington, DC: U.S. EPA, 1997), 49.

4. John Tierney, "Recycling Is Garbage," New York Times Magazine, June 30, 1996.

5. William Rathje and Cullen Murphy, Rubbish! The Archaeology of Garbage (New York: HarperCollins, 1992), 34–37.

6. Charles Gunnerson, "Debris Accumulation," Journal of the Environmental Engineering Division, American Society of Civil Engineers (June 1973), as cited in Rathje and Murphy, Rubbish!, 35.

7. Ibid.

8. Frank Ackerman, Why Do We Recycle? Markets, Values, and Public Policy (Washington, DC: Island Press, 1997), 14.

9. Rathje and Murphy, Rubbish!, 37; Louis Blumberg and Robert Gottlieb, War on Waste: Can America Win Its Battle With Garbage? (Washington, DC: Island Press, 1989), 10.

10. U.S. EPA, Characterization of Municipal Solid Waste: 1996 Update, 2. It was once a popular pastime to come up with picturesque images of how much trash American households produce. For example, according to a

1989 report by the President's Council on Environmental Quality, the amount produced annually in the country would fill a convoy of ten-ton trucks stretching halfway from the earth to the moon. Such estimates are not very precise, however, and there is usually no way of finding out how the authors came up with them. A critical factor is the total volume of garbage (as distinct from the total weight), which depends on what is in the garbage, how much it is compressed in trucks and by landfilling, and how much moisture it retains.

11. Judd H. Alexander, *In Defense of Garbage* (Westport, CT: Praeger, 1993), 5; also Rathje and Murphy, *Rubbish!*, 50.

12. U.S. Environmental Protection Agency, *Report to Congress: Solid Waste Disposal in the United States*, vol. 2 (October 1988), 3–19 to 3–35.

13. Franklin Associates, Ltd., *Resources and Environmental Profile Analysis of Foam Polystyrene and Bleached Paperboard Containers* (June 1990), I-1, prepared for the Council for Solid Waste Solutions; also U.S. EPA, *Characterization of Municipal Solid Waste: 1996 Update*, 67.

14. *Life* (1955), as cited in Rathje and Murphy, *Rubbish!*, 41.

15. Blumberg and Gottlieb, *War on Waste*, 10–14.

16. As cited in ibid., 12.

17. U.S. EPA, *Characterization of Municipal Solid Waste: 1996 Update*, 61–64.

18. Cited in Blumberg and Gottlieb, *War on Waste*, 20.

19. U.S. EPA, *Characterization of Municipal Solid Waste: 1995 Update*, 11.

20. Bureau of Solid Waste Management report, as cited in Blumberg and Gottlieb, *War on Waste*, 17.

21. "Garbage Odyssey Proves Embarrassing," *New York Times*, May 3, 1987, sec. 21, p. 1.

22. "With No Room at the Dump, U.S. Faces a Garbage Crisis," *New York Times*, June 29, 1987, B8.

23. William L. Rathje, "Rubbish!" *Atlantic Monthly* (December 1989), 101.

24. National Solid Wastes Management Association (NSWMA), Environmental Industry Associations, *Municipal Solid Waste Disposal Trends: 1996 Update* (Washington, DC: Environmental Industry Associations, 1996), 2.

25. Blumberg and Gottlieb, *War on Waste*, 20.

26. "Curbside Recycling," *Wall Street Journal*, 1.

27. "Waste Is a Terrible Thing to Mind," *Discover* (January 1988), 76. Although the *Mobro*'s voyage took on almost mythic proportions, another case, that of the *Khian Sea*, involved far more drama and intrigue. The *Khian Sea* was a cargo ship contracted in 1987 by the city of Philadelphia to take fourteen thousand tons of incinerator ash to a foreign dump. Unable to find a port to accept the load, the ship wandered for two years, its owners becoming increasingly frustrated. In the end the ash mysteriously disappeared, most likely dumped somewhere in the Indian Ocean. Blumberg and Gottlieb, *War on Waste*, 4–5.

28. NSWRA, *Municipal Solid Waste Disposal Trends: 1996 Update*, 4.

29. Ackerman, *Why Do We Recycle?*, 66–7.
30. Franklin Associates, *Characterization of Municipal Solid Waste: 1990 Update*, 43.
31. Blumberg and Gottlieb, *War on Waste*, 199–201.
32. Ibid., 203.
33. Ibid., 182.
34. Blumberg and Gottlieb, *War On Waste*, 208.
35. U.S. EPA, *Characterization of Municipal Solid Waste: 1996 Update*, 49.
36. Goldstein, "The State of Garbage," 62.
37. "State Recycling Laws Update" (Raymond Communications, April 1995).
38. Ackerman, *Why Do We Recycle?* 10.
39. Tierney, "Recycling Is Garbage."
40. U.S. EPA, *Unfinished Business: A Comparative Assessment of Environmental Problems* (February 1987), 77.
41. Report of the Council on Environmental Quality, chap. 1A, 3.
42. Ackerman, *Why Do We Recycle?* 10.
43. "Curbside Recycling," *Wall Street Journal*, 1.
44. Chris Hendrickson, Lester Lave, and Francis McMichael, "Time to Dump Recycling?" *Issues in Science and Technology* (Spring 1995), 81.
45. Ackerman, *Why Do We Recycle?* 70–71, 79.
46. The average net cost = the average cost of recycling ($174/ton)—average avoided landfill tipping fees ($31/ton)—average revenues from sales of recycled materials ($100/ton) = $43/ton.
47. Ackerman, *Why Do We Recycle?*, 69.
48. Roger W. Powers, "Curbside Recycling: Energy and Environmental Considerations," *Solid Waste Technologies* (September/October 1995), 32. See also Franklin Associates, *The Role of Recycling in Integrated Solid Waste Management to the Year 2000* (Stamford, CT: Keep America Beautiful, Inc., 1994), 6–27.

Chapter 3

1. U.S. Environmental Protection Agency; *Reducing Risk: Setting Priorities and Strategies for Environmental Protection*, Report of the Science Advisory Board to William K. Reilly, Administrator (September 1990). California Comparative Risk Project, *Toward the 21st Century: Planning for the Protection of California's Environment*, Summary Report, Submitted to the California Environmental Protection Agency (May 1994).
2. Several other pollutants are important precursors in the creation of ozone and particulates, however. A large fraction of fine particulate pollution is made up of condensed aerosols from both volatile organic compounds and sulfur; and ozone is created through photochemical reactions involving volatile organic compounds and nitrogen oxides.
3. Natural Resources Defense Council, *Breath Taking: Premature Mortality Due to Particulate Air Pollution in 239 American Cities* (New York: May 1996), 1, 55–56.

4. The Intergovernmental Panel on Climate Change concluded that "the balance of evidence from changes in global mean surface air temperature and from changes in geographical, seasonal, and vertical patterns of atmospheric temperature suggests a discernible human influence on global climate." The various findings and conclusions of the Panel's most recent major assessment were published in three massive volumes—*Climate Change 1995* (Cambridge, UK: Cambridge University Press, 1996) and are available via the internet at www.ippc.ch.

5. Union of Concerned Scientists, "World Scientists Call for Action at the Kyoto Climate Summit" (September 1997).

6. A. J. McMichael et al., eds, *Climate Change and Human Health* (Geneva: World Health Organization, 1996), xvi, 57.

7. Malcolm W. Browne, "The Decline of Songbirds," in Nicholas Wade et al., eds., *The New York Times Book of Scientific Literacy: The Environment from Your Backyard to the Ocean Floor,* vol. 2 (New York: Times Books, 1994), 51.

8. Gretchen C. Daily, "Introduction: What Are Ecosystem Services?" in Gretchen C. Daily, ed., *Nature's Services: Societal Dependence on Natural Ecosystems* (Washington, DC: Island Press, 1997), 4–5.

9. U.S. Department of Agriculture, Economic Research Service, *Agricultural Resources and Environmental Indicators: 1996–97,* chap. 2: "Water" (July 1997), 91.

10. Passenger-mile and vehicle-mile data are from *National Transportation Statistics 1997,* 222 and 225, and are for 1995.

11.

Table 3.5. The Share of Total Consumer Impacts Attributable to Cars and Light Trucks

	Global Warming	Air Pollution		Water Pollution		Habitat Alteration	
	GREENHOUSE GASES	COMMON	TOXIC	COMMON	TOXIC	WATER USE	LAND USE
Manufacturing	3%	3%	3%	2%	9%	1%	1%
Driving	24	19	44	4	3	1	12
Maintenance	2	2	2	1	9	0	1
Fraction of all impacts	29%	24%	48%	6%	21%	2%	13%

12. The actual amounts of pollution for our baseline of one passenger mile traveled by bus are 35.7 grams of greenhouse gases, 2.0 grams of common air pollutants, 0.1 gram of toxic air pollutants, 0.5 gram of common water pollutants, 0.0 gram of toxic water pollutants, 0.1 gallon of water used, and 1.9 acres of land used per year. To find out the actual amounts of the

other forms of transportation, you can multiply these baseline numbers by the numbers in the table for the other methods of transportation.

13. Emissions controls on locomotives will be phased in soon. The EPA is promulgating emission standards and associated regulatory requirements for the control of emissions from locomotives and locomotive engines as required by the Clean Air Act. The primary focus of this rule is the reduction of emissions of oxides of nitrogen (NO_x). The standards will take effect in 2000 and, according to the EPA, will ultimately result in a more than 60 percent reduction in NO_x from locomotives. U.S. EPA, *Locomotive Emissions Final Rulemaking* (December 1997).

14. The average Amtrak train has nine cars and carries eighteen passengers per car, a very modest loading indeed. *National Transportation Statistics 1997*, 238.

15. U.S. Environmental Protection Agency, Office of Air and Radiation, *Nonroad Engine and Vehicle Emission Study*, EPA-21A-2001 (November 1991), xii. (Available from the National Technical Information Service.) Compare with *National Transportation Statistics 1997*, 191.

16. *Statistical Abstract of the United States 1995*, table 1140, 690, and table 1145, 692.

17. Alan Durning, *How Much Is Enough?* (New York: W.W. Norton, 1992), 69–77.

18.

Table 3.6. Impacts of Food Processing, Packaging, and Transportation

	Global Warming	Air Pollution		Water Pollution		Habitat Alteration	
	GREENHOUSE GASES	COMMON	TOXIC	COMMON	TOXIC	WATER USE	LAND USE
Cultivation	4%	52%	39%	73%	17%	99%	82%
Food processing	16	6	1	4	8	0	1
Packaging	8	4	9	5	11	0	9
Transportation	26	15	19	0	0	0	7
Retail	1	1	5	1	0	0	1
Other	46	22	26	17	63	1	1
Total for fruit, vegetables, & grains	100%	100%	100%	100%	100%	100%	100%
As fraction of all impacts	2%	5%	3%	3%	5%	30%	6%

19. Our definition of wood heat includes both casual use of fireplaces and the use of wood as a principal source of heat in wood stoves.

20. It is difficult to estimate residential land use precisely. The Economic Research Service of the U.S. Department of Agriculture estimates there were 58 million acres of urban or built-up land in 1992 (*Agricultural Resources and Environmental Indicators: 1996–97*, chap. 1: "Land," 3). However, some of this land was occupied by roads, rail lines, utility lines, shopping centers, parks, golf courses, and other uses. From data on the distribution of urban land in fast-growth counties, we estimate that about 62.5 percent of such land, or 36 million acres, was actually occupied by residential housing (including farmsteads). This works out to 0.39 acre per household. For comparison, the average lot size of new single-family houses built in 1985 was about 0.25 acre. See Marlow Vesterby, Ralph E. Heimlich, and Kenneth S. Krupa, *Urbanization of Rural Land in the United States,* USDA, Economic Research Service, AER 673 (March 1994), 18, 59.

21. A simple way to do this, since we don't really know the life span of houses being built today, is to divide the land-use figure by the total number of existing households. Measured that way, the land used to produce wood and other materials in homes is about 1.75 acres per household per year, or five times the land physically occupied by the housing. When you adjust for ecological significance, the construction share shrinks to about 18 million acres, or 0.2 acre per household per year.

22. To compare the impacts of building a typical single-family house with those of manufacturing a typical mobile home, we started by gathering some basic cost figures. In 1995 the average new single-family home cost $170,000, while the average price of a mobile home was $33,500. When we ran these figures through our model, we got estimates of the one-time impact of the construction of each. But a single-family home usually lasts much longer than a mobile home. We assume that an average new house will last one hundred years and a new mobile home thirty years. After running the information through our model, we find the impacts *per year* to be as shown in the table below.

Table 3.7. Impacts of Building a Single-Family House Versus a Mobile Home

	Global Warming	Air Pollution		Water Pollution		Habitat Alteration	
	GREENHOUSE GASES	COMMON	TOXIC	COMMON	TOXIC	WATER USE	LAND USE
	kg/yr	kg/yr	kg/yr	kg/yr	kg/yr	gal/yr	acres
Single-family house	354	17.6	0.55	38.2	0.033	3,162	0.092
Mobile home	120	5.3	0.31	5.6	0.015	684	0.032

23. The average rate of yard use is inferred from data on average indoor use (without conservation measures) and total household use. See American Water Works Association, *1990 Residential Water Use Summary*, at http://www.waterwiser.org. Surveys of individual communities indicate outdoor water use fractions as high as 50 or 60 percent.

24. U.S. EPA, *Nonroad Engine and Vehicle Emissions Study*, vi, viii–ix.

Chapter 4

1. U.S. Department of Commerce, *Statistical Abstract of the United States 1995*, table 1214, 729.

2. Jacqueline Blix et al., *Getting a Life: Real Lives Transformed by Your Money or Your Life* (New York: Viking, 1997) and Juliet B. Schor, *Overspent: Upscaling, Downshifting, and the New Consumer* (New York: Basic Books, 1998).

3. U.S. Department of Transportation, *National Transportation Statistics 1997*, 80.

4. U.S. Department of Transportation, *Transportation Statistics Annual Report 1997*, 148.

5. Ibid., 167.

6. Ibid., 149

7. *Transportation Statistics Annual Report 1997*, 87–88.

8. Ibid., 89.

9. Ibid., 156.

10. Molly D. Anderson, "The Economics of Organic and Low-Input Farming in the United States of America," in N. H. Lampkin and S. Padel, *The Economics of Organic Farming: An International Perspective* (Wallingford, UK: CAB International, 1994), 161–84.

11. National Research Council, *Alternative Agriculture* (Washington, D.C.: National Academy Press, 1989).

12. Judd H. Alexander, *In Defense of Garbage* (Westport, CT: Praeger, 1993), 176.

13. For more information on this house, see Donald W. Aitken et al., "The Barritt House: Nevada's First PV Net-Metered Tract Home," *Proceedings of 1998 Annual Conference of the American Solar Energy Society* (1998): 181–186. For other examples of affordable eco-houses, see Alice Horrigan, "Affordable by Design," *E Magazine* (July/August 1997): 29–35.

Chapter 5

1. U.S. Environmental Protection Agency, Office of Air and Radiation, Office of Mobile Sources, "EPA Consumer Information: Boating Pollution Prevention Tips" (July 1966).

2. U.S. EPA Office of Air and Radiation, *Nonroad Engine and Vehicle Emission Study* (Washington, D.C.: U.S. EPA, 1991), vi.

3. Andre Mele, *Polluting for Pleasure* (New York: W.W. Norton & Co., 1993), 26.

4. Ibid., 30.

5. U.S. EPA, "EPA Environmental Fact Sheet: Emission Standards for New Gasoline Marine Engines" (August 1996).

6. F. Herbert Bormann et al., *Redesigning the American Lawn* (New Haven: Yale University Press, 1992), 99, 103–4, 97.

7. Sara Stein, *Noah's Garden: Restoring the Ecology of Our Own Back Yards* (Boston: Houghton Mifflin Co., 1993), 9. In this book Stein tells the story of the various transformations to her yard.

8. Ibid., 15.

9. Ibid., 18.

10. A. C. S. Hayden, "Fireplaces: Studies in Contrasts," *Home Energy Magazine* (September–October 1994), 27–29.

11. Ibid., 29.

12. *Hearthwarming: Guide to Hearth Products* (Guilford, NH: Village West Publishing, 1994), 7–8.

13. Hayden, "Fireplaces," 32.

14. Robert H. Webb and Howard G. Wilshire, *Environmental Effects of Off-Road Vehicles* (New York: Springer-Verlag, 1983), 144.

15. For information on the purchase of endangered plants and animals, see *Traffic USA,* a newsletter put out by the World Wildlife Fund on international trade in wildlife and wildlife products.

16. Charles A. S. Hall et al., "The Environmental Consequences of Having a Baby in the United States," *Population and Environment* 15 (July 1994): 505–24.

17. Thomas Hylton, *Save Our Land, Save Our Towns: A Plan for Pennsylvania* (Harrisburg: RB Books, 1995), 42.

18. President's Council on Sustainable Development, *Population and Consumption Task Force Report* (Washington, DC: President's Council on Sustainable Development, 1996).

Chapter 6

1. "The King of Cools," *Consumer Reports* (January 1998), 50, 52.

2. Gary C. Woodard and Todd C. Rasmussen, "Residential Water Demand: A Micro Analysis Using Survey Data," in *Hydrology and Water Resources in Arizona and the Southwest,* volume 14 (Tucson: Arizona Section of the American Water Resources Association, 1994).

3. EarthWorks Group, *50 Simple Things You Can Do to Save the Earth* (Berkeley, CA: Earthworks Press, 1989), 68.

4. David Stipp, "Life-Cycle Analysis Measures Greenness, but Results May Not Be Black and White," *Wall Street Journal,* February 28, 1991, B1; "Reassessing Costs of Keeping Baby Dry," *Science News,* December 1, 1990, 347.

5. Stipp, "Life Cycle Analysis," B5.
6. Beverly J. Sauer et al., "Resource and Environmental Profile Analysis of Children's Diaper Systems," *Environmental Toxicology and Chemistry* 13, no. 6 (1994): 1003–9.
7. Franklin Associates, *Resource and Environmental Profile Analysis of Polyethylene and Unbleached Paper Grocery Sacks,* Report prepared for the Council for Solid Waste Solutions, June 1990.
8. Ibid., 4-8–4-9.
9. Quoted in Paul Schneider, "The Cotton Brief," *New York Times,* June 20, 1993, sec. 9, 1.
10. Simpson's experiences and advice are described in Walter Simpson, *Recipe for an Effective Campus Energy Conservation Program* (Cambridge, MA: Union of Concerned Scientists, 1991).
11. Alex Wilson and John Morrill, *Consumer Guide to Home Energy Savings,* rev. ed. (Washington, DC: American Council for an Energy-Efficient Economy, 1996), 191–92.
12. Harwood Group, *Yearning for Balance: Views of Americans on Consumption, Materialism, and the Environment* (Takoma Park, MD: Merck Family Fund: 1995), 1–2.
13. Ibid., 5–6.

Chapter 7

1. Roland Hwang, *Money Down the Pipeline* (Cambridge, MA: Union of Concerned Scientists, 1995), 1–2.
2. John T. Preston, "Technology Innovation and Environmental Progress," in Marian R. Chertow and Daniel C. Esty, eds., *Thinking Ecologically: The Next Generation of Environmental Policy* (New Haven: Yale University Press, 1997), 140.
3. Sandra Postel, *Last Oasis: Facing Water Scarcity,* rev. ed. (New York: W.W. Norton & Co., 1997), 99–113.
4. John A. Baden, "An Economic Perspective on the Use of Land," in Henry L. Diamond and Patrick E. Noonan, *Land Use in America* (Washington, DC: Island Press, 1996), 320.
5. On the German and other producer responsibility laws, see Jim Motavalli, "The Producer Pays," *E Magazine* (May/June 1997), 36–41; and Frank Ackerman, *Why Do We Recycle? Markets, Values, and Public Policy* (Washington, DC: Island Press, 1997), 105–22.
6. Paul Krugman, "Earth in the Balance Sheet: Economists Go for the Green," *Slate* (an internet magazine; www.slate.com) (April 17, 1997), 4.
7. Robert Repetto et al., *Green Fees: How a Tax Shift Can Work for the Environment and the Economy* (Washington, DC: World Resources Institute, 1992); M. Jeff Hamond et al., *Tax Waste, Not Work* (San Francisco: Redefining Progress, 1997).
8. Krugman, "Earth in the Balance Sheet," 5.

9. President's Council on Sustainable Development, *Population and Consumption Task Force Report* (Washington, D.C.: President's Council on Sustainable Development, 1996).

10. Alliance to Save Energy et al., *Energy Innovations: A Prosperous Path to a Clean Environment* (Washington, DC: Alliance to Save Energy, 1997).

11. Frances Cairncross, *Costing the Earth: The Challenge for Governments, the Opportunities for Business* (Boston: Harvard Business School Press, 1993), 100.

12. Ibid., 107.

13. "Bottle and Can Recycling Rates," *Container and Packaging Recycling Update* (Spring 1996), 3; Container Recycling Institute press release, April 11, 1997.

14. Ackerman, *Why Do We Recycle?* 123–41.

15. On unit pricing for garbage, see Ackerman, *Why Do We Recycle?* 30–34.

16. The price differences and energy savings from purchasing an efficient versus and inefficient refrigerator are based on "The Kings of Cool," *Consumer Reports* (January 1998), 50, 52.

17. Christine A. Ervin, testimony, in *Federal Energy Efficiency Standards for Consumer Products,* Hearings before the Subcommittee on Energy and Power of the Committee on Commerce, House of Representatives (July 25, 1996), 11.

18. Ibid., 11.

19. Howard Geller, *National Appliance Efficiency Standards: Cost-Effective Federal Regulations* (Washington, DC: American Council for an Energy-Efficient Economy, 1995), 8.

20. Howard Geller et al., "Recommendations Concerning Tax Incentives for Energy Efficiency Measures," American Council for an Energy-Efficient Economy policy paper (November 26, 1997).

21. U.S. Department of Energy, "Refrigerator Energy Efficiency Standards," DOE Factsheet (1997).

22. See, for example, Sustainable Energy Budget Coalition, *America Speaks Out on Energy: A Survey of Public Attitudes on Sustainable Energy Issues* (Washington, DC: Sustainable Energy Budget Coalition, 1996).

23. Alan Nogee and Paul Jefferiss, *Renewable Energy and Electric Utility Restructuring in New York: Risks and Opportunities* (Cambridge, MA: Union of Concerned Scientists, 1997), 24–27.

24. Terry Parker et al., *The Land Use–Air Quality Linkage: How Land Use and Transportation Affect Air Quality* (Sacramento: California Air Resources Board, 1997), 3.

25. John Turner and Jason Rylander, "Land Use: The Forgotten Agenda," in Marian R. Chestow and Daniel C. Esty, *Thinking Ecologically: The Next Generation of Environmental Policy* (New Haven: Yale University Press, 1997), 61.

26. William K. Reilly, "Across the Barricades," in Henry L. Diamond and Patrick P. Noonan, *Land Use in America* (Washington, DC: Island Press, 1996), 188.

27. Ibid.

28. Diamond and Noonan, *Land Use in America,* 68.

29. Jean W. Hocker, "Patience, Problem Solving, and Private Initiative: Local Groups Chart a New Course for Land Conservation," in Diamond and Noonan, *Land Use in America,* 248, 256–58.

30. Turner and Rylander, "Land Use," 72.

31. Diamond and Noonan, *Land Use in America,* 35.

32. On impact fees, see Douglas R. Porter, *Managing Growth in America's Communities* (Washington, DC: Island Press, 1997), 135–41.

33. Thomas Hylton, *Save Our Land, Save Our Towns: A Plan for Pennsylvania* (Harrisburg: RB Books, 1996), 110; Peter Pollock, "Controlling Sprawl in Boulder: Benefits and Pitfalls," *Land Lines: Newsletter of the Lincoln Institute of Land Policy* (January 1998), 1–3; Porter, *Managing Growth,* 32.

34. To learn more about value of natural ecosystems for human well-being, see Gretchen C. Daily, ed., *Nature's Services: Societal Dependence on Natural Ecosystems* (Washington, DC: Island Press, 1997).

35. Turner and Ryland, "Land Use," 67.

Epilogue

1. Henry David Thoreau, *Walden* (New York: Harper & Row, 1961), 16.

2. *Last Whole Earth Catalog* (Menlo Park, CA: Portola Institute, 1971), 37.

3. Thoreau, *Walden,* 5.

4. Ibid., 33.

5. David Shi, *The Simple Life: Plain Living and High Thinking in American Culture* (New York: Oxford University Press, 1985), 143.

6. Thoreau, *Walden,* 45.

7. Shi, *The Simple Life,* 140–41.

8. Daniel Horowitz, *The Morality of Spending: Attitudes Toward the Consumer Society in America, 1875–1940* (Baltimore: Johns Hopkins University Press, 1985), 2, 6.

9. Ibid., 8.

10. Shi, *The Simple Life,* 144.

11. See Horowitz, *Morality of Spending,* p. 16.

12. Susan Strasser, *Satisfaction Guaranteed: The Making of the American Mass Market* (New York: Pantheon Books, 1989), 1–28, 89–123.

13. Horowitz, *The Morality of Spending,* 33; Simon J. Bronner, "Reading Consumer Culture," in Bronner, ed., *Consuming Visions: Accumulation and Display of Goods in America, 1880–1920* (New York: W.W. Norton & Co., 1989), p. 25.

14. Susan Strasser, *Never Done: A History of American Housework* (New York: Pantheon Books, 1982), 210–23.

15. William Leach, *Land of Desire: Merchants, Power, and the Rise of a New American Culture* (New York: Pantheon Books, 1993), 192.

16. Sinclair Lewis, *Babbitt* (London: Cape, 1922), 7, 81.

17. Robert Lynd and Helen Merrell Lynd, *Middletown: A Study in Contemporary American Culture* (New York, Harcourt, Brace & World, 1929), 80–81.

18. Ibid., 83.

19. Ibid., 232.

20. Ibid., 255.

21. In 1931 market researchers for Time, Inc., estimated that 90 percent of American families had no refrigerators. Time, Inc., *Markets by Incomes: A Study of the Relationship of Income to Retail Purchases in Appleton, Wisconsin* (New York: Time, Inc., 1932), 22; Roland S. Vaile, *Research Memorandum on Social Aspects of Consumption in the Depression* (New York: Social Science Research Council, 1937), 19.

22. R.O. Eastman, Inc., *Zanesville and 36 Other American Communities: A Study of Markets and of the Telephone as a Market Index* (New York: The Literary Digest, 1927), 108; Stanley Lebergott, *Pursuing Happiness: American Consumers in the Twentieth Century* (Princeton, NJ: Princeton University Press, 1993), 130.

23. Lebergott, *Pursuing Happiness,* 130.

24. Ibid., 152, 157.

25. John Kenneth Galbraith, *The Affluent Society* (Boston: Houghton Mifflin, 1958), x.

26. Ibid., 153.

27. Lebergott, *Pursuing Happiness,* 157.

28. Barry Commoner, *The Closing Circle: Nature, Man and Technology* (New York: Alfred A. Knopf, 1971), 125.

29. Ibid., 295.

30. Wendell Berry, *The Unsettling of America: Culture and Agriculture* (San Francisco: Sierra Club Books, 1977), 18.

31. Ibid., 24.

32. Lebergott, *Pursuing Happiness,* 157–63.

33. Juliet Schor, *The Overworked American: The Unexpected Decline of Leisure* (New York: Basic Books, 1991), 33.

34. Ibid., 9.

35. Ibid., xv–xvi.

36. Joseph R. Dominguez and Vicki Robin, *Your Money or Your Life: Transforming Your Relationship with Money and Achieving Financial Independence* (New York: Viking, 1992), 54.

37. Thoreau, *Walden,* 39.

38. Dominguez and Robin, *Your Money or Your Life,* xix.

Appendix A

1. To clarify the terminology, *risk assessment* generally refers to the process of ranking environmental problems of the same general type, for instance, in order to assign priorities to the cleanup of hazardous waste dumps. *Comparative risk assessment* attempts to compare and assess problems of different types. For example, it tries to determine whether urban air pollution is a more serious health hazard than contaminated drinking water.

2. Economists often attempt to reduce risks to dollar figures so that risks of different types can be compared, but this approach is highly controversial. One method is to survey people to find out how much they are willing to pay to protect something they value, such as a park or an endangered species. Another is to estimate how much society is willing to pay based on the costs of regulations and laws it has passed. Yet a third is to estimate the actual dollar value of the impact, such as the lost value of timber in a degraded forest. Often the three approaches lead to very different results.

3. For a range of views on the usefulness and accuracy of comparative risk assessments, see Adam M. Finkel and Dominic Golding, eds., *Worst Things First? The Debate over Risk-Based National Environmental Priorities* (Washington, DC: Resources for the Future, 1994).

4. Paul Slovic, "The Legitimacy of Public Perceptions of Risk," *Journal of Pesticide Reform* (Spring 1990), 13–15.

5. Unfortunately, placing too much reliance on the technique is exactly what some critics of past U.S. environmental regulation would like to do, by forcing the government to base every significant regulatory decision on the outcome of an analysis weighing benefits against costs, which for environmental regulations would invariably mean a risk assessment. Worse, these assessments would be subject to judicial challenge, which given the uncertainties in the techniques could tie up proposed regulations in courts for years. See, for example, William K. Stevens, "Congress Asks, Is Nature Worth More Than a Shopping Mall?" *New York Times,* April 25, 1995, G3; Warren Leon, "House Risks Too Much in Regulatory Reform," *Los Angeles Times,* March 1, 1995, A11.

6. U.S. Environmental Protection Agency, *Reducing Risk: Setting Priorities and Strategies for Environmental Protection,* Report of the Science Advisory Board to William K. Reilly, Administrator (September 1990).

7. California Comparative Risk Project, *Toward the 21st Century: Planning for the Protection of California's Environment,* Summary Report, Submitted to the California Environmental Protection Agency (May 1994). Other states besides California have conducted comparative risk assessments, but none have been as comprehensive or detailed. For information on the various state assessments, see Richard A. Minard, Jr., "CRA and the States: History, Politics, and Results," in J. Clarence Davies, ed.,

Comparing Environmental Risks: Tools for Setting Government Priorities (Washington, DC: Resources for the Future, 1996), 23–61.

8. Lisa Y. Lefferts, "Risks," *E Magazine* (January/February 1993), 39; "Not So Hot for Tots," *Psychology Today* 25 (September 1, 1992), 15; J. L. Jacobson and S. W. Jacobson, "Dose-Response in Perinatal Exposure to Polychlorinated Biphenyls (PCBs): The Michigan and North Carolina Cohort Studies," *Toxicology and Industrial Health* (May–August 1996), 435–45.

9. California Comparative Risk Project, *Toward the 21st Century*, 21.

10. In particular, the water pollution and air pollution categories include a variety of pollutants and pollutant sources, not all of which are of equal concern.

11. H. A. Stark, *Ward's Automotive Yearbook* (Detroit, MI: Ward's Communications, 1996), 24.

12. A general description of LCA is given in Paul Portney, "The Price Is Right: Making Use of Life Cycle Analysis," *Issues in Science and Technology* (Winter 1993–94), 69–75. For more extensive discussions, see J. A. Fava et al., *A Technical Framework for Life-Cycle Assessments*, Society of Environmental Toxicology and Chemistry (November 1991), and George A. Keoleian et al., *Product Life Cycle Assessment to Reduce Health Risks and Environmental Impacts* (Park Ridge, NJ: Noyes, 1994). The technique is not without its critics. See Mark Duda and Jane S. Shaw, *A New Environmental Tool? Assessing Life Cycle Assessment*, Center for the Study of American Business, Contemporary Issues Series 81 (August 1996).

13. The diaper studies are discussed in chapter 6. For packaging, one of the most extensive and well-regarded studies was the Tellus Institute, *Packaging Study* (Boston: Tellus Institute, 1992).

14. We are not the first to think of applying input-output models to environmental analysis, but ours is the first such model of the U.S. economy to cover so many industry sectors and to analyze consumer expenditures and environmental impacts in a comprehensive manner. For examples of other, related applications of input-output analysis, see Faye Duchin and Glenn-Marie Lange, *The Future of the Environment: Ecological Economics and Technological Change* (New York: Oxford University Press, 1994); Duchin and Lange, "The Use, Disposal, and Recycling of Plastics in the U.S.," Report to the AT&T Industrial Ecology Faculty Fellowship Program (New York University, Institute for Economic Analysis, June 1995); J. M. Breuil, "Input-Output Analysis and Pollutants Emissions in France," *Energy Journal* (1992); and Lester B. Lave et al., "Using Input-Output Analysis to Estimate Economy-Wide Discharges," *Environmental Science and Technology* 29, no. 9 (1995), 420A–26A.

15. The data source is U.S. Department of Energy, *Emissions of Greenhouse Gases in the United States* (1995). Quantities of methane are multiplied by a factor of 11 to account for the greater direct global warming potential of this gas over a hundred-year period. The adjustment factor is

from Intergovernmental Panel on Climate Change, *Climate Change 1992: The Supplementary Report to the IPCC Scientific Assessment* (Cambridge, UK: Cambridge University Press, 1992), 15. Other greenhouse gas emissions in the United States contribute comparatively little to the problem and are ignored.

16. The data come from the U.S. Environmental Protection Agency, *National Emissions Trends Viewer CD-ROM* (1995). The quantities of 10-micron particulate matter (PM) in this database were converted to 2.5-micron PM using adjustment factors from another database, the draft *National Emissions Inventory* (Doug Solomon, E.H. Pechan & Associates, personal communication).

17. For a given source of pollution (such as automobiles), the amount of each pollutant emitted was divided by the total emissions of that pollutant, then multiplied by the total emissions of all four pollutants. The resulting four quantities (one for each pollutant) were then averaged to yield the combined pollution index. The rationale for this weighting method is that all four pollutants appear to pose roughly comparable threats to public health. VOCs and NO_x contribute approximately equally to the formation of ozone, while VOCs and SO_2 contribute substantially to particulate matter formation, as do, of course, direct particulate emissions.

18. The source of data was the draft EPA *National Toxics Inventory* (1997), which was provided on disk by Dave Epperson of Eastern Research Group. Some of the data in this inventory are preliminary and undergoing review, and the year of emissions is not specified, but by and large they reflect conditions in the early 1990s.

19. Research by the World Bank suggests that weighting pollutants by toxicity would not greatly affect the results of our analysis, although it could change the rank ordering of some consumer purchases. Toxic pollution indicators similar to our own were created for the manufacturing industries using several different methods of toxicity weighting. When the industry pollution rankings using the different methods were compared, the rank correlation coefficients ranged from 0.8 to 0.99, indicating that most of the industries that rank high according to one weighting method also rank high according to others. See Hemamala Hettige, Paul Martin, Manjula Singh, and David Wheeler, *The Industrial Pollution Projection System* (Policy Research Department, World Bank, 1997), 24. It should be noted that persistence in the environment and human exposure are just as important as toxicity to determining the overall human or ecological health impact, but relatively little reliable data on such characteristics of chemicals are available.

20. Point source data for 1995 from the Permit Compliance System were provided on disk through a Freedom of Information Request to the U.S. Environmental Protection Agency. Data on sources of water quality impairment were from U.S. Environmental Protection Agency, *National*

Water Quality Inventory 1994 Report to Congress, appendix A, tables A-5 and A-6 (December 1995). This inventory cites hydroelectric and other types of dams as one source of harm to water quality. To determine how these effects should be distributed among the various uses of dams, we relied on the U.S. Army Corps of Engineers, *National Inventory of Dams (Updated Data: 1995–96),* on CD-ROM. On the basis of acre-feet of impounded water, the leading uses of dams are flood control, hydroelectric power, drinking water supply, irrigation, navigation, and recreation.

21. U.S. Environmental Protection Agency, *Toxic Release Inventory 1987–1994* (August 1996), CD-ROM.
22. D. A. Goolsby and W. A. Battaglin, "Occurrence, Distribution, and Transport of Agricultural Chemicals in Surface Waters of the Midwestern United States," in Goolsby et al., *Selected Papers on Agricultural Chemicals in Water Resources of the Midcontinental United States,* Open-File Report 93-418, U.S. Geological Survey (1993), 1–25.
23. Curtis H. Flather, Linda A. Joyce, and Carol A. Bloomgarden, *Species Endangerment Patterns in the United States,* General Technical Report RM-241, Rocky Mountain Forest and Range Experiment Station, U.S. Forest Service (January 1994), 11.
24. Acreage by crop type from the U.S. Department of Commerce, *1992 Census of Agriculture,* CD-ROM. Other land use from Arthur B. Daugherty, *Major Uses of Land in the United States 1992,* Agricultural Economic Report No. 723, Economic Research Service, U.S. Department of Agriculture (November 1995), 3, 4, 17.
25. For example, suppose household purchases of beef result in cattle being grazed on 100 acres of range land. On our index that would translate into 100 / 17 = 6 acres of urban-equivalent land use.
26. Wayne B. Solley, *Preliminary Estimates of Water Use in the United States, 1995,* Open-File Report 97-645, U.S. Geological Survey (1997), 3–6. We distributed water use for irrigation among different crop types using data from the *1992 Census of Agriculture.* Water use in manufacturing and mining was distributed on the basis of the U.S. Department of Commerce, *1982 Census of Manufactures: Water Use in Manufacturing* (1986) and *1982 Census of Mineral Industries: Water Use in Mineral Industries* (1985). Unfortunately, the water-use surveys were discontinued after the 1982 census.
27. W. Leontief, *Review of Economic Statistics* 52, no. 3 (1970), 262–71. See also W. Leontief, *Input-Output Economics* (New York: Oxford University Press, 1986).
28. Minnesota IMPLAN Group, Inc., *IMPLAN Pro User's Guide* (1996).
29. Total carbon emissions from automobiles and trucks are from Energy Information Administration, *Annual Energy Review 1996,* table 12.3, 338. (The underlying data are from the DOE, *Emissions of Greenhouse Gases in the United States.*) Commercial and industrial use of passenger

cars is assumed to be negligible compared with household use. Emissions from personal use of trucks are derived from truck miles and fuel efficiencies, as reported in U.S. Department of Commerce, *1992 Truck Inventory and Use Survey,* table 10, 118–29.

30. This includes 1.54 trillion vehicle miles by passenger cars (U.S. Department of Transportation, *National Transportation Statistics 1997,* 222) and 0.46 trillion vehicle miles by personal light trucks (*1992 Truck Inventory and Use Survey,* 118–29).

31. The remaining amounts break down as follows: wholesale trade—$612; motor vehicle freight transport and warehousing—$253; railroads and related services—$159; other—$112.

32. As an example of respending effects, suppose that in producing a $1 roll of toilet paper, a manufacturer pays $0.25 to its paper supplier, $0.15 to its cardboard roll supplier, and $0.05 to its packaging supplier. The total of immediate and upstream expenditures is $1.45. An input-output model would actually take the upstream effects even further, counting payments by the paper manufacturer to its logging contractors, for instance.

33. The appearance of "car manufacturers" on the list means that some of the money spent by manufacturers goes to establishments that are also classed as manufacturers. Probably most is for car parts, such as engines or transmissions (Rolls-Royce buys transmissions from General Motors, for example, even though General Motors is classed as a manufacturer of cars, not car parts).

34. The analysis is not quite complete, since we haven't considered the upstream impacts of everyday purchases of fuel, tires, brake fluid, and all of the other materials needed to keep a car running. But they're a small factor when it comes to carbon emissions, so we ignore them in this example. Such impacts are included in the results presented later in this chapter.

35. The household expenditure data, which are part of the IMPLAN model, are derived from the U.S. Census Bureau's consumer expenditure survey. A summary of the data can be found in U.S. Department of Commerce, *Statistical Abstract of the United States 1995,* 465.

36. For an interesting case study of how practices and environmental impacts can vary greatly from place to place, see Claude E. Boyd and Jason W. Clay, "Shrimp Agriculture and the Environment," *Scientific American* (June 1998): 58–65.

ABOUT THE UNION OF CONCERNED SCIENTISTS

The Union of Concerned Scientists (UCS) has been working for a healthier environment and a safer world since 1969. UCS's scientific analysis forms the basis for its advocacy work on energy, transportation, global warming, biodiversity, agriculture, and arms control.

UCS experts work together with people from across the country to help implement innovative ideas and transform science into policy solutions. This powerful partnership is currently working to encourage responsible stewardship of the global environment and life-sustaining resources; promote energy technologies that are renewable, safe, and cost-effective; reform transportation policy; curtail weapons proliferation; and promote sustainable agriculture. An independent nonprofit organization, UCS conducts technical studies and public education, and seeks to influence government policy.

You can learn more about the organization and find extensive environmental information by visiting the UCS web site, www.ucsusa.org. To become a sponsor of UCS's work, go to "Join UCS" on the web site, call 617-547-5552, or write to UCS, Two Brattle Square, Cambridge, MA 02238-9105.

§ 279

Thomas H. Stone
Chair, Saul Stone and Company

Ellyn R. Weiss
Former Deputy Assistant Secretary, U.S. Department of Energy

Victor F. Weisskopf
Institute Professor of Physics Emeritus, MIT
Former Director-General, European Center for Nuclear
Research

INDEX